ALEXANDER HAMILTON AND
THE IDEA OF REPUBLICAN GOVERNMENT

ALEXANDER HAMILTON
AND THE IDEA OF
REPUBLICAN GOVERNMENT

BY

GERALD STOURZH

STANFORD UNIVERSITY PRESS
STANFORD, CALIFORNIA
1970

Stanford University Press
Stanford, California
© 1970 by the Board of Trustees of the
Leland Stanford Junior University
Printed in the United States of America
ISBN 0-8047-0724-3
LC 69-18496

TO THE MEMORY OF
DOUGLASS ADAIR

CONTENTS

INTRODUCTION   1

I. "RESORT TO FIRST PRINCIPLES"   9
BLACKSTONE, HAMILTON, AND THE NATURAL RIGHT TO
REVOLUTION
The Climate of British Political Thought on the Eve of the
American Revolution, 9. The Role of Natural Law in the Amer-
ican Revolution, 11. The Natural Right of Self-Preservation, 17.
Hamilton's Image of the Social Contract: Blackstone Contra
Locke, 24. Beyond Legality: "Resort to First Principles" After
the Revolution, 30. A Machiavellian Tradition and Revolu-
tionary Political Thought, 34.

II. THE MEANING OF REPUBLICAN GOVERNMENT   38
POPULAR SOVEREIGNTY, FREEDOM, AND VIRTUE
Republican Government—A Transitory Stage?, 38. "Free"
vs. "Arbitrary" Government, 40. In Quest of "Republican"
Government, 44. Republican Government as "Government by
the People," 48. Republican Government as the Rule of
Law, 56. Virtue as the Principle of Republican Government, 63.
Hamilton, Hume, and the Replacement of Virtue by Self-
Interest: The Victory of the Moderns, 70.

III. THE SPRINGS OF REPUBLICAN GOVERNMENT   76
PRIVATE PASSIONS, PUBLIC INTEREST, AND THE LOVE OF FAME
The Age of Human Nature, 76. The Meaning of Interest and
the Rise of Utilitarian Morality, 80. Human Nature and Social
Classes, 87. The Ambiguity of Self-Interest and the Hier-
archy of Passions, 90. The Love of Power, Demagoguery,

and "The Ruling Passion of the Noblest Minds," 95. Nation-Building Without Patriotism: The Danger of "Foreign Corruption in Republics," 106. Factions, Parties, Sections, and the Extent of Territory: Hamilton vs. Madison, 110. Hamilton's Discovery of Collective Emotions, 120.

IV. THE FOREIGN POLICY OF REPUBLICAN
    GOVERNMENT   126

The Peacefulness of Republics: Charles Pinckney vs. Alexander Hamilton, 126. Peace and the Good Society in Classical Political Thought, 130. Early Modern Thought on Foreign Policy: Empirical Study and Natural Law, 132. Montesquieu's Concept of International Relations, 138. Montesquieu's Second Contribution: The Political Theory of International Commerce, 140. Free Trade, Sea Power, and American Independence, 145. Alexander Hamilton and the Primacy of Foreign Policy, 148. The Optimum Size of Nations: Montesquieu, Hamilton, and the Meaning of "Confederation," 153. Foreign Policy, Military Policy, and the Concept of Unitary Government, 161. The End of an Age-Old Debate: Once More the Victory of the Moderns, 166.

V. THE PURSUIT OF GREATNESS   171

Liberty and Greatness, 171. The Scale of Greatness, 174. Power and Responsibility: Hamiltonianism vs. Jeffersonianism, 180. The Scope of Responsibility: Public Interest and Reasons of State, 186. The Meaning of Empire, 189. The Pursuit of Greatness, 201.

LIST OF SHORT TITLES   207

NOTES   213

ACKNOWLEDGMENTS   269

INDEX   271

ALEXANDER HAMILTON AND
THE IDEA OF REPUBLICAN GOVERNMENT

The station of a member of C-----ss, is the most illustrious and important of any I am able to conceive. He is to be regarded not only as a legislator, but as the founder of an empire. A man of virtue and ability, dignified with so precious a trust, would rejoice that fortune had given him birth at a time, and placed him in circumstances so favourable for promoting human happiness. He would esteem it not more the duty, than the privilege and ornament of his office, to do good to mankind; from this commanding eminence, he would look down with contempt upon every mean or interested pursuit.

Alexander Hamilton, November 16, 1778

INTRODUCTION

This essay is concerned with the political thought of a statesman who used the discussion of political and constitutional issues as a constant and important instrument in the pursuit of his political design. By studying Alexander Hamilton's political thought in the context of his and his contemporaries' understanding of republican government, I have tried to contribute to our knowledge of the political ideas of the Founders of the American Republic. By relating Hamilton's political thought to his statesmanship, I hope to contribute to our understanding of the way Hamilton understood himself and the tasks he did or hoped to accomplish.

Before we start assessing whether and in what way a historical figure may have thought new thoughts or done new deeds, we ought to remember that he was molded by preceding, older ways of thought and speech and action. An awareness of earlier traditions is especially appropriate to a study concerned with the American Founding Fathers. The very name given to that group of American statesmen—who seem even to the foreign observer, unmoved by patriotic attachment, a most uncommon lot of men—indicates how much these men have been regarded as the originators rather than the receivers of political traditions.

The continuity of American history since the late eighteenth century, partly to be explained by the longevity of the Constitution of 1787, is responsible for the fact that the Founders remain living partners in a dialogue on the purpose and destiny of Amer-

ican politics that is renewed in every generation.[1] The closeness
of the Founders to the American present—which finds no par-
allel in the history of Europe—may, however, have hindered
rather than helped to illuminate their political views. Otherwise
it could hardly be explained that the impact of the radical Whig
tradition in England on eighteenth-century America was virtually
discovered only a few years ago—witness the work of Bernard
Bailyn and others. Nor could it be explained that the meaning
of republican government to the generation of the Founders has
just begun to be investigated—witness, for instance, the scarcity
of research available on the meaning and implications of the
Federal Constitution's guarantee to every state in the union of
a "republican form of government." Recently it has been rightly
observed, with particular reference to the development of civil
liberties, that we need an analysis of republican thought in America between 1776 and 1800—that we need, in other words, to
know more about the nature of republican government and its
relationship to the people.[2]

This book is intended to contribute to the growing discussion
about the meaning of republican government to the generation
of the Founders by analyzing both Alexander Hamilton's understanding of republican government and the direction he wished to
give it in America. The issues raised point beyond Hamilton's
career to the core of the problems confronting the Founders between about 1760 and 1800. These issues, rather than specific
stages of Hamilton's life, are discussed in the five chapters that
follow. Accordingly, a topical rather than a chronological arrangement has been used.

Three assumptions or convictions about the political thought
of the generation of the Founders underlie this study and should
be explained at the outset.

First, for the reasons just indicated, I have been concerned with
the origins and background of political concepts that were significant for Alexander Hamilton and his contemporaries. This emphasis does necessitate, on occasion, explorations of certain earlier
stages of political thought in Europe. These explorations I believe
to be meaningful for the following reason: the political thought of

the Founders was secular, not religious. Hamilton may represent an extreme example of this secular character, owing to his origins and upbringing (though peculiar modifications occurred toward the end of his life), but he was by no means an exception. With the gradual slackening of the Puritan hold on political discourse, European secular political thought, symbolized by a range of names from Machiavelli, Bacon, Sidney, Locke, and Montesquieu, to Hume and Blackstone, not to forget the lesser lights of the English radical Whig tradition, hit the American shores with particular impact. Never before or since the second half of the eighteenth century has the Atlantic Ocean been less a barrier to the communication of political and constitutional ideas, a situation that made possible what Robert Palmer has called the Age of Democratic Revolution.

Second, this study expresses a view of the character of political thought that, though here applied to the analysis of Hamilton and the Founders, seems relevant for the whole of early modern political thought from the sixteenth century to the eighteenth and perhaps even in a wider context. This must be explained in some detail. It is possible to discern two main concerns of political thought: concern for the principles of political obligation and concern for the empirical conditions of stability and decay, freedom and tyranny, peace and war, greatness and weakness. The first concern has been expressed on three levels of discourse, the theological, the philosophical, and the juridical, depending on where the sources of political obligation were to be located—in divine revelation, in the nature of man according to human reason, or in a particular constitutional system (a constitutional system could, in turn, be justified by recurring to theological or philosophical axioms). In the seventeenth and eighteenth centuries this concern was expressed primarily through the natural rights tradition of political thought. The second concern inquires into specific forms of government (government taken in its old, all-encompassing meaning) by way of comparative analysis, accessible through the empirical investigation of both past and present states. The German term *Staatsformenlehre* approximates (though rather too narrowly) a tradition best called the comparative study of political regimes, unmistakably identified by evoking the names of Aristotle, Machiavelli, Harrington, Montesquieu, and Tocqueville. This empirical tradition has combined the examination of the domestic institutions, the foreign policies, and the moral properties of societies.[3] Distinguishing between these two concerns may supply a criterion for understanding two different branches of political thought of which great political thinkers of early modern times have been quite aware. Hugo Grotius, representing the natural rights tradition, has explained with admirable conciseness his own task:

I have refrained from discussing topics which belong to another subject, such as those that teach what may be advantageous in practice. For such topics have their own special field, that of politics, which Aristotle rightly treats by itself, without introducing extraneous matters into it. Bodin, on the contrary, mixed up politics with the body of law with which we are concerned. In some places nevertheless I have made mention of that which is expedient, but only in passing, and in order to distinguish it more clearly from what is lawful.[4]

John Locke put essentially the same distinction even more succinctly: "Politics contains two parts, very different the one from the other. The one, containing the original of societies, and the rise and extent of political power; the other, the art of governing men in society."[5] In America, this distinction did not go unnoticed by members of the revolutionary generation. Benjamin Rush put it this way:

It is one thing to understand the *principles*, and another thing to understand the *forms* of government. The former are simple; the latter are difficult and complicated. There is the same difference between principles and forms in all other sciences. Who understood the principles of mechanics and optics better than Sir Isaac Newton? and yet Sir Isaac could not for his life have made a watch or a microscope. Mr. Locke is an oracle as to the *principles*, Harrington and Montesquieu are oracles as to the *forms* of government.[6]

The distinction between these two concerns of political thought may profitably be applied to the interpretation of American political thought between roughly 1760 and 1790. The controversy over the true nature of the British Constitution, with the issue of representation at its center, was essentially a debate on the basis of political obligation (or disobedience). Although the appeal to legal precedent, drawn from constitutional history, was predominant, recurrence to principles of natural law was not unknown, since eighteenth-century constitutionalism was deeply imbued with the natural rights tradition. As the break with the mother country became irrevocable, the issue of legitimacy above and beyond allegiance to Great Britain prevailed. In the same way, the first principles of political obligation, symbolized by the image of the social compact and the rights of man, now became the center of interest. But beyond a new statement of the principles of political obligation, as embodied in the first Bills of Rights and in the Declaration of Independence, new *forms* of government were to be established. This grand effort ranged on the state level from New Hampshire, in late 1775, to Massachusetts, in 1780; it culminated in the drafting and ratification of the Federal Constitution. The task of setting up new forms of government consisted in the endeavor to reach, as Hamilton told the New York Ratifying Convention of 1788, "the perfect balance between liberty and power," since "good constitutions are formed upon a comparison of the liberty of the individual with the strength of government."[7] The search for this balance, it goes without saying, was at the core of Hamilton's political thought and practice.

The third assumption basic to this study has to do with this "perfect balance between liberty and power." The attainment of this balance required, in Hamilton's eyes, a measurement of the needs of a government with regard to the rest of the world. Thus we are inevitably led to an assessment of the role of international politics in political thought. The writings of great political thinkers, with the exception of Machiavelli, have been constantly probed for what they have to say on the proper structuring of a society, on the good life within society. What they have to say on relations among societies, on "politics among nations," has remained considerably more in the background, except for some notable recent studies.[8] The great "empirical" thinkers mentioned above were always aware that the domestic structure of a society and the society's place within a world of nations were but two sides of the same coin. The interdependence of forms of government and the conduct of foreign policy is one of the great issues in the debate on the nature of republican government, and Hamilton has been very much in the middle of this debate. Consequently, the nature of the interdependence between domestic and foreign affairs, between constitutional structures and a nation's place in the world, is a main theme of this inquiry.

The chapters that follow reflect the assumptions just outlined. The first chapter deals with "principles" rather than "forms" of government, i.e., with the fundamentals of political obligation (or disobedience), called, in eighteenth-century parlance, "first principles." It so happens that there is a motive of chronology as well as of topical arrangement for dealing with "first principles" first, since Hamilton's early writings were part of the debate about the grounds of political obligation that preceded and culminated in the break with the mother country. Hamilton's attitude toward the natural rights tradition will be examined in close connection with the position of William Blackstone. To recall Benjamin Rush's words, if Hamilton needed an "oracle" on principles of government, it was Blackstone rather than Locke. First principles might, however, be "first in history," as well as "first in nature" or reason, as has rightly been observed.[9] In that sense, "first principles" refer to the original principles, or the original ordering of a given government. The assumption of a political theory thinking in terms of decay to be arrested or slowed rather than in terms of progress to be speeded was, of course, that original principles were identical with right principles. Accordingly, the connection of the American revolutionaries' use of "first principles" with a tradition going back to Machiavelli's teachings will be thrown into relief.

Chapters II through V deal with the meaning and implications of that form of government which, according to a general consensus (general perhaps because it rested on vague premises) was alone suitable to America—republican government. In Chapter II, various alternative interpretations of republican government, as well as Hamilton's own stand, are investigated. It should emerge that the debate on the meaning of republican government was linked to the battle between ancients and moderns, which, various crosscurrents notwithstanding, was to end with the victory of the moderns. In Chapter III, the springs of a "modern" republican government, according to Hamilton's understanding, are examined. I have stressed what Hamilton considered the most frightening, as well as the most redeeming features of republican government—demagoguery and "foreign corruption" on one side, the "ruling passion of the noblest minds" on the other. In addition, I have discussed the strange modification of Hamilton's political psychology in his last years of disappointment and bitterness. Chapter IV discusses the interdependence between forms of government and the conduct of foreign policy. Here the roots of the Founding Fathers' ideas need to be explored in considerable detail. In Chapter V, finally, Hamilton the statesman takes precedence over Hamilton the political thinker. It should become clear that Hamilton was not, as it has been claimed so often, far ahead of his times; rather he seems very much in tune with his times, if we look at them from an angle encompassing the international scene. Then we shall grasp how very much Great Britain's ascendancy as the leading maritime and industrial nation of the age provided the example for Hamilton's vision of the future United States. To make a second England of America, eventually to take over Britain's ascendancy, that was a pursuit of national greatness that Hamilton linked to his own striving for enduring fame.

Is it worthwhile to try to lay bare the origins and the frequently tortuous development of the ideas with which one of America's first great statesmen wrestled, rejecting some of them with the same vigor with which he espoused others? I believe that for the realm of political and constitutional concepts, especially if they have entered into policies and institutions, Sir Henry Maine's argument retains all the force it has for the domain of law: "Nothing in law springs entirely from a sense of convenience. There are always certain ideas existing antecedently on which the sense of convenience works, and of which it can do no more than form some new combination; and to find these ideas is exactly the problem."[10]

I

"RESORT TO FIRST PRINCIPLES"

BLACKSTONE, HAMILTON, AND THE NATURAL RIGHT TO REVOLUTION

The Climate of British Political Thought on the Eve of the American Revolution

William Blackstone's *Commentaries on the Laws of England* began to appear in print in 1765. They were the perfect expression of English constitutional thought in an age when England prided herself on the balance and harmony of her free government, received as a heritage from the struggles of previous generations. The upheavals of the seventeenth century were not very remote, but Blackstone, who was closely read by Americans as well as Englishmen, tried hard to push the seventeenth century's feverish quest for first principles back into the mythical past. Touching on the cornerstone of the established order, the deposition of James II and the Glorious Revolution, Blackstone exhorted his readers:

... Care must be taken not to carry this inquiry farther, than merely for instruction or amusement. The idea, that the consciences of posterity, were concerned in the rectitude of their ancestors' decisions, gave birth to those dangerous political heresies, which so long distracted the state, but at length are all happily extinguished. I therefore rather chuse to consider this great political measure upon the solid footing of authority, than to reason in it's favour from it's justice, moderation, and expedience: because that might imply a right of dissenting or revolting from it, in case we should think it to have been unjust, oppressive, or inexpedient.[1]

Thus the great teacher of the laws of England drew a veil of reverence over the first principles of his society. Administrative

practice and constitutional interpretation largely took the place
of political theory and speculation. To a contented country England's great political theorist, David Hume, presented the bulk
of his political thought in the pleasant, fragile, and somewhat
noncommittal form of short essays, not in pamphlets or political
treatises. Englishmen on both sides of the Atlantic were satisfied
that the first principles of government had been settled in the
previous century, when to their surprise and dismay they were
called upon to argue about the true nature of the British Constitution, to fight a war, to wrestle anew with the first principles of
political obligation, and eventually to see the establishment of
a new form of government in America.

First principles, in the parlance of the eighteenth century, referred to the fundamentals of political society. Two meanings,
however, must be distinguished. In one sense they meant the
principles of natural law and the rights derived therefrom. The
protection of those rights alone conferred legitimacy on government, and violation of them by a ruler might justify recourse
to extralegal, indeed revolutionary, action. This view was expounded by the radical philosopher Joseph Priestley in his *Essay
on the First Principles of Government*, published in 1768; Priestley's arguments proved valuable to Americans in succeeding
years.[2] Yet a conservative jurist could entertain the same notion
as William Blackstone did when he spoke of "those extraordinary recourses to first principles, which are necessary when the
contracts of society are in danger of dissolution, and the law
proves too weak a defence against the violence of fraud or oppression."[3] And with the same argument, young Alexander Hamilton proclaimed, in his second revolutionary pamphlet, the right
to revolution: When the first principles of civil society are violated, and the rights of a whole people are invaded, the common
forms of municipal law are not to be regarded. Men may then
betake themselves to the law of nature; and, if they but conform
their actions, to that standard, all cavils against them, betray
either ignorance or dishonesty."[4]

There is, however, a second meaning for "first principles":

"first" not in nature or reason only, but first in time, in history, in origins as well. English political thought in the seventeenth and eighteenth centuries was yet largely informed by the ancients' assumption, imbued with renewed vigor in the Renaissance, that the origins of states were good, whether owing to the greatness of founders or to the simplicitiy and purity of the people's manners or both. A tendency toward decay could be halted or slowed, it was hoped, by stabilizing measures like the famous Polybian balance of mixed government; but if decline and corruption went far, the surgeon's knife might be required to restore the state to its original purity and goodness.[5] There is a suggestion of this second meaning in Blackstone's understanding of history. "We find from history," the learned jurist said, that "in the infancy and first rudiments of almost every state, the leader, chief magistrate, or prince, hath usually been elective." and, Blackstone continued wistfully, revealing his adherence to a view of history in terms of decline rather than progress, "if the individuals who compose that state *could always continue true to first principles*, uninfluenced by passion or prejudice, unassailed by corruption, and unawed by violence, elective succession were as much to be desired in a kingdom, as in other inferior communities."[6] In times of upheaval and discontent with present conditions, recurrence to first principles according to nature *and* according to history, i.e., the (pretended) original purity of the constitution, might imperceptibly merge into a doubly powerful justification for discarding legal remedies in favor of revolution. In this chapter, I shall first discuss the role of first principles in the natural rights tradition and then turn to their import in terms of historical origin.

The Role of Natural Law in the American Revolution

What else but resorting to first principles was it when Alexander Hamilton, in February 1775, cried out: "The sacred rights of mankind are not to be rummaged for, among old parchments, or musty records. They are written, as with a sun beam, in the whole *volume* of human nature, by the hand of the divinity itself; and can never be erased or obscured by mortal power."[7] This exclamation, reminiscent of Tom Paine's *Common Sense*, was neither merely the expression of youthful exuberance nor propaganda. Its florid wording notwithstanding, it did not depart radically from accepted ways of constitutional reasoning. Compare the similar words of the venerable Sir Edward Coke, in a case actually used by Hamilton in the same pamphlet. Coke invoked *"Lex aeterna*, the moral law, called also the law of nature . . . written with the finger of God in the heart of man."[8]

Interpretations of the American Revolution as a conservative movement have stressed the colonists' concern with the true nature of the British Constitution, deprecating or leaving unexplained the role of political theory, in particular the theory of natural law and natural rights.[9] As a result, legal and philosophical levels of argument have been opposed, the importance of political theory has been slighted, and a cleavage between constitutional and natural law is suggested where none exists.

The theory of natural law served, as it were, as the connecting arch between the society the Americans broke away from and the new society, or societies, they formed. John Adams's recollection of the drafting of the Declaration of Rights in 1774 illuminates the thinking of the colonists as matters approached a crisis: it was discussed "whether We should recur to the Law of Nature, as well as to the British Constitution and our American Charters and Grants. Mr. Galloway and Mr. Duane were for excluding the Law of Nature. I was very strenuous for retaining and insisting on it, as a Resource to which We might be driven, by Parliament much sooner than We were aware."[10] Blackstone himself, eminently respectable as well as eminently up to date, provided an opening for the colonists' resort to first principles that was anticipated by John Adams and expressed by Hamilton in the startling words given above, and that culminated in the preamble to the Declaration of Independence. The wise Blackstone admitted, with a candor and modesty for which he deserves more credit than he has received;

Indeed, it is found by experience, that whenever the unconstitutional oppressions, even of the sovereign power, advance with gigantic strides and threaten desolation to a state, mankind will not be reasoned out of their feelings of humanity; nor sacrifice their liberty by a scrupulous adherence to those political maxims, which were originally established to preserve it. And therefore, though the positive laws are silent, experience will furnish us with a very remarkable case, wherein *nature* and *reason* prevailed. . . . [Reference to the abdication of James II] In these therefore, or other circumstances, which a fertile imagination may furnish, since both law and history are silent, it becomes us to be silent too; leaving to future generations, whenever necessity and the safety of the whole shall require it, the exertion of those *inherent (though latent) powers of society, which no climate, no time, no constitution, no contract, can ever destroy or diminish.*[11]

A recent student of the political thought of the American Revolution tells us that "a South Carolinian spoke of 'those *latent*, though *inherent* rights of SOCIETY, which *no climate, no time, no constitution, no contract*, can ever destroy or diminish.' " The historian Claude Van Tyne, commenting on these words inciting to revolution, said that "to a mind that venerated the Constitution such ideas were poisonous, and pointed plainly to anarchy." It is shocking indeed to learn that these ideas were taken by the South Carolinian writer John Mackenzie straight out of the work of "a mind that venerated the Constitution"—with the psychologically illuminating substitution of "rights" for "powers"![12]

Hamilton relied on Blackstone more than any other writer in composing his revolutionary pamphlets, *A Full Vindication of the Measures of Congress*, December 1774, and *the Farmer Refuted*, February 1775. It reads like a comment on Blackstone when Hamilton says: "When human laws contradict or discountenance the means, which are necessary to preserve the essential rights of any society, they defeat the proper end of all laws, and so become null and void."[13]

The arguments of people like John Adams, John Mackenzie of South Carolina, Hamilton, and Blackstone himself should point out the extremism of an interpretation of the American Revolution that neglects the role of the resort to first principles. Daniel Boorstin, who takes a "legal" and "conservative" view of the Revolution, has taken issue with Carl Becker's explanation of the role of natural law in the Revolution as follows:

According to this view, the colonists *began* their argument on a low legalistic level, finding it convenient to debate first within the framework of the imperial constitution and the common law; but they gradually and inevitably climbed the ladder of abstraction until, by mid-1776, they were thinking and talking in the arid heights of natural law.... [Becker's account] supposes a kind of intellectual mobility—near disingenuousness—which enabled the Americans to shift their grounds to suit their needs. It takes for granted ... that the colonists could as readily abandon the legal for the philosophical level of argument as a hired counsel could alter his plea from guilty to not guilty.[14]

This criticism fails to consider John Adams's reasoning, illustrated above, and the role of natural rights in Alexander Hamilton's two pamphlets written before independence. It might seem a paradox that Hamilton advocated natural rights more strongly in his contributions to the great debate on the nature of the British Constitution than did Thomas Jefferson in his *Summary View of the Rights of British America*. But the paradox turns out to be apparent rather than real when we are reminded, by Hamilton himself, that New York, where he was writing, had no royal charter, and that his careful arguments for the charter rights of other colonies did not apply to New York—although "if it could support its claim to liberty in no other way, it might, with justice, plead the common principles of colonization: for, it would be unreasonable, to seclude one colony, from the enjoyment of the most important privileges of the rest." There was no need, however, for this plea, because Hamilton now proclaimed that the "sacred rights of mankind" were not to be found among old parchments or musty records, as we have seen above, but were written in human nature "by the hand of divinity itself."[15] Hamilton's reasoning shows that an element of prudence, not necessarily disingenuousness, prompted Americans to suit their arguments to their needs; these needs were different in 1774 and 1776, as they were different in New York and Virginia.[16]

Yet a more fundamental consideration invalidates the strict

separation of the "legal" and the "philosophical" levels of argument. This separation denies the interdependence of legal and philosophical thinking in the eighteenth century's understanding of the British Constitution. It transposes into the age of the American Revolution a positivistic, "Austinian" conception of law and sovereignty that developed only during the nineteenth century. The first Resolve of the Massachusetts House of Representatives of October 29, 1765, proclaimed "that there are certain essential rights of the *British* Constitution of Government, which are founded in the Law of God and Nature, and are the common Rights of Mankind."[17] This argument was by no means "invented" by the ingenious mind of Sam Adams to suit a particular need, even if it proved more and more frequently helpful and finally indispensable to the colonial cause. It embodies an ancient element of the British Constitution going back to the supremacy, in the Middle Ages, of a law that could be discerned and applied, but never be made, by men.[18] It was this element of the Constitution that was expressed in 1768 by the Massachusetts Circular Letter which insisted that the "essential, unalterable right, in nature"—viz. "what a man has honestly acquired is absolutely his own"—was "engrafted into the British Constitution, as a *fundamental law.*"[19]

In homage to this tradition, Blackstone wrote in his *Commentaries*, in a passage quoted by Hamilton, that the law of nature, "being co-eval with mankind and dictated by God himself, is of course superior in obligation to any other. It is binding over all the globe, in all countries, and at all times: No human laws are of any validity, if contrary to this; and such of them as are valid derive all their force, and all their authority, mediately or immediately, from this original."[20] Hamilton fully exploited Blackstone's statement. He contrasted it with the doctrines of the sinister "Mr. Hobbes" and charged his pamphleteering opponent Samuel Seabury with the heinous crime of Hobbesianism:

[Hobbes's] opinion was, exactly, coincident with yours, relative to man in a state of nature. He held, as you do, that he was, then, perfectly free from all restraint of *law* and *government.* Moral obligation, according to him, is derived from the introduction of civil society; and there is no virtue, but what is purely artificial, the mere contrivance of politicians, for the maintenance of social intercourse. But the reason he run into this absurd and impious doctrine, was, that he disbelieved the existence of an intelligent superintending principle, who is the governor, and will be the final judge of the universe.[21]

There is a good deal of irony in this contest between Blackstone and Hamilton, on the one hand, and Hobbes and Seabury on the other. After all, Blackstone was a firm adherent of the Hobbesian view of law as command rather than as pure right reason (though this oversimplifies both Blackstone's and Hobbes's concern for the principles of political obligation). Hamilton's polemic against Hobbes and Seabury did not prevent him from agreeing, in the very same pamphlet, to Seabury's Blackstonian idea that "in every government, there must be a supreme absolute authority lodged somewhere." Hamilton added: "This position when properly explained, is evidently just. In every civil society there must be a supreme power, to which all the members of that society are subject; for, otherwise, there could be no supremacy, or subordination, that is no government at all."[22]

Yet Hamilton avoided Seabury's conclusion, supremacy of the British Parliament over the colonies, by positing the supremacy of every single legislature within the Empire over its own territory, the king alone being the single common bond. For the present argument, Hamilton's affirmation of the principle of supremacy is more important than the twist he gave it in the debate on the true nature of the British Constitution. It is a Hobbesian view of government and laws, which Hamilton put most powerfully and succinctly in No. 33 of *The Federalist*: "A LAW by the very meaning of the term includes supremacy. It is a rule which those to whom it is prescribed are bound to observe. This results from every political association. If individuals enter into a state of society the laws of that society must be the supreme regulator of their conduct. . . . It would otherwise be a mere treaty, dependent on the good faith of the parties, and not a government; which is only another word for POLITICAL POWER AND SUPREMACY."[23] Striking is Hamilton's positive attitude to Blackstone's (quite Hobbesian) doctrine of the sovereignty of Parliament at the Federal Convention, notwithstanding the difficulties that doctrine had created for the colonists prior to 1776. Combating the "small state" views of Luther Martin of Maryland who demanded an equality of votes for small and big states alike, Hamilton used the example of the British Parliament that "asserted a supremacy over the whole empire, and the celebrated Judge Blackstone labors for the legality of it, although many parts were not represented. This parliamentary power we opposed as contrary to our colonial rights. With that exception, throughout that whole empire it is submitted to."[24]

This impressive evidence of Hamilton's Hobbesian view of law is further corroborated by his disdain for a formula enjoying a great reputation among adherents of free government and republicanism—the formula of "a government of laws, not of men" as the essence of good government. Hamilton did not care to conceal his low opinion of "the idea of governing at all times by the simple force of law (which we have been told is the only admissible principle of republican government)." It had "no place but in the reveries of those political doctors, whose sagacity disdains the admonitions of experimental instruction."[25]

Do we, then, have to discount Hamilton's appeal to the law of nature in his revolutionary pamphlets as an argument prepared for a particular occasion? Or were Hamilton and Blackstone positivists who employed the language of natural law improperly? The answer to this puzzle is neither a charge of disingenuousness nor a charge of muddled thinking. Rather, our understanding of the Founding Fathers' political thought is likely to remain defective if we continue to view it in terms of a simple distinction between "natural" and "positive" laws.

The Natural Right of Self-Preservation

This distinction mentioned above fails to recognize the three elements in what the founders of the nation called "the laws of nature and nature's God." First, there were principles of common law, like the right of trial by a jury of one's peers, that were sacred and "natural" by the very antiquity of their tradition. The merger of rights under common law and rights under natural law was consummated in the declarations of rights incorporated in several of the revolutionary state constitutions and in the Bill of Rights of the Federal Constitution.[26] Second, there were rules of moral conduct ordained by God and revealed in the Christian scriptures, or, in Coke's words, "written with the finger of God in the heart of man." The writers on natural law within the Christian tradition considered the laws of nature to emanate from God, to be susceptible of human recognition, since God had created man in His own Image, and to consist in those duties of moral conduct whose fulfillment led toward virtue and perfection.[27] Third, and most important for our consideration of American revolutionaries, were rules of behavior that defined the rights of men—without any necessary connection with those standards of perfection enjoined by classical or Christian political thought. Regardless of all their references to the God of Christianity, both Thomas Hobbes and, though less obviously, John Locke found the most fundamental law of nature in the desire for *mere* self-preservation.[28] From this they deduced the right of every man to pursue a course most conducive to the preservation of his own life. The proclamation of the desire for self-preservation as the basis of all reasoning on things social and political was responsible for the development of one of the most striking tenets of seventeenth- and eighteenth-century political philosophy: the doctrine of the radical selfishness of man. This doctrine was of paramount significance for the thought of Alexander Hamilton.

This radical selfishness was the source of Hobbes's and Locke's fundamental distinction between the state of nature and the state of society; it explained the necessity of the social contract.[29] The state of nature, in which everyone was held to be judge of his own cause, was actually or potentially a state of war. Hobbes admitted it openly, and even Locke's explicit denial does not stand up under a thorough analysis of his writings.[30] In the eighteenth century's speculations on the state of nature, Locke's denial does not seem to have been taken too seriously. David Hume, in his essays, which were closely read and cherished by Alexander Hamilton, regarded the political philosophers' state of nature as being "full of war, violence, and injustice."[31] Sam Adams, in America, wrote in 1771: "In the state of nature there was subordination: The weaker was *by force* made to bow down to the more powerful."[32] Even more striking is the description of the state and law of nature in the debates of the Massachusetts Ratifying Convention of 1788. Without a confederacy, a speaker observed, "the several states, being distinct sovereignties, would be in a state of nature, with respect to each other; and the law of nature, which is the right of the strongest, would determine the disputes that might arise."[33]

There seems to be every reason to adopt a less enthusiastic attitude toward laws and rights of nature than many students of the American Revolution have done. "A right implies a remedy," as Madison put the juristic axiom in *The Federalist*.[34] The exercise of the natural right to self-preservation, then, turns out to be a fairly grim expedient. It belongs to the realm of power politics, though of power politics pursued with a clear conscience. "No method to redress the infringements" of the law of nature existed, according to Blackstone, "but the actual exertion of private force."[35]

The foregoing considerations are confirmed if we listen to Alexander Hamilton in 1774: "Self-preservation is the first principle of our nature. When our lives and properties are at stake, it would be foolish and unnatural to refrain from such measures as might preserve them, because they would be detrimental to others."[36] Among the protective measures in Hamilton's mind was the breach of the navigation laws to enable the colonies to get goods from France and Holland. Since he had denounced "unlawful trade" previously, Hamilton felt compelled to justify his resort to it: "I despise the practice of avaricious smugglers, very heartily; but when a whole people are invaded, there can be no law of any force, against their procuring every needful succours."[37] He held to this principle long after the occasion for its first enunciation had passed. Thirteen years later, concerned with stability and "good government," Hamilton declared with no less conviction than before, "If the representatives of the people betray their constituents, there is then no resource left but in the exertion of that original right of self-defence which is paramount to all positive forms of government."[38]

In conformity with the generally accepted principles of his time, Hamilton held that "self-interest" was "the most powerful incentive of human actions." He saw it operating in the conflict between the colonies and England—to the detriment of the colonies, since the House of Commons saw oppression of the colonies as a means of alleviating the burdens of Englishmen at home.[39]

Owing to America's Christian heritage, self-interest has not received public approbation. The rights of man, on the other hand, have received the fervent salute of American idealism. Yet the natural right to self-preservation joins a "realistic" self-interest and an "idealistic" adherence to the rights of man. The principle of a natural equality of rights was built upon every person's interest in his self-preservation. Thus Hamilton argued that no one in Great Britain had a "right to the life, property, or liberty of a freeholder, citizen, or any other man in America . . . because nature has distributed an equality of rights to every man."[40] Hamilton echoes here Blackstone's doctrine that the cessation of legitimate government "reduces all the members to their original state of equality."[41] Hamilton considered it the purpose of representation in the British House of Commons "to preserve the life, property, and liberty of the subject, from the encroachments of oppression and tyranny." He reasoned that this purpose was accomplished because of "the *intimate connexion* of interest, between those members and their constituents, the people of Great-Britain." With respect to the people of America, however, he saw no such intimate connection of interest, but the contrary.[42] Thus he came to the conclusion given above that human laws which contradicted or discountenanced the means "necessary to preserve the essential rights of any society" were null and void.

The seeming contradiction between Blackstone's and Hamilton's simultaneous adherence to a Hobbesian view of law and to the doctrine of natural rights disappears in the light of a rather sober conception of the fundamental right of self-preservation. The resort to first principles was a resort to extrajudicial, extralegal acts against the established authority, with the support of a clear conscience. Hamilton's frequent reliance on Blackstone (with the possible exception of Hume, quoted more than any other writer) makes it legitimate to establish in this context the consistent logic of Blackstone's principles, allegedly so contradictory.[43] We have mentioned above Blackstone's admission that "extraordinary recourses to first principles" were necessary if the social contract were "in danger of dissolution."[44] But he opposed Locke's assertion that the people had the inherent power to "remove or alter the legislative, when they find the legislative act contrary to the trust reposed in them."[45] Blackstone added:

But however just this conclusion may be in theory, we cannot adopt it, nor argue from it, under any dispensation of government at present actually existing. For this devolution of power, to the people at large, includes in it a dissolution of the whole form of government established by that people; reduces all the members to their original state of equality; and, by annihilating the sovereign power, repeals all positive law whatsoever before enacted. No human laws will therefore suppose a case, which at once must destroy all law, and compel men to build afresh upon a new foundation; nor will they make provision for so desparate an event, as must render all legal provisions ineffectual.[46]

Blackstone explicitly referred his readers from this to a subsequent passage which concludes his argument:

The supposition of *law* therefore is, that neither the king nor either house of parliament (collectively taken) is capable of doing any wrong; since in such cases the law feels itself incapable of furnishing any adequate remedy. For which reason all oppressions, which may happen to spring from any branch of the sovereign power, must necessarily be out of the reach of any *stated rule*, or *express legal* provision: but, if ever they unfortunately happen, the prudence of the times must provide new remedies upon new emergencies.[47]

The predicament of the American Revolution has found no more forthright description, none more helpful to and in conformity with the "prudence" of the colonists, and none more completely disregarded by posterity, than William Blackstone's anticipation of "new emergencies."

Hamilton's spirited defense of the colonies in *The Farmer Refuted* shows his debt to Blackstone's reasoning: "When the first principles of civil society are violated, and the rights of a whole people are invaded, the common forms of municipal law are not to be regarded. Men may then betake themselves to the law of nature; and, if they but conform their actions, to that standard, all cavils against them, betray either ignorance or dishonesty. There are some events in society, to which human laws cannot extend; but when applied to them lose all their force and efficacy."[48]

Thus the seeming contradiction between the Hobbesian and Blackstonian concept of law and sovereignty on the one hand and the doctrine of the rights of man on the other—so disturbing and even scandalous to students of political theory—disappears.[49] In other words, Blackstone's (and Hobbes's) theory of sovereignty strictly distinguishes between absolute and arbitrary power. Sovereign power is by definition absolute.[50] Yet since sovereign power is also by definition legitimate power, the use of power in arbitrary or illegitimate ways divests it of the quality of sovereignty. One of the biggest obstacles to our understanding of the political theory of the American Revolution has been the tendency to confuse absolute with arbitrary power (a tendency which, incidentally, was encouraged by the rhetorical blasts of *Common Sense* against the arch-villain of the last stage of the Revolution, George III).

The foregoing analysis points the way to a second conclusion: resort to the first principles of natural rights holds a genuine place in the development of the American Revolution. Both the conservative, constitution-minded interpreters of the Revolution and the historians who represent the appeal to natural rights in the Declaration of Independence as a propaganda device do injustice to the most important function of first principles. It has been said that the Declaration of Independence implied a shift "to another audience and with another appeal."[51] America did appeal to continental Europe; yet it is misleading to regard the Declaration of Independence as "an attempt to rephrase English rights in such a way that they would appeal to contemporary European intellectuals."[52] The American leaders certainly knew that they would have to deal with the ministers of an absolute monarch, not with *philosophes*. The chief use of the recourse to first principles concerned the Americans themselves. To judge one's own cause is not easy. Yet this is the meaning of the appeal to natural rights, since, according to Locke, outside the civil state everyone has the right to be "executioner of the Law of Nature."[53] It seems indeed likely that the American leaders, embarking upon an act of the utmost gravity, wanted to proceed upon principles firmly held, and used the argument from natural rights to persuade their countrymen as much as public opinion abroad.

The example of Alexander Hamilton demonstrates the vast difference between the radicalism of an ultimate resort to first principles and social radicalism, i.e. the leveling and more truly democratic spirit apparent in certain stages of the American Revolution considered as a social movement. The social conservatism of both Blackstone and Hamilton should place their "recourse to first principles" in its proper light. With regard to Hamilton, it would be a grave mistake indeed to see in the revolutionary writings of 1774 and 1775 a youthful, reckless enthusiasm, that was later supplanted by exhortations about "good government" and "social order." Hamilton was as much an advocate of social order in 1775 as in 1787 or 1800. An episode of mob violence in the fall of 1775—the attack on James Rivington's printing press in New York—provoked the earliest expression of Hamilton's social conservatism. As he complained to John Jay:

Though I am fully sensible how dangerous and pernicious Rivington's press has been, and how detestable the character of the man is in every respect, yet I cannot help disapproving and condemning this step.

In times of such commotion as the present, while the passions of

men are worked up to an uncommon pitch there is great danger of
fatal extremes. The same state of the passions which fits the multitude,
who have not a sufficient stock of reason and knowledge to guide them,
for opposition to tyranny and oppression, very naturally leads them to
a contempt and disregard of all authority. . . . In such tempestuous
times, it requires the greatest skill in the political pilots to keep men
steady and within proper bounds, on which account I am always more
or less alarmed at every thing which is done of mere will and pleasure,
without any proper authority.[54]

Hamilton's clear distinction between legitimate revolution and
arbitrary violence testifies to the socially conservative bent of his
mind; it foreshadows his scorn for the multitude and for demagogues who would use it.

Hamilton's Image of the Social Contract: Blackstone Contra Locke

"Recourse to first principles" resembles a familiar idea: the
dissolution of the social contract. Alexander Hamilton shared the
belief of most of his contemporaries in the social contract as the
source of political obligation. There were a few writers, like
James Otis, James Winthrop, and Fisher Ames who disputed
the historical probability of an actual contract and therefore rejected the concept wholesale.[55] But Hamilton was not bothered
by the doubtful historical accuracy of that hypothesis, and in this
instance he leaned toward Blackstone rather than toward his other
great master, David Hume. Before Rousseau and Kant, with
whom the formal, non-historical theory of the social contract is
usually associated,[56] Blackstone's common sense had admirably
clarified the situation:

Not that we can believe, with some theoretical writers, that there ever
was a time when there was no such thing as society; and that, from the
impulse of reason, and through a sense of their wants and weaknesses,
individuals met together in a large plain, entered into an original contract, and chose the tallest man present to be their governor. This
notion of an actually existing unconnected state of nature, is too wild
to be seriously admitted. . . . But though society had not it's formal

beginning from any convention of individuals, actuated by their wants and their fears; yet it is the *sense* of their weakness and imperfection that *keeps* mankind together . . . and this is what we mean by the original contract of society.[57]

Blackstone's argument, it becomes readily apparent, reduces to a minimum the differences between the contractual and utilitarian schools of liberalism. In substance, Blackstone is not so far removed from Hume, the first great critic of the social contract on both historical and philosophical grounds. Hume argued that "the general obligation which binds us to government is the interest and necessities of society."[58]

Hume's utilitarian foundation of the principles of political obligation was echoed in Hamilton's observation that "utility is the prime end of all laws."[59] There was no need, however, to sacrifice the image of the social contract to utilitarian considerations, as Blackstone's example proved; besides, the contest between the colonies and Great Britain made that traditional image more useful than ever.

Hamilton's use of the social contract as the source of political obligation shows an ambiguity that he shared with many contemporaries, including Blackstone. It was the lack of distinction between the *pactum societatis* and the *pactum subiectionis*, that is, between the contract that welded individuals into one society and the contract that exchanged the ruler's protection for the obedience of the ruled.[60] John Locke knew only the first; the setting up of government in Locke's theory involved a subtle transaction analogous to the establishment of a trust, involving trustor, trustee, and beneficiary.[61] Blackstone's explanation of the social contract also corresponds, on the most fundamental level, to the first concept—of individuals joining together to form a society—and Hamilton too on occasion talked of the social contract in these terms.[62] Yet, when evoking the significant precedent of the Glorious Revolution, Blackstone spoke of the original contract between king and people, broken by the former; he merely echoed the formula of the Convention Parliament of 1689. The American Declaration of Independence, too, denounced a contract between ruler and ruled; the fact that it was issued jointly by the United States in Congress Assembled—i.e. by an organized society—prevents us from seeing in that act a dissolution of Locke's kind of social contract.

Hamilton argued in terms of a contract between the ruled and the ruler even before actual independence. In 1775, Hamilton declared that "the origin of all civil government, justly established, must be a voluntary compact, between the rulers and the ruled; and must be liable to such limitations, as are necessary for the security of the *absolute rights* of the latter."[63] He bolstered his argument with a quotation from Blackstone: "the first and primary end of human laws, is to maintain and regulate these *absolute rights* of individuals."[64] Hamilton then stated that the king of Great Britain was "King of America, by virtue of a compact between us and the Kings of Great-Britain."[65] Here it is the *pactum subiectionis* rather than the *pactum societatis* with which Hamilton was concerned. Apart from Blackstone's influence, Hamilton reveals on this occasion his legal training in pre-Lockean English constitutional thought, which was still steeped in medieval conceptions of law and authority. He quoted from Sir Edward Coke's opinion in *Calvin's Case* (1608): "Legiance is the mutual bond and obligation between the King and his subjects, whereby subjects are called his liege subjects, because they are bound to obey and serve him; and he is called their liege lord, because he is bound to maintain and defend them."[66]

Hamilton's un-Lockean interpretation of the social contract was influenced by the peculiar predicament of the final stage of the British-American contest before independence, from 1774 to 1776. It was that period in which Hamilton began his career as political writer. It was the period when leading colonial advocates like John Adams, Thomas Jefferson, James Wilson, and Alexander Hamilton himself espoused a dominion theory of the British Empire.[67] While they now denied the supremacy of the British Parliament in which they were not represented, they continued to see in the king of England their sovereign ruler. Hamilton's interest in a medieval conception of the social contract now appears in its proper context: "The law of nature and the British constitution both confine allegiance to the person of the King; and found it upon the principle of protection. . . . Hence it is evident, that while we enjoy the protection of the King, it is incumbent upon us to obey and serve him, without the interposition of parliamentary supremacy."[68] Difficulties arose, of course, with respect to the sovereignty of Parliament, supposedly securely anchored in Blackstone's *Commentaries*. Yet Hamilton circumvented that obstacle very cleverly indeed:

Those, who aver, that the independency of America on the British Parliament implies two Sovereign authorities in the same state, deceive themselves or wish to deceive others in two ways; by confounding the idea of the same state with that of the same individual society, and by losing sight of that share which the King has in the sovereignty, both of Great-Britain and America. Perhaps, indeed, it may with propriety be said, that the King is the only Sovereign of the empire. The part which the people have in the legislature, may more justly be considered as a limitation of the Sovereign authority, to prevent its being exercised in an oppressive and despotic manner: Monarchy is universally allowed to predominate in the constitution.[69]

Even for this daring attack on the doctrine of Parliamentary sovereignty Hamilton found some support in Blackstone; the king's "sovereign prerogative" was of vast importance in his system, surpassing the domain of a mere "executive." One might wonder whether Blackstone was not inconsistent, sometimes placing sovereignty in Parliament, and when discussing the royal prerogative placing it in the king alone.[70] But we may safely absolve him of such a contradiction. When he wrote with regard to the treaty-making power that "in England the sovereign power, *quo ad hoc* [for that purpose], is vested in the person of the king," he displayed a subtler understanding of sovereignty than he has been given credit for—namely, the understanding that sovereignty may inhere for different purposes in differently constituted bodies.[71] Insofar as Hamilton identified the king as the sovereign, it was logical for him to regard the social contract as an agreement between the king and the people. Apart from

Coke, that pre-Lockean formulation was, of course, advocated by Blackstone, who repeatedly referred in the *Commentaries* to "that original contract, which in all states impliedly, and in ours most expressly, subsists between the prince and the subject."[72] It was that contract which James II had broken. And it was that contract which George III had broken with all the measures catalogued in the Declaration of Independence. Precisely because the king was the last constitutional link with the empire recognized by the colonists, George III was bound to become the final scapegoat (which he has remained in American folklore ever since Tom Paine poured his invective on the "Royal Brute of Great Britain").

Hamilton's understanding of the social contract as an agreement between ruler and ruled emerges also from his retrospective interpretation of what exactly happened in July 1776. In the Federal Convention, Hamilton denied "the doctrine that the States were thrown into a State of nature" at the time of the Declaration of Independence, thus concurring with his two predecessors in debate, Rufus King and James Wilson, who also had claimed the character of a sovereign nation for the union of the colonies as of the time of Independence.[73] In the same year, in a speech in the New York State legislature, Hamilton read the final paragraph of the Declaration of Independence and commented: "Hence we see that the union and independence of these states are blended and incorporated in one and the same act; which, taken together clearly, imports, that the United States had in their origin full power to do all acts and things which independent states may of right do; or, in other words, full power of sovereignty."[74] Hamilton's theory of national sovereignty independent of the Constitution of 1787 first entered judicial doctrine in 1795 and was finally adopted by a majority of the Supreme Court in 1936.[75] A doctrine of national sovereignty that was born from the exigencies of foreign policy and derived from the law of nations rather than constitutional law was bound to raise most awkward questions with respect to the status of the states both before and after the adoption of the Federal Constitution. Not surprisingly, Hamilton did not care to repeat his argument in *The Federalist*.[76]

Hamilton's concept of sovereignty did not change in later years. In a polemic against the faction led by Governor George Clinton of New York in 1789, Hamilton inveighed against Clinton's alleged purpose of fostering "the spirit of opposition in the people" against the Federal Constitution until desired amendments or even a new convention might be obtained. Hamilton pointed out that "the United States are to determine on the propriety of amendments, and on the expediency of a convention. Both must be referred to their judgment. If they think both improper, or unnecessary, it is the duty of a particular member to acquiesce. This is the fundamental principle of the social compact."[77] The "United States" in the sense of this polemic was the ruler, whose sovereignty consisted in the exclusive possession of the amending power. If "sovereignty is a legal competence to change the rules of a system of law,"[78] then the essence of sovereignty rests jointly in all those whose concurrence is required to amend the constitution.

The same usage appears in Hamilton's report on "Spirits, Foreign and Domestic" of 1792. His argument for an excise on domestic spirits was based on the expectation that the growth of domestic production would reduce the quantity of duties derived from the imports of such articles. "If the Government cannot then resort to internal means for the additional supplies which the exigencies of every nation call for, it will be unable to perform its duty, or, even to preserve its existence. The community must be unprotected, and the social compact be dissolved."[79] The levying of the excise produced the Whisky Rebellion in Pennsylvania, which Hamilton was determined to crush by force. On that occasion again, the social contract was seen from the point of view of the ruler: "You have already seen that the merits of excise laws are immaterial to the question to be decided, that you have prejudged the point by a solemn constitutional act, and that until you shall have revoked or modified that act, resistance to its operation is a criminal infraction of the social compact."[80]

Hamilton's debt to the teachings of Hobbes, Blackstone and Hume has become apparent and should caution us against viewing Hamilton as an American Burke.[81] Hamilton never formulated anything akin to Burke's famous concept of the social contract as the partnership of past, present, and future generations. For Hamilton, the social contract remained that convenient image of the grounds of political obligation (and disobedience) that he shared with the other leaders of the revolutionary generation.

Beyond Legality: "Resort to First Principles" After the Revolution

Hamilton and his contemporaries possessed then an excellent awareness of the vital distinction between legitimacy and legality. This awareness was not limited to the revolutionary period; in Hamilton's case the distinction retained its impact on his political thought right to the end of his career. There might be infringements upon the constitutional and legal order from below, like the mob violence so distasteful to Hamilton; there also might be infringements much more difficult to handle with the ordinary remedies of government, i.e., those from above, on the part of the rulers, violating the purpose of government and its original structure embodying that purpose. Both, according to Hamilton, should be prevented, or at any rate remedied, by resorting to first principles. In a historical or empirical sense, we may define resort to first principles as reestablishing, if need be by extralegal but "legitimate" means, the conditions of rule originally designed to guarantee the purpose of government.

The actual experience of resorting to first principles on the grand scale in the American Revolution was bound to reveal the ultimate precariousness of the stablest political order. This perception is mirrored in Hamilton's thoughtful and lucid commentary in *The Federalist*: "And as to those mortal feuds, which in certain conjunctures spread a conflagration through a whole nation, or through a very large proportion of it, proceeding either from weighty causes of discontent given by the government, or from the contagion of some violent popular paroxism, they do not fall within any ordinary rules of calculation. When they happen, they commonly amount to revolutions and dismemberments of empire."[82] This grim picture assures us of Hamilton's loathing of a frequent resort to first principles, an idea not unknown to some of the revolutionists. There is every indication that Hamilton felt strongly about the "sacred reverence which ought to be maintained in the breast of rulers toward the constitution of a country."[83] Yet in a Cabinet paper addressed to President Washington in 1790, Hamilton admitted that a resort to first principles could be justified by "some urgent public necessity, some impending national Calamity, something that threatens direct and general mischief to the Society, for which there is no adequate redress in the established course of things . . ." Hamilton's statement was occasioned by a rather complicated legal matter concerning payments of arrears of pay to officers and soldiers, putting assignees of such debts at a disadvantage by the provisions of a joint congressional resolution. Hamilton advised Washington against endorsing it, since it was an "overleaping of the ordinary and regular bounds of Legislative discretion; and is in the nature of a resort to first principles."[84]

Two years later, Hamilton again advised against "resort to first principles." This time New York state politics and the fate of the Federalist party were involved. The Federalists had lost an election, apparently through the machinations of the Board of Canvassers of New York, controlled by Governor Clinton's faction. Hamilton wrote to Rufus King who had consulted him in this matter: "It is not for the friends of good government to employ extraordinary expedients, which ought only to be resorted to in cases of great magnitude and urgent necessity." He rejected the idea of a convention as well as any use of force.[85]

After another two years, Hamilton found again the opportunity to stress that "a state of revolution and subversion of the established Government is inadmissible, except in those great cases, which justify a nation in resuming its delegated powers and changing its civil constitution."[86] The masterful *Camillus* letters, written in 1796, reveal further the constancy of Hamilton's principles. "The cases must be very extraordinary that can ... be of a kind to authorize a revolution in government; for every resort to original principles, in derogation from the established Constitution, partakes of this character."[87] The time was to come, though, when Hamilton felt that such an extraordinary situation existed. His stature as a conservative leader throws into striking relief his abiding belief in the right of revolution.

In the spring of 1800, election returns from New York City and some other places resulted in the virtual certainty of an anti-Federalist or Jeffersonian majority in the state legislature. At that time, the presidential electors of the State of New York were chosen by the two houses of the legislature. In the national context, it very likely assured Jefferson's ascendancy to the Presidency of the United States, which it seemed to Hamilton would undo his own lifework—the creation of a united political fabric, the establishment of the United States as a nation. As he had put it in the last number of *The Federalist*, "a NATION without a NATIONAL GOVERNMENT is, in my view, an awful spectacle."[88] It was this threat that stirred up the idea of resorting to first principles. The letter Hamilton wrote to Governor John Jay of New York is one of the most remarkable documents of his political correspondence. The "very high probability" that the composition of the new state legislature would bring "Jefferson into the chief magistracy" suggested to Hamilton "the immediate calling together of the existing Legislature." "I am aware," Hamilton told Jay, "that there are weighty objections to the measure, but the reasons for it appear to me to outweigh the objections; and in times like these in which we live, it will not do to be over-scrupulous. It is easy to sacrifice the substantial interests of society by a strict adherence to ordinary rules." He wanted the existing pro-Federalist legislature to meet in special session to provide for the election of new presidential electors by the people in districts; this legally doubtful exercise in "electoral mathematics" might ensure Federalist electors. Hamilton felt that this would not be anything that integrity should forbid, and that "the scruples of delicacy and propriety, as relative to a common course of things, ought to yield to the extraordinary nature of the crisis. They ought not to hinder the taking of a *legal* and *constitutional* step to prevent an atheist in religion, and a fanatic in politics, from getting possession of the helm of state." That there was no more than a semblance of legality about the step Hamilton was candid enough to admit when he distinguished between "delicacy and propriety" on the one hand and "integrity" on the other. It is permissible to recognize in Hamilton's distinction an analogy to the differentiation of legality and legitimacy. Hamilton argued that "as to its intrinsic nature," the plan was "justified by the unequivocal reasons of PUBLIC SAFETY." "The reasonable part of the world will, I believe, approve it. They will see it as a proceeding out of the common course, but warranted by the particular nature of the crisis and the great cause of social order." "In weighing this suggestion," Hamilton exhorted Jay, "you will doubtless bear in mind that popular governments must certainly be overturned, and, while they endure, prove engines of mischief, if one party will call to its aid all the resources which vice can give, and if the other (however pressing the emergency) confines itself within all the ordinary forms of delicacy and decorum."[89]

Hamilton's father-in-law, Philip Schuyler, a prominent conservative, urged Jay to accept Hamilton's proposal. Somewhat surprisingly, there is a hint in Schuyler's letter that John Marshall may have been agreeable to this suggestion.[90] Governor Jay rejected Hamilton's proposal by noting that it was made for "party purposes, which I think it would not become me to adopt." He did not even bother to reply.

Posterity has followed Jay's judgment,[91] and has failed to place Hamilton's attitude within the larger frame of his thought. Hamilton knew there were occasions when the statesman's sense of responsibility might force him to act against the letter of the law. With hindsight we may pronounce a statesman's resort to first principles in any particular case right or wrong. Hamilton's plan of 1800 has been judged wrong. Jefferson's knowing disregard of the Constitution in the Louisiana Purchase has been considered right. It is interesting to note that Jefferson's self-justification for

his breach of the letter of the law is based on Hamilton's principles: "A strict observance of the written law is doubtless *one* of
the high duties of a good citizen, but it is not *the highest*. The
laws of necessity, of self-preservation, of saving our country when
in danger, are of higher obligation. To lose our country by a
scrupulous adherence to written law, would be to lose the law
itself, with life, liberty, property and all those who are enjoying
them with us; thus absurdly sacrificing the end to the means."[92]

A Machiavellian Tradition and Revolutionary
Political Thought

There is one difference between Hamilton's and Jefferson's
thought that impels us to search for a yet more precise and full
understanding of "resort to first principles." Jefferson was actually much more in favor of frequently resorting to first principles.
Jefferson's complacent reaction to Shays's Rebellion no less than
to the bloodshed of the French Revolution has been regarded
as one of the more puzzling and less admirable features of his
complex makeup. "Tumults" or "irregular interpositions of the
people," he wrote, would keep the governors of society "to the
true principles of their institution."[93] The "turbulence" to be
found in republics prevented "the degeneracy of government."
"A little rebellion" now and then was a good thing, "as necessary
in the political world as storms in the physical." Such rebellions
were "a medicine necessary for the sound health of government."[94]

If we look for the sources of Jefferson's ideas, we are first led
to a well-known formula. Article XV of the Virginia Declaration
of Rights states that "no free government, or the blessing of
liberty, can be preserved to any people but by a firm adherence to
justice, moderation, temperance, frugality, and virtue, and by
frequent recurrence to fundamental principles." This article was
substantially received into a number of other states' bills of
rights.[95] Its author was George Mason; a further clue to the
origin and meaning of "recurrence to fundamental principles" is
furnished in an earlier paper of Mason's in which he remarked
that "it has been wisely observed by the deepest politician who

ever put pen to paper, that no institution can be long preserved, but by frequent recurrence to those maxims on which it was formed."[96]

It is likely that George Mason's "deepest politician" was Machiavelli. Some of the political writers most popular in revolutionary America all pointed to Machiavelli. James Burgh, for example, wrote in his *Political Disquisitions*: "*Machiavel* says, that to render a commonwealth long lived, it is necessary to correct it often, and reduce it towards its first principles, which is to be done by punishments and examples."[97] Perhaps more likely to have influenced Mason was an older classic of colonial political readings, *Cato's Letters* by Thomas Gordon and John Trenchard.[98] It states: "*Machiavel* tells us, that no Government can long subsist, but by recurring often to its first Principles." *Cato* went on to tell his readers what the "great Authority just quoted" proposed for the circumstances that made a state's being reduced to first principles appropriate.[99] Finally, an earlier and more famous author than either Burgh or Gordon and Trenchard, Algernon Sidney, who had died the martyr's death for the cause of liberty, had dealt with this question in detail: "All human constitutions are subject to corruption, and must perish, unless they are timely renewed, and reduced to their first principles." "There must therefore be a right of proceeding judicially or extrajudicially against all persons who transgress the laws," he said, "or else those laws, and the societies that should subsist by them, cannot stand; and the ends for which governments are constituted, together with the governments themselves, must be overthrown. Extrajudicial proceedings, by sedition, tumult, or war, must take place, when the persons concerned are of such power, that they cannot be brought under the judicial." All governments "that deserve to be examples to us, did arise from the consent of the respective nations, and were frequently reduced to their first principles, when the princes endeavoured to transgress the laws of their institution."[100] Sidney told his readers that Machiavelli had proposed "reducing every state, once in an age or two, to the integrity of its first principle."[101]

The era of the American Revolution and the framing of the

Constitution witnessed the last glowing of the Renaissance tradition of political philosophy that regarded decay and corruption as the basic rule of historical change. Before the idea of social perfectibility started its Icarian flight of a century and a half, the deepest concern of political thinkers was the purging of those poisons which forever crept into the body politic to threaten corruption and disintegration. Thus we find the sober Blackstone speculating on the form of government that would be best "if the individuals who compose that state could always continue true to first principles, uninfluenced by passion or prejudice, unassailed by corruption, and unawed by violence."[102] This preoccupation with the recovery of first principles must ultimately be traced back to Machiavelli.[103] The first chapter of the third book of Machiavelli's *Discourses* was entitled: "To insure a long existence to religious sects or republics, it is necessary frequently to bring them back to their original principles." Said Machiavelli: "And those are the best-constituted bodies, and have the longest existence, which possess the intrinsic means of frequently renewing themselves, or such as obtain this renovation in consequence of some extrinsic accidents. . . . Thus, the doctors of medicine say, in speaking of the human body, that 'every day some ill humors gather which must be cured.' "[104] Apart from great external crises that might cause a salutary recurrence to first principles, internal devices were available: "they are either the result of a law, that obliges the citizens of the association often to render an account of their conduct; or some man of superior character arises amongst them, whose noble example and virtuous actions will produce the same effect as such a law."[105] Algernon Sidney regarded both frequent elections *and* popular tumults as remedies against the insolence of office and the corruptions of power.[106]

We are here at the source of two ideas of paramount significance for the intellectual outlook of the Founding Fathers. First the ideas of "rotation in office," of frequent elections, of short Parliaments, which dominated English political debate in the eighteenth century, entered the Federal Constitution as well as the state constitutions; and, in America, further devices for constitutional revision were developed, such as the amending process, or the institutionalized convention, so that "the people might recurr to first principles in a Regular Way, without hazarding a Revolution in the Government."[107] Second, the expectation of extralegal resort to first principles, or, legitimate resort to force, was regarded by both Hamilton and Jefferson with more equanimity than we are generally willing to admit or to suspect, though it is true that Hamilton's soberer political imagination saved him from the excesses of Jefferson's somewhat bookish admiration for "little rebellions."

The recognition of first principles beyond sovereign power—in fact, of principles that can alone confer a "sovereign" or public character upon any wielder of physical power—now leads us to a closer examination of different forms of government. The Founders, even Hamilton with his paramount interest in administration, were forced to wrestle with problems of nation building that involved more than appeal to legal precedent or to the simple image of the social contract as the source of political obligation. Establishing a new form of government required reasoning on the proper direction and distribution of public power, proper, that is, in relation to certain presuppositions, like human nature in a given environment, as well as in relation to certain ends, like the blending of liberty with stability, and perhaps even with greatness. To this quest for the right form of government as it was perceived by Alexander Hamilton the following chapters are devoted.

THE MEANING OF
REPUBLICAN GOVERNMENT
POPULAR SOVEREIGNTY, FREEDOM, AND VIRTUE

Republican Government—A Transitory Stage?

The Constitution of the United States guarantees to every state "a republican form of government."[1] Few provisions of the Constitution, through all the vicissitudes of American history, have been more fully taken for granted, few have been less subject to challenge or interpretation. And yet, this guarantee was a commitment of historic significance, especially in the light of the gloomy predictions on the subject of republican government made by many of the Founding Fathers. In the Federal Convention of 1787, Hugh Williamson of North Carolina said that "it was pretty certain . . . that we should at some time or other have a King; but he wished no precaution to be omitted that might postpone the event as long as possible."[2] Benjamin Franklin, justly considered one of the most democratic of the Founders, agreed. He felt that "there is a natural inclination in mankind to Kingly Government." He was "apprehensive," he said, "that the Government of these States may in future times end in a Monarchy. But this Catastrophe," he hoped, might yet be "long delayed."[3] John Adams predicted in his famous *Defence of the Constitutions of Government of the United States of America* that the growth of wealth and the ascendancy of America to greatness, power, and luxury would influence Americans to adjust their governments "to a nearer resemblence of the British constitution," including a hereditary king and a hereditary senate.[4] The more democratic James Madison was less content with this trend, but his expectations were akin to Adams's. In fact, Madison at one time thought that the United States would reach a population density similar to that of Great Britain and France about the 1930's, and that this would necessitate a new constitution.[5] George Washington, just before assuming the chairmanship of the convention that framed a guarantee of republican government, spoke of that form in less than flattering terms. "I am fully of opinion that those, who lean to a monarchical government, have either not consulted the public mind, or that they live in a region, which (the levelling principles in which they were bred being entirely eradicated) is much more productive of monarchical ideas, than are to be found in the southern States. . . . I am also clear, that, even *admitting the utility; nay, necessity*" of monarchy, "yet that the period is not arrived for adopting the change without shaking the peace of this country to its foundation."[6]

And Alexander Hamilton? There remains little doubt about his attitude. In his outline to what was probably the greatest speech of his political career, his plan of government for America presented to the Federal Convention on June 18, 1787, he put it baldly: "It is said a republican government does not admit a vigorous execution. It is therefore bad; for the goodness of a government consists in a vigorous execution."[7]

Fifteen years later, after the end of his public career, despair had indeed caught up with Hamilton. His was "an odd destiny," he told his friend Gouverneur Morris. "Perhaps no man in the United States has sacrificed or done more for the present Constitution than myself; and contrary to all my anticipations of its fate, as you know from the very beginning, I am still laboring to prop the frail and worthless fabric." Every day proved more and more that "this American world" was not made for him. What better could he do "than withdraw from the scene"?[8] When he wrote these bitter words, Hamilton had little more than two years to live. In truth, he had not quite withdrawn from the scene; he continued to advise, to counsel, to push, and to plead. On the day before he met Aaron Burr in his mortal duel, Hamilton put down in a letter what amounted to a political testament.

In it was a fervent wish for the preservation of the Union, but the reasons were somewhat unorthodox: "Dismemberment of our empire will be a clear sacrifice of great positive advantages without any counterbalancing good, administering no relief to our real disease, which is *democracy*, the poison of which, by a subdivision, will only be the more concentrated in each part, and consequently the more virulent."[9]

What was at the basis of Hamilton's skepticism, of what posterity can only call an unrealistic assessment of America's future? What were the assumptions from which Hamilton's dread of republican government arose? In this chapter I will examine two questions. First, how did the concept of republican government emerge in the revolutionary period, and what was Hamilton's stand? Second, what were the crucial assumptions of republican government, and how did Hamilton react to them? To sketch Hamilton's attitude toward these isues is essential for any attempt to understand how he tried to shape the character of the new nation according to his ambitions and convictions.

"Free" vs. "Arbitrary" Government

Whether the monarchical or the republican form of government was superior, a question that caused the Founding Fathers so much anxious soul-searching, was a question of little significance prior to 1776, when the decision for independence ushered in an era of constitution-building. Before the Declaration of Independence of the United States of America in Congress Assembled—and not, the point is worth making, of the United Republics of America—the simplest distinction in the vocabulary of political discussion was between free and arbitrary government. The limpid language of David Hume, much admired by Hamilton, summed up to perfection the idea of a free government: "The government which, in common appellation, receives the appellation of 'free' is that which admits of a partition of power among several members whose united authority is no less, or is commonly greater, than that of any monarch, but who, in the usual course of administration, must act by general and equal laws that are previously known to all the members and all their subjects."[10] This description beautifully fitted the notion that Englishmen on both sides of the Atlantic Ocean had of their "mixed," "balanced," "limited," or "free" constitution. There is no reason to question the genuineness of Hamilton's sentiments when he assured readers of his second revolutionary pamphlet in February 1775 that he was "a warm advocate for limitted monarchy, and an unfeigned well-wisher to the present Royal Family."[11]

Hamilton's declaration of loyalty sets us on the strange detour that led Americans to identify free with republican, and arbitrary with monarchical government. The disturbing fact that, contrary to all traditional notions about the seat of liberty, Parliament rather than the king was the source of "arbitrary" measures, produced a peculiar outburst of "monarchism" in America. As we have noted, in the last stage of colonial political thought, the only hope of imperial unity was the king, who might rule the different parts of the empire with the help of a plurality of coordinated representative bodies. This phase of colonial thinking, from 1774 to 1775 (though some Americans including Benjamin Franklin conceived the idea in the late 1760's) is represented by John Adams's *Novanglus*, by James Wilson's *Considerations on the Authority of Parliament*, by Thomas Jefferson's *Summary View of the Rights of British North America*. This distinguished group was joined in New York by young Alexander Hamilton. Hamilton's two pamphlets *A Full Vindication of the Measures of Congress* and *The Farmer Refuted* showed that at this stage of the colonial argument, the quest for free government was more remote than ever from the quest for republican government. Hamilton, in fact, indignantly rejected an imputation that he favored republican government. What motives could men have, he cried, to suspect that "the commotions in America originate in a plan, formed by some turbulent men to erect it into a republican government?"[12] The king, he predicted, would be "the great connecting principle."[13]

The traditional distinction between free and arbitrary governments was at the core of Hamilton's reasoning. In his first pamphlet, he put it simply as follows: "The only distinction between freedom and slavery consists in this: In the former state, a man is governed by the laws to which he has given his consent, either in person, or by his representative: In the latter, he is governed by the will of another. In the one case his life and property are his own, in the other, they depend upon the pleasure of his master."[14] In his second pamphlet, the argument is more specific and original. Hamilton told his opponent Samuel Seabury:

You are mistaken when you confine arbitrary government to a monarchy. It is not the supreme power being placed in one, instead of many, that discriminates an arbitrary from a free government. When any people are ruled by laws, in framing which, they have no part, that are to bind them . . . without, in the same manner, binding the legislators themselves, they are in the strictest sense slaves, and the government with respect to them, is despotic. Great Britain is itself a free country; but it is only so because its inhabitants have a share in the legislature.[15]

At this point of the argument, Hamilton called in "Mr. Hume," who happily could provide historical observations most pertinent to the perplexing predicament of the colonies. Hamilton asserted that the authority of the British Parliament over America would probably "be a more intolerable and excessive species of despotism than an absolute monarchy." Impressed with Hume's political maxims ("which will be eternally true"), Hamilton cited his remark that free governments, while being most happy for those who partook of their freedom, were yet most ruinous and oppressive to their provinces; and that a free state necessarily sharply distinguished between itself and its provinces " 'till men learn to love their neighbours as well as themselves." Ireland under the English, as compared with the colonies of France, provided a telling example.[16] In his earlier pamphlet as well, Hamilton had looked at "the page of history" with Hume's help (though unacknowledged) and had observed that Rome, the "nurse of freedom," was "celebrated for her justice and lenity; but in what manner did she govern her dependent provinces? They were made the continual scene of rapine and cruelty.

From thence let us learn, how little confidence is due to the wisdom and equity of the most exemplary nations."[17] Hume, on whose *Essays* Hamilton drew so heavily on this as on other occasions, had gleaned this idea from Machiavelli's *Discourses*[18]—one more example of the relevance of Machiavelli's thought for the political ideas of the American Revolution.

As the failure of reconciliation between England and her colonies became increasingly apparent, the Americans' concern with the first principles of legitimate government increased; and it roused their interest in forms of government as well. It was the reluctant decision for independence that brought about the shift of thought and terminology that turned advocates of "free government" into "republicans." After an Indian summer of virtual Tory philosophy, playing off the goodness of the king against the encroachments of Parliament,[19] George III was turned into a despot, because the expectations of those who had adhered to the Commonwealth theory had been disappointed and also because the final measures of repression were acts of the executive.

Thomas Paine's *Common Sense*, that trailblazer of independence, fixed in the minds of Americans the identification of "monarchical" (or "absolute") with "arbitrary" government and of "free" with "republican" government—an identification that was to assume tremendous importance in the acrimonious debate between Federalists and Republicans in the 1790's. Paine found it somewhat difficult to find "a proper name" for the government of England.

Sir William Meredith calls it a republic; but in its present state it is unworthy of the name, because the corrupt influence of the crown, by having all the places in its disposal, hath so effectually swallowed up the power, and eaten out the virtue of the House of Commons (the republican part in the constitution) that the government of England is nearly as monarchical as that of France or Spain. . . . Why is the constitution of England sickly but because monarchy hath poisoned the republic, the crown has engrossed the commons?[20]

There is a wide gulf between Paine's indictment of the king, published in January 1776, and Hamilton's efforts to enhance

the king's power at the expense of Parliament, made only eleven
months earlier! Paine, to be sure, even if the most influential, was
not the only apostle of republican government. It is hardly surprising that among prominent American leaders, John Adams,
that lover of the "divine science of the politics," addressed himself perhaps more insistently than anyone else to the question of
forms of government. Almost simultaneously with the appearance of *Common Sense*, John Adams inquired of a friend whether
she was "for an American Monarchy or Republic."[21]

In Quest of "Republican" Government

The idea of republican government implied a number of postu-
lates. Disagreement could be found on any single issue concerned
—a state of affairs that drove John Adams once to the despairing
observation that a republic might mean "any thing, every thing,
or nothing."[22] Hamilton, too, observed that the word was "used
in various senses."[23] Hamilton's notes for his defense of the Constitution in the New York Ratifying Convention testify to the
morass of conflicting historical traditions regarding the nature of
republican government. He enumerated cases in which the word
"republic" had been applied to aristocracies and monarchies.

1. To Rome under the Kings.
2. To Sparta though a Senate for life.
3. To Carthage though the same.
4. To United Netherlands, though Stadtholder, Hereditary nobles:
5. To Poland though aristocracy and monarchy
6. To Great Britain though Monarchy &c[24]

I shall attempt to disentangle the confusion on this account
that baffled and sometimes misled the generation of the Founders
as well as later students by sorting out different connotations of
republican government. The meaning of republican government
has often been sought without asking sufficiently distinct questions. Answers to the following questions should help to define
the criteria for republican government.

First: In order to qualify a regime as republican, who is to rule it? This question calls for specification in two different directions: one in relation to the number of rulers (one, a few, or many); the other in relation to the mode of succession (hereditary or non-hereditary). The most common answers to these questions are well known and need not be suggested at this point.

Second: In order to qualify a regime as republican, are there limitations imposed on the ruler regardless of who rules? An answer suggested by important writers of the eighteenth century was that the rule of law was such a limitation.

Third: In order to qualify a regime as republican, must it contain certain substantive principles, reflected in the conduct of the people who live in it? An answer enjoying wide currency in the eighteenth century named the principle of political virtue.

The remainder of this chapter will analyze the answers of the Founders, especially those of Alexander Hamilton, to the questions posed. Some of the definitions given in response to these questions were of little significance and will not engage our attention; others, with considerable bearing on the task of nation-building and constitution-building, will be dealt with in more detail.

With regard to the question of who was to rule in a regime to qualify it as republican, it may be convenient first to dispose of the criterion of heredity. From the rise of medieval communes and city-states to the present day, the absence of a hereditary monarchy has been regarded as one, if not the single, distinguishing feature of republican government. In the Anglo-American world of the eighteenth century, this criterion of republican government was widely accepted. Englishmen had experienced republican government under Cromwell after the execution of Charles I. That experience gave republicanism a negative reputation in the eighteenth century, when Englishmen took pride in the glories of the British Constitution.[25] But the evaluation of "republican" in the sense of non-hereditary government was bound to change in America at the very moment when the colonists capped links not merely to the British Parliament, but to King George as well. In an America seething with resentment against the "tyrant

George," the stress on this criterion of republican government was bound to be particularly strong.

If this were the only criterion, however, an aristocracy like Venice or even the elective monarchy of Poland would be counted among republics, putting the newly independent American states in a neighborhood they did not approve of. It was for this reason that at least one opponent of the Federal Constitution was not impressed by its guarantee to the states of a republican form of government: "It is vain to tell us, that the proposed government guarantees to each state a republican form. Republicks are divided into democraticks and, aristocraticks."[26] Before exploring this view we ought to examine Hamilton's stand on republican government as defined by the lack of hereditary rulers. "In his private opinion," as Madison's notes record Hamilton's great speech in the Federal Convention, "he had no scruple in declaring, supported as he was by the opinions of so many of the wise & good, that the British Govt. was the best in the world: and that he doubted much whether any thing short of it would do in America."[27] Hamilton's attachment to Great Britain's mixed government, including its hereditary components, King and Lords, would seem to place him squarely in the anti-republican camp. Insofar as the Jeffersonians' frequent reproaches of Hamilton as a "monarchist" aimed at his preference for a British type of government, they were justified; Hamilton was not, however, an advocate of absolute monarchy of the French type; nor did he seriously envisage or think possible the introduction of hereditary elements into the Constitution of the United States. The nearest thing to a mixed government of the British type was Hamilton's sketch of a "high-toned" government including life tenure for the President as well as for the Senate. Even this plan, put forward in the secrecy of the Federal Convention, did not, in Hamilton's eyes, have any real chance of being adopted. It was "republican," however, in excluding the element of heredity; and to that extent Hamilton could—and, with justification, did—defend himself against the charge of "monarchism."

Let us now turn from the mode of succession to the question of how many rule in a republic. John Adams once put it this way: "The strict definition of a republic is, that [form of government] in which the sovereignty resides in more than one man. A democracy, then, is a republic, as well as an aristocracy, or any mixture of both."[28] Even mixed governments with hereditary elements, like England's, could be "placed on the list of republics," as James Madison noted with displeasure in the *Federalist*, referring to "the extreme inaccuracy" with which the term "republic" was used in political disquisitions.[29] The subsumption of aristocracies and democracies under the general category of republics, by virtue of their plurality of rulers, can be traced back to the political terminology of the city-states of Renaissance Italy; in the eighteenth century its most prominent, though by no means unambiguous expression, was in Montesquieu's *Spirit of the Laws*.[30]

There was, however, another answer to the question of who rules in a republican government. This answer was the result of adding the criterion of the *major part* to the previously mentioned criteria of lack of heredity and of plurality. Sloppiness that confused a plurality of rulers with majority or "popular" rule was prevalent—it even crept into that distinguished work of English letters, Samuel Johnson's *Dictionary*, first published in 1755. Under Johnson's entry "Republick," one would find a definition of it as "Commonwealth; state in which the power is lodged in more than one." Yet under the entry "Commonwealth," the criterion of popular rule was added to that of plurality: it was defined (apart from the more general connotations "polity" and "the publick") as "a government in which the supreme power is lodged in the people; a republick."[31] It remains to be investigated to what extent, if at all, English historical experience with the simultaneous proclamation of the Commonwealth and the abolition of the House of Lords in 1649, and the ensuing rule of the rump House of Commons, favored Johnson's definition of Commonwealth as a government in which the supreme power was "lodged in the people." For the Americans, after their emancipation from the British Constitution, the conception of republican government as "Government by the People" enjoyed by far the widest currency.[32]

Republican Government as "Government by the People"

When the Americans broke away from Great Britain, they found themselves without a king, and this alone, according to a widely held view, made them "republican." They had never had a hereditary nobility; their representative assemblies corresponded most closely to what was known as the popular or democratic part of the British Constitution, the House of Commons, except that they were more widely representative of their constituents than the British Commons. The provisional governments developing in the various colonies-turned-states represented "the people" in the eighteenth-century meaning of that term.[33] That notable production of an unknown laborer from Massachusetts, William Manning's *The Key of Libberty*, is more representative of traditional thinking on republican government than its unorthodox spelling might lead us to suppose: "Their are also sundry names by which free governments are described, such as Democratical, Republican, Elective, all which I take to be senominus tarmes, or that all those nations who ever adopted them aimed at nearly the same thing, viz. to be governed by known Laws in which the hole nation had a Voice in making, by a full and fair Representation, & in which all the officers in every department of Government are (or aught to be) servents & not masters."[34]

Alexander Hamilton strove to impose some order on the prevailing confusion, as the notes for his speech to the New York Ratifying Convention show:

Again great confusion about the words. Democracy, Aristocracy, Monarchy

    I. Democracy defined by some[,] Rousseau &c
       A government exercised by the collective body of the People
      2 Delegation of their power has been made the criterion of

Aristocracy [This is both Hobbes's and Rousseau's definition of aristocracy]
II. Aristocracy has been used to designate governments.
  1. Where an independent few possessed sovereignty.
  2. Where the representatives of the people possessed it.
III. Monarchy, where sovereignty in the hands of a single man.

Hamilton then redefined the terms in a manner more logical to
him, and indeed more like our way of thinking.

Democracy in my sense, where the whole power of the government in
the people
I. Whether exercised by themselves, or
2 By their representatives chosen by them either mediately or immediately and legally accountable to them.
Aristocracy where whole sovereignty is permanently in the hands of a
few for life or hereditary
Monarchy where the whole sovereignty is in the hands of one man for
life or hereditary.
Mixed government when these three principles unite.

In this survey of forms of government, one pattern clearly corresponded most closely to the situation of America: it was that
variety of democracy in which the power of government was exercised, as Hamilton put it with a lawyer's precision, by the people's
"representatives chosen by them either mediately or immediately
and legally accountable to them." Thus the conclusion of Hamilton's survey was inevitable: "*Consequence*, the proposed government a *representative democracy*."[35] Though the term "representative democracy" is commonplace in our day, it was novel then,
and Hamilton, who as early as 1777 had referred to the government of New York State as a representative democracy, was
among the first, if not the first, to use it.[36] The idea of representative democracy would have appeared self-contradictory to philosophers like Hobbes, Locke, Algernon Sidney, and Rousseau.
Traditionally, whoever had the power of legislation was the ruler,
or the sovereign; even Hamilton agreed that this was essentially

true.[37] Yet the growth of representative government in England had led to an as yet insufficiently investigated distinction between the "collective" body of the people and the "representative" body, that is, the House of Commons. This distinction was at the root of the concept of representative democracy; yet it was in revolutionary America rather than in the mother country that the concept apparently made its first appearance. The British formula distinguishing between the collective and the representative body of the people (of particular significance in the political writings of Daniel Defoe and of Bolingbroke) was an engine of opposition to a House of Commons accused of oligarchic tendencies or of corruption through royal "influence."[38] This distinction was echoed across the Atlantic at the time of the Stamp Act crisis, when John Adams felt impelled to add a fourth part to the three traditional components of legislative power: "king, lords, commons, and the people."[39] One year after independence, when Americans had neither king, nor Lords, nor Commons to contend with, it was reflected in Alexander Hamilton's analysis of the constitution of New York. When the "deliberative or judicial powers" were vested "wholly or partly in the collective body of the people," he argued, "you must expect error, confusion and instability. But a representative democracy," he continued, "where the right of election is well secured and regulated" and the exercise of legislative, executive, and judicial authority was vested in select persons "chosen *really* and not *nominally* by the people," would in his opinion be "most likely to be happy, regular and durable." Hamilton thus anticipated by fifteen years Thomas Paine's famous description of the American system of government as "representation ingrafted upon democracy," eliminating the "inconvenience of simple democracy."[40]

The concept of representative democracy, liberated from the weight of king and Lords, boosted the idea of popular sovereignty, encouraging the rather novel distinction—by no means generally understood—between sovereign (the whole people's collective body, as it were) and legislator (the people's elected representatives). The idea of popular sovereignty increased opportunities for rhetorical abuse, for the deliberate blunting of contradictions, for misleading explanations of the true sources of power. Hamilton eyed the phenomenon of representative democracy with greater skepticism in 1787 than he had done a decade earlier, and he was to avail himself, it would be absurd not to admit, of the vastly expanded field for skillful propaganda with considerable ease. Democracy, popular government, or, as it was often synonymously said, republican government might now be put into a Procrustean bed. With an infinite variety of devices such as election, representation, and the separation of powers, the controlling power of the "sovereign" people became an amorphous thing indeed. Even a "high-toned" government, that is, one in which popular control was remote and indirect, could still be regarded as "popular" or "republican." This is what Hamilton did in his Convention speech of June 18. His sketch of a Constitution provided for an Assembly elected triennially, a Senate of members elected for life (on "good behavior"), and a supreme Executive also elected for life. "But is this a Republican Govt. it will be asked?" Hamilton added rhetorically. "Yes, if all the Magistrates are appointed, and vacancies are filled, by the people, or a process of election originating with the people."[41]

Sixteen years later, on the request of Timothy Pickering, who was anxious to protect him from the accusation of monarchism, Hamilton repeated his formula for republican government:

The highest toned propositions, which I made in the Convention, were for a President, Senate and Judges during good behaviour—a house of representatives for three years. . . . This plan was in my conception conformable with the strict theory of a Government purely republican; the essential criteria of which are that the principal organs of the Executive and Legislative departments be elected by the people and hold their offices by a *responsible* and temporary or *defeasible* tenure.[42]

Hamilton went on to say that Madison, too, had advocated an Executive to serve during good behavior—"Thus, if I sinned against *Republicanism*, Mr. Madison was not less guilty." And then Hamilton added an inexplicable extenuation of his constitutional propositions which is not in accord with facts. He told

Pickering that he had toned down his plans for the President from life tenure to a tenure of three years, in a draft constitution that he had given to Madison toward the end of the Federal Convention. The modified plan was based on the following: "1. That the political principles of the people of this country would endure nothing but republican government—2. That in the actual situation of the country, it was in itself right and proper that the republican theory should have a fair and full trial—3. That to such a trial it was essential that the Government should be so constructed as to give all the energy and stability reconcileable with the principles of that theory."[43] Hamilton hoped it would not someday be discovered that "through want of sufficient attention to the last idea, the experiment of Republican Government, even in this country," had not been "as complete, as satisfactory and as decisive as could be wished." The draft that Hamilton gave to Madison toward the close of the Convention exists—but it does not reduce the tenure of the Executive.[44]

What Hamilton was willing to defend as republican government, and what he called in his notes a representative democracy, he actually regarded as a mixed government—one that combined the principles of democracy, aristocracy, and monarchy. This was precisely what he recommended to the Federal Convention, not for wholesale acceptance, but as a yardstick of good government.[45] In Convention, Hamilton spoke bluntly; he was quite willing to consider a "monarch" an actual possibility for America, even if hereditary succession was not in his mind. If an Executive for good behavior might be called an "elective monarch," Hamilton replied to a rhetorical objection, "He wd. reply that *Monarch* is an indefinite term. It marks not either the degree or duration of power."[46]

Remote indeed from his arguments in Convention is Hamilton's stress in *The Federalist* on the sovereignty of the "people" as the ultimate creator of government. Ironically, except for a few passages by Hamilton indicative of the mixed character of the new government,[47] the anti-majoritarian emphasis of *The Federalist* is stronger in Madison's than in Hamilton's essays. Hamilton, as has been well said, turned "the formulas and stereotypes of popular government against the logic of popular government."[48] It was Hamilton who justified judicial review as an exaltation of popular over legislative omnipotence. It was Hamilton who proclaimed as "the fundamental maxim of republican government" that "the sense of the majority should prevail."[49] It was Hamilton, above all, who developed an argument against a Federal Bill of Rights that is one of the most ingratiating praises of popular sovereignty in American political literature. Bills of Rights were originally stipulations between kings and their subjects, Hamilton argued.

It is evident, therefore, that, according to their primitive signification, they have no application to constitutions, professedly founded upon the power of the people, and executed by their immediate representatives and servants. Here, in strictness, the people surrender nothing; and as they retain every thing they have no need of particular reservations. "WE, THE PEOPLE of the United States, to secure the blessings of liberty to ourselves and our posterity, do *ordain* and *establish* this Constitution for the United States of America." Here is a better recognition of popular rights, than volumes of those aphorisms which make the principal figure in several of our State bills of rights, and which would sound much better in a treatise of ethics than in a constitution of government.[50]

Hamilton's rhetoric, for once, was too smooth. A close observer of his political utterances—and even a careful reader of *The Federalist*—might have noted that Hamilton fundamentally remained more old-fashioned than his talk of representative democracy and popular sovereignty promised. He had remained enough of a Blackstonian—and therefore Hobbesian—to retain the identification of sovereignty with legislative power, which Locke and the exigencies of the American Revolution had shattered in the popular imagination. For him, the delegation or surrender of the legislative power (or of the executive power, with respect to foreign affairs) meant the delegation or surrender of sovereignty.[51] The people remained "sovereign" only through the carefully guarded and complex machinery of election. Even in *The Fed-*

eralist, Hamilton baldly spoke of "the authority of the sovereign or legislature,"[52] and defined laws as "rules prescribed by the sovereign to the subject."[53] Similarly Hamilton had argued a strictly Hobbesian theory of sovereignty in 1787 with respect to the proposed independence of Vermont from New York. The opponents of Vermont's severance from the State of New York had made the point that no express power to dismember the state was given to the legislature; the silence of the constitution was a tacit reservation of that power to the people. "To all this I answer," Hamilton retorted, "the sovereignty of the people by our constitution is vested in their representatives in senate and assembly, with the intervention of the council of revision ... ; the power of dismembering the state under certain circumstances is a necessary appendage of the sovereignty."[54]

The examples of Hamilton's thinking just offered strongly suggest that he had a clear understanding of sovereignty. Professor C. H. McIlwain, who claimed that he had not, has observed:

Popular sovereignty is, in fact, possible only in a pure democracy without representative institutions. As usually employed the phrase contains a contradiction in terms. In choosing a legislature, whether we like it or not, we are choosing a master and because we choose it, it is legally no less a master than a monarch with hereditary title. ... Yet it is curious how persistently men have deceived themselves on this point. They confuse the people with the legislature, power with authority. Probably the most striking instance of this confusion in our own history appeared in the debates in 1788 over the ratification of the federal constition.

Professor McIlwain then presents Hamilton's argument against a federal Bill of Rights, just cited, as a pertinent example of that confusion. In truth, however, Hamilton is guilty of rhetorical distortion rather than of muddled thinking.[55] The confusion that Professor McIlwain deplores so justly, and that has bedeviled American political thought and debate to the present day, is more appropriately accounted for by a superficial though handy Lockeanism that interprets the principle of "the people shall be judge" as a legal rather than extralegal device.[56]

Though Hamilton stressed the representative variety of popular government, he never committed himself to the definition of republican government propounded in *The Federalist* by his collaborator James Madison. Madison is the creator and sole advocate of the idea of republican government as one "in which the scheme of representation takes place." Thus it was distinguished from a democracy, which was "a society consisting of a small number of citizens, who assemble and administer the Government in person."[57] Madison thus chose *representation* as the essential criterion of republican government. Therefore his definition amounts to a *fourth* concept of republican government, if we recall the previously discussed definitions based on the criteria of lack of heredity, plurality of rulers, and majority rule. Madison preserved indeed the traditional meaning of democracy; but the contrast he drew between democratic and republican government ran counter to a number of widely current notions about the meaning of "republic." John Adams took him to task for this. "Mr. Madison's part" in *The Federalist* was "as respectable as any other," Adams commented in 1819, "but his distinction between a republic and a democracy, cannot be justified. A democracy is really a republic as an oak is a tree, or a temple a building."[58]

It is appropriate to pause for a moment and to speculate on the reasons that may have led Madison to that careful distinction while Hamilton covered a multitude of sins with the concept of republican government. First of all, the Founders were confronted with a task we are hardly able to appreciate anymore—the difficult task of reconciling the classical scheme of three forms of government with the "modern" system of representation (often called "Gothic" because of its supposed origins in the assemblies of feudal lords of the Germanic nations). John Locke was notably unsuccessful in this effort. Of all political theorists known to the generation of the Founders, Algernon Sidney and Montesquieu came closest to clearly formulating the problem.[59] Furthermore, Madison and Hamilton preferred a "republic" over a "representative democracy" or a "mixed government" because republicanism could best be made acceptable to fairly diverse and even conflicting groups of people. Everyone, of course, was against sin, against arbitrary government; everyone was for a "free" government.[60] But as to the form and substance of freedom, opinions varied greatly. A "republic" appealed to the democratic majority of Americans, who hated "monarchism" (George III) and "aristocracy" (royal officials and the supremacy of the British Parliament),[61] as well as to the conservatives, who feared a despotism of the vulgar. This point may best be illustrated by juxtaposing the views of two Bostonians, a radical and a conservative. The radical, Benjamin Hichborn, put popular sovereignty supreme: "I define civil liberty to be, not a 'government by laws,' made agreeable to charters, bills of rights or compacts, but a power in the people at large, at any time, for any cause, or for no cause, but their own sovereign pleasure, to alter or annihilate both the mode and essence of any former government, and adopt a new one in its stead."[62] The conservative, Judge Joseph Story, was of the opinion that "in a republican government the fundamental truth is, that the minority have indisputable and inalienable rights; that the majority are not everything, and the minority nothing; that the people may not do what they please."[63]

These two statements, in their starkly contrasting views on the power of the people, shift the quest for the meaning of republican government away from the concern over who rules in a republic to the second question raised at the beginning of this chapter: What are the limitations of republican government?

Republican Government as the Rule of Law

The question regarding the limitations of republican government was answered in the eighteenth century with the ancient and majestic formula of a "government of laws and not of men" as it was embodied in Art. XXX of the Massachusetts Declaration of Rights of 1780. Its greatest protagonist in America was John Adams, who acknowledged his indebtedness to James Harrington's *Oceana*. In his *Defence of the Constitutions of Government of the United States of America* Adams observed that some writers, instead of identifying a republic with a democracy, regarded a republic as "a government, in which all men, rich and poor, magistrates and subjects, officers and people, masters and servants, the first citizens and the last, are equally subject to the laws. This, indeed," said Adams, "appears to be the true and only true definition of a republic."[64]

The ideal of the Rule of Law, which eliminated arbitrariness from the conduct of government, was derived from residues of classical thought, the medieval supremacy of law over the ruler, and the seventeenth-century English struggle against the pretensions of monarchy. It reached its finest flower in British constitutional thought in the eighteenth century.[65] No other than John Adams himself, before his decision for independence, had paid the British Constitution this magnificent tribute: "If Aristotle, Livy, and Harrington knew what a republic was, the British constitution is much more like a republic than an empire. They define a republic to be a *government of laws, and not of men*."[66] Alexander Hamilton, steeped in the same legal and constitutional tradition as Adams, seemed to consent when he observed that "the obedience of a free people to general laws, however hard they bear, is ever more perfect than that of slaves to the arbitrary will of a prince."[67] The period of the Articles of Confederation, which suffered from frequent arbitrary legislative interference with the obligation of contracts through special legislation and *ex post facto* laws, sharpened Hamilton's awareness of the possible abuses of sovereign power.

Hamilton's most forceful defense of a government of laws was made in New York before the Federal Constitution was conceived. Yet his "Phocion" essays of 1784 remain to this day among the most notable documents of American constitutionalism.[68] Hamilton's fight against the post-revolutionary proscription of Tories very naturally legitimized itself by an appeal to the "spirit of Whiggism": that spirit, Hamilton said, "cherishes legal liberty, holds the rights of every individual sacred, condemns or punishes no man without regular trial and conviction of some crime declared by antecedent laws, reprobates equally the punishment of the citizen by arbitrary acts of legislature, as by the lawless combinations of unauthorised individuals."[69] Hamilton denied the power of the state legislature to pass discriminatory "partial" or "unequal" legislation on two different grounds. First, there was its legal incompatibility with the obligations incurred by the Peace Treaty with Great Britain. This treaty had been concluded by "the United States in Congress" and Great Britain; the legislature of the State of New York was not sovereign with respect to treaties.[70] There were, Hamilton said, "reasonable limits" even to the "prerogatives of the Union"; but these were none other than "the general safety and the *fundamentals* of the Constitution." These fundamentals are defined as the principles of a "republican government." Hence the second ground on which he opposed legislative omnipotence: "The rights too of a republican government are to be modified and regulated by the *principles* of such a government. These *principles* dictate, that no man shall lose his rights without a hearing and conviction, before the proper tribunal; that previous to his disfranchisement, he shall have the full benefit of the laws to make his defence; and that his innocence shall be presumed till his guilt has been proved."[71]

Imperceptibly, those principles of "republican" government turn into principles of "free government":

Cases indeed of extreme necessity are exceptions to all general rules; but these only exist, when it is manifest the safety of the community is in imminent danger. Speculations of possible danger never can be justifying causes of departures from principles on which in the ordinary course of things all private security depends—from principles which constitute the essential distinction between free and arbitrary governments.[72]

The identification of republican with free government is here complete; none of the principles of republican government as presented by Hamilton were absent from the Whig view of the British Constitution. "Phocion"-Hamilton of 1784 echoes the ideas of "Novanglus"-Adams of 1775. Hamilton did not try to reconcile this view of republican government with his more frequently expressed conception of republican as "popular" government.

Hamilton energetically fought his opponents' argument—

"their last resting-place," as he called it—that "this is a new case, the case of a revolution." Hamilton rightly perceived that allowing the argument would mean entering a "wilderness through all the labyrinths of which" it was impossible to find one's way.[73] The legislature, Hamilton concluded, was "a creature of the Constitution."[74] To disregard these principles would convert the "government into a government of will not of laws."[75]

This essay of Hamilton's is of exceptional interest. It points to one of the most significant of Hamilton's contributions to *The Federalist*, the doctrine of judicial review and the sovereignty of the Constitution. "Phocion" is the origin for his assertion, in No. 71, that "it is one thing to be subordinate to the laws, and another to be dependent on the legislative body," whose tendency to absorb every other authority "in governments purely republican" was "almost irresistible."[76] There were such things as "unjust and partial laws" that might injure "the private rights of particular classes of citizens."[77]

Hamilton's pamphlet of 1784 also allows us to recognize an ingredient of his understanding of constitutionalism which is, doubtless for rhetorical reasons, somewhat obscured in No. 78 of *The Federalist*. In No. 78, which was chiefly designed to convince "democrats" of the harmlessness of the Federal Constitution, he stressed the creation of the Federal Constitution by "the power of the people," expressing "the intention of the people,"[78] though Hamilton is as suspicious of the "momentary inclination" of "a majority" of constituents as of the legislatures proper.[79]

The problem is one of overwhelming complexity. The Founders saw three different entities competing for the title of sovereign: the legislature, the community, and natural law. Sir Ernest Barker has aptly observed that the Americans chose a fourth—the sovereign constitution.[80] The sovereignty of the Constitution is most clearly expressed in Hamilton's observation in the 78th *Federalist*: "Every act of a delegated authority, contrary to the tenor of the commission under which it is exercised, is void. No legislative act, therefore, contrary to the Constitution, can be valid. To deny this, would be to affirm, that the deputy is greater than his principal."[81] That the Constitution is superior to the legislature, which is constituted according to the rules of the Constitution, is obvious enough. Yet whence does the Constitution derive its sovereign character? The answer is bound to remain ambiguous—the ambiguity is apparent in Hamilton's essay itself. On the one hand, we know that the Constitution is superior to the Legislature because the people are superior to their representatives, and the people have made the Constitution without the intermediary of any legislature. In this respect, what Sir Ernest calls the sovereignty of the community asserts itself. Yet on the other hand, natural law is deemed sovereign. Hamilton regarded the American Constitution, like the British, as a limited constitution. "By a limited Constitution, I understand one which contains certain specified exceptions to the legislative authority; such, for instance, as that it shall pass no bills of attainder, no *ex-post-facto* laws, and the like."[82] The question arises as to what Hamilton would have said about a constitution that did not contain these "limitations." There can be little doubt that Hamilton regarded prohibitions of bills of attainder and of ex post facto laws as good *per se*, regardless of popular sanction or its lack.

The moral, rather than physical, impact of sovereign power depends on a title of legitimacy attached to it. The tremendous strength of the Constitution as the true sovereign of America derives from the fact—transparent in No. 78—that two distinct and not necessarily compatible titles support it: principles of natural law as well as "the people." It is true that in the 78th *Federalist*, the balance inclines in favor of the sovereignty of the community. Yet all the more important are the "Phocion" papers, in which the "fundamentals" of a Constitution or the "principles" of republican government convey the impression of enduring and general principles of reason and justice that remain true and valid regardless of popular approval or disapproval. The underlying assumption seems to be that arbitrariness is never legitimate or, for that matter, legal. Our contemporary addiction to legal positivism has led us to see in every act of the legislature a "law." A command issued by the legislator we have come to regard as law. Yet Hamilton was steeped in an older legal tradition of which even Hobbes and Blackstone were a part. Only general rules promulgated by the sovereign legislator were considered laws. It was the generality inherent in the nature of a rule that, to the Founding Fathers, insured the impartial or equal character of a law, that indeed conferred the character of law upon an act of the sovereign. This is expressed in Hamilton's lucid definition: "The essence of the legislative authority is to enact laws, or in other words to prescribe rules for the regulation of the society."[83] Hamilton was to avail himself of the idea of free government as a government of laws in his journalistic contribution to the quelling of the Whisky Rebellion of 1794 in Pennsylvania:

If it were to be asked, What is the most sacred duty, and the greatest source of security in a republic? the answer would be, An inviolable respect for the Constitution and the laws—the first growing out of the last. . . .

Government is frequently and aptly classed under two descriptions— a government of FORCE, and a government of LAWS; the first is the definition of despotism—the last, of liberty.[84]

A number of grave reservations, though, have to be entered against any precipitate conclusions about Hamilton's stand on this matter. Hamilton was perfectly able to recognize the limitations of any given sphere of discourse, and he was not tempted to take *pars pro toto*, to regard even the best system of laws as a guarantee that the claims of the public good had been settled. Hamilton was a lawyer by profession—and a good one—yet he was a statesman by vocation, and his perception of the irreducible passions, interests, and prejudices of the political arena prevented his ever succumbing to a legalistic approach to politics.

The ideal of a government of laws was for Hamilton a point of departure, not of arrival. Hamilton was aware that behind the formal notion of a rule of law, behind the elimination of arbitrariness—important a safeguard of freedom as it was—there loomed a vaster problem that was beyond the ken of jurisprudence and logic: What social and political structure of society was most apt to minimize arbitrariness and maximize liberty?[85] The abuse of sovereign authority, whatever its source, was an experience that had dominated the formative years of Hamilton's career. The awareness of the truly extraordinary difficulties involved in founding a nation, furthermore, left a deep imprint on his political consciousness, as will become clearer in the course of this inquiry. Even the rhetorical requirements of the enterprise to which *The Federalist* was dedicated did not prevent Hamilton from stating bluntly the facts as he saw them: "The idea of governing at all times by the simple force of law (which we have been told is the only admissible principle of republican government), has no place but in the reveries of those political doctors whose sagacity disdains the admonitions of experimental instruction."[86] One notices the impatience of the practitioner of politics in Hamilton's question whether republics, as well as monarchies, were not administered by men![87]

There remained, then, the quest for the political and social conditions of a free government, i.e., a government free from tyranny and despotism. Basically, the Founders were confronted with two radically different approaches. One predominated in England during the late seventeenth and the eighteenth centuries, and it was hardly challenged in America up to the very eve of Independence: balanced, or mixed government. David Hume's definition of free government given at the beginning of this chapter beautifully demonstrates that freedom as a lack of arbitrariness depends upon "a partition of power among several members." Examples of Hamilton's indebtedness to that conception have been given, and our subsequent discussion of his blueprint for America will put his approach to mixed or balanced government into clearer light. Suffice it to say at this point that Hamilton really presented the obverse of Hume's concept of free government when he spoke at the New York Ratifying Convention of "despotism; . . . a government, in which all power is concentr[at]ed in a single body."[88]

There existed, however, an important tradition of political theory in disagreement with the famed ideal of British liberty achieved through a balance of estates, classes, interests, or powers.

It posited social equality, rather than balanced diversity, as the main, indeed the essential, condition of freedom. In the notion of government by laws rather than by men, there is a formalism that veils the complexity of freedom as it was perceived by the Founders. This complexity will be fully apparent only after a close examination of what remains now as the *sixth*, and last description of republican government: a government informed by the principle of *virtue*.

Virtue as the Principle of Republican Government

This conception has only recently begun to be studied by students of American political thought; its significance has remained more obscure than that of all the other notions just reviewed. Yet it was at the center of discussion when the foundations for American independence were laid. John Adams wrote to a friend in January 1776: "As Politicks ... is the Science of human Happiness and human Happiness is clearly best promoted by Virtue, what thorough Politician can hesitate who has a new Government to build whether to prefer a Commonwealth or a Monarchy?"[89] And in the Federal Convention, John Dickinson said that he "had always understood that a veneration for poverty & virtue, were the objects of republican encouragement."[90] From the pamphlets of the crucial year 1776 to the debates on the Federal Constitution and to the acrimonious polemics of the 1790's, virtue appeared to be the key to the success of republican government. But perhaps just because it became such a commonplace, the image of the virtuous republican obscured rather than illuminated the far-reaching implications of virtue in the Founders' political speculations.

Virtue, or the "virtuous life," was meaningful in at least three different ways. First, it might refer to the Christian virtues of fear of God, brotherly love, and humility. These Christian virtues had strong political relevance in the early history of the Puritan and Quaker colonies; but by the time of the Revolution and the framing of the Constitution their significance had subsided. Second, there was the teaching of the ancient philosophers on the identity of virtue with highest wisdom, to be approached through a slow process of education. Its political expression was the classi-cal philosophers' design for the state best suited to the good life, which meant life within society. This complex of ideas only briefly survived the fundamental change from the classical—and Chris-tian—conception of nature and human nature to the modern a-tele-ological view of men as driven by urges and passions rather than by any striving for wisdom or redemption. When David Hume boldly stated that reason was, and ought to be, the slave of the passions, he attacked the traditions of classical antiquity, as well as Christianity, head-on.

Yet Hume was not the first to proclaim the physical and moral primacy of the passions. There was a group of political theorists with views vastly different from Hume's, who endeavored to combine a "classical" commitment to civic virtue as the central principle of the good society with their modern psychology of man's *essentially* passionate nature. These writers whose ideals were republican regarded virtue as a passion for the public good. Niccolò Machiavelli, Baron de Montesquieu, the Abbé Mably, and Jean-Jacques Rousseau were the most prominent and out-spoken ones, while in England, James Harrington, Algernon Sid-ney, and the other "classical republicans" of the seventeenth cen-tury, as well as their followers, the "Commonwealthmen" of the late seventeenth and eighteenth centuries, reflected classical and Machiavellian elements in varying degrees.[91]

Third, then, virtue was a passion for the public good. As such, it was a strange hybrid of ancient and modern ways of thought. It was based both on the desire to build a public-spirited common-wealth on the model of the real or ideal republics of antiquity and on a conception of human nature that denied any genuine public-spiritedness to man. Since the goal of a noble or good life had been replaced by the value of life itself, striving for perfection necessar-ily was replaced by the mere struggle for self-preservation.

Under these circumstances, drastic means were required to achieve "virtue." To keep the state rich, but the citizens poor, was Machiavelli's often repeated advice in the *Discourses*.[92] The very core of his teaching, and of Montesquieu's, was that a republic, i.e.

a public-spirited, free government, was possible only if an equality of fortunes, based on general frugality, turned the private and selfish passions for enrichment and aggrandizement into zeal for the public good. In other words, virtue became a function of external institutional contrivances rather than of an intrinsically perfectible human nature. No one revealed the primacy of the private passions more strikingly than Montesquieu:

The less we are able to satisfy our private passions, the more we abandon ourselves to those of a general nature. How comes it that monks are so fond of their order? It is owing to the very cause that renders the order insupportable. Their rule debars them from all those things by which the ordinary passions are fed; there remains therefore only this passion for the very rule that torments them. The more austere it is, that is, the more it curbs their inclinations, the more force it gives to the only passion left them.[93]

It will remain to the credit of John Adams that he sensed the artificial and negative character of the early modern notion of virtue and contrived to define his objections more concisely than others. At first, in 1776, with much enthusiasm and without much discrimination, he had accepted Montesquieu's principles of government.[94] His imagination fired, he had written: "There must be a positive Passion for the public good, the public Interest, Honour, Power, and Glory, established in the Minds of the People, or there can be no Republican Government, nor any real Liberty; and this public Passion must be Superior to all private Passions. ... The only reputable principle and doctrine must be that all things must give way to the public."[95] By 1787, however, Adams had second thoughts on Montesquieu's kind of virtue: "It is not the classical virtue which we see personified in the choice of Hercules, and which the ancient philosophers summed up in four words,—prudence, justice, temperance, and fortitude. It is not Christian virtue, so much more sublime, which is summarily comprehended in universal benevolence. What is it then? According to Montesquieu, it should seem to be merely a negative quality; the absence only of ambition and avarice."[96]

Few Americans carried the anatomy of virtue to the extent that Adams did. In general, Montesquieu's teaching that virtue was the true principle of republican government found a fertile and well-prepared soil in revolutionary America. Adam Smith, in the *Wealth of Nations*, had commented on the greater equality of the American colonists as compared with Englishmen at home, and he added that "their manners are more republican, and their governments, those of three of the provinces of New England in particular, have hitherto been more republican too."[97] Many Americans, especially after 1763, saw in the corruption of the English Parliament and the general venality of English political life, with its unchecked scramble for enrichment and aggrandizement, one of the chief causes for the oppression of the colonies and the outbreak of conflict.[98] If for no other reason, virtue was the appropriate banner for those in revolt against England. Then, too, many conditions suited for the prevalence of virtue seemed to exist in America. Frugality rather than luxury distinguished the social scene even before a special premium was put on the virtue of frugality during the non-importation campaign against England. Most inhabitants were middling people, and their employment in agriculture assured the continuing mediocrity of their fortune—or so it seemed to many.

This receptive soil had been watered, for about five decades prior to independence, with a popularized (and for several reasons somewhat diluted) version of early modern republican writing: *Cato's Letters* by Thomas Gordon and John Trenchard, two writers who stood, as it were, on the left wing of the Whig spectrum, and who are best described as "radical Whigs" rather than as "Commonwealthmen" or "libertarians"; their thought is deeply indebted to Algernon Sidney and ultimately to the Machiavelli of the *Discourses*.[99] *Cato's Letters* castigated the corruption in England; they preached virtue and public spirit, which was for them a "passion" as it was for Machiavelli. However, *Cato's Letters*, though at the left of the Whig spectrum, accepted the mixed monarchy established in the Glorious Revolution; while fighting the abuses of the Whig settlement, they did not advocate republican government, despite their indebtedness to a republican tradition of political ideas. James Burgh, whose *Political Disquisitions* were published in London in 1774–75 and immediately reprinted in Philadelphia, stood in the same tradition of radical Whiggism; he also protested his respect for the British Constitution, though his sympathies for republican government were but thinly disguised.[100] When independence came, however, Americans searching for a textbook on republican government found it in Montesquieu's *Spirit of the Laws* as much as in *Cato's Letters* or even Burgh's *Disquisitions*; Montesquieu was an "oracle" for forms of government, as Benjamin Rush put it.[101]

After independence, the connection between virtue, a noncommercial society, and republicanism was affirmed most impressively in Thomas Jefferson's *Notes on Virginia*. The independence of the husbandman was conducive to "substantial and genuine virtue," whereas dependence on others begot "subservience and venality," suffocated "the germ of virtue," and prepared "fit tools for the designs of ambition." Corruption was inevitable in rich trading or manufacturing communities.[102] America fortunately could choose to rely on European manufactures, thereby preserving the integrity of its agricultural development and a degree of equality sufficient for the existence of virtue. Americans, Jefferson wrote a little later, would remain virtuous "as long as agriculture is our principal object, which will be the case, while there remains vacant lands in any part of America. When we get piled upon one another in large cities, as in Europe, we shall become corrupt as in Europe."[103] Similar arguments reverberated through the debates on the Constitution in 1788.[104]

It is a testimony to the influence of Montesquieu's theory of republicanism, with its stress on social and political equality, that even Alexander Hamilton should temporarily have abandoned his faith in balanced government, so strong both prior to independence and again in 1787 and 1788. In the spring of 1777, in the wake of the enthusiasm evoked by independence and the framing of free state constitutions, Hamilton did just that. From Washington's headquarters at Morristown, New Jersey, Hamilton wrote his comments on the new constitution of New York to a prominent New York politician, Gouverneur Morris. His criticisms strike an unexpected tone, indeed, unique in his political writings.

That instability is inherent in the nature of popular governments, I think very disputable; unstable democracy, is an epithet frequently in the mouths of politicians; but I believe that from a strict examination of the matter, from the records of history, it will be found that the fluctuation of governments in which the popular principle has borne a considerable sway, has proceeded from its being compounded with other principles and from its being made to operate in an improper channel. Compound governments, though they may be harmonious in the beginning, will introduce distinct interests; and these interests will clash, throw the state into convulsions & produce a change or dissolution.[105]

Hamilton dreaded the bicameralism of the New York legislature not so much because of the "delay and dilatoriness" that might be expected, but because the Senate, "from the very name and from the mere circumstances of its being a separate member of the legislature," would be "liable to degenerate into a body purely aristocratical." He added in the vein in which he had begun, "I think the danger of an abuse of power from a simple legislature would not be very great, in a government where the equality and fulness of popular representation is so wisely provided for as in yours.[106]

In the decade between 1777 and 1787, Hamilton extended his views from the narrow range of New York politics to the whole United States. During this decade he went through a school of politics whose lessons he never forgot. The "different interests" whose birth he had dreaded in 1777 he found already in existence; the equality of outlook that he had deemed essential for popular government he found wanting. There were ample reasons to doubt whether the conditions for the reign of virtue existed even within individual states.[107] As to the United States *in toto*, Hamilton's trenchant mind was not deceived either by an illusion of uniformity or, for that matter, by the windmill battle of the small against the large states that threatened to deadlock the Federal Convention in 1787. Hamilton recognized the decisive effect of the cleavage between the Eastern states, occupied in navigation and trade, and the Southern states, primarily engaged in agriculture.[108] In the New York Ratifying Convention he repeated this point and defended the compromise on the commerce clause that had been struck in the Federal Convention:

It was a delicate point; and it was necessary that all parties should be indulged. Gentlemen will see, that if there had not been a unanimity nothing could have been done: For the Convention had no power to establish, but only to recommend a government. Any other system would have been impracticable. Let a Convention be called to-morrow. Let them meet twenty times; nay, twenty thousand times; they will have the same difficulties to encounter; the same clashing interests to reconcile.[109]

If we look at Hamilton's reflections in the larger context of the crosscurrents of political theory, the climate of opinion in which America's new forms of government were framed, we find that his realistic insights were shared in a quarter where one might have expected them least. There was one *philosophe*, at the time ranked with Montesquieu or Voltaire, who cherished the political ideals associated with antiquity even more exclusively than Montesquieu. The Abbé Mably's devotion to the political institutions recommended by Plato or realized in the laws of Sparta and Crete made him the arch-defender of the policy of the ancients in the eighteenth century. Yet Mably, some of whose writings were used by Hamilton in *The Federalist*, was skeptical regarding the applicability of the principles of a virtuous republic to America. Mably considered Switzerland the only modern country that fulfilled the necessary conditions for the reign of virtue. Swiss people were happier than any other people in Europe, because their "impartial" laws brought them closer to "natural equality." Fortunes neither too small nor too large bred neither the spirit of tyranny nor of servitude, and their very lack of wealth protected them from foreign enmity.[110] In the sea ports and trading centers of America luxury and class distinctions were not unknown. America, Mably feared, had been connected with England too long not to have been infected by British manners and principles—diametrically opposed to republican virtue. Furthermore, the fertility of the American soil contained the promise of greater prosperity than was compatible with the frugal ways practiced in poor and mountainous Switzerland, where the people condemned to silence "those passions most natural to the human heart."[111]

Hamilton, Hume, and the Replacement of Virtue by Self-Interest: The Victory of the Moderns

Alexander Hamilton, so intimately involved in the debates on the shape and structure of the emerging nation, could not possibly ignore theories accepted by many distinguished men and by the public as well; but his flirtation with them had been brief and fleeting. As early as 1782, in his series of articles called *The Continentalist*, Hamilton attacked the core of the argument on republican virtue.

We may preach till we are tired of the theme, the necessity of disinterestedness in republics, without making a single proselyte. The virtuous declaimer will neither persuade himself nor any other person to be content with a double mess of porridge, instead of a reasonable stipend for his services. We might as soon reconcile ourselves to the Spartan community of goods and wives, to their iron coin, their long beards, or their black broth. There is a total dissimulation in the circumstances, as well as the manners, of society among us; and it is as ridiculous to seek for models in the simple ages of Greece and Rome, as it would be to go in quest of them among the Hottentots and Laplanders.[112]

Hamilton, it is worth pointing out, did not refute the feasibility of a regime based on social equality and productive of public-spiritedness, but he did deny the feasibility—and the desirability—of social equality and uniformity of interests here and now. With the background of the public debate on "republican virtue," a celebrated statement in Hamilton's speech to the Federal Convention takes on new significance: "In every community where industry is encouraged, there will be a division of it into the few & the many. Hence separate interests will arise."[113] A few days later, he reminded the delegates: "The difference of property is already great amongst us. Commerce and industry will still increase the disparity. Your government must meet this state of things, or combinations will in process of time, undermine your system."[114] And soon afterward, in the New York Ratifying Convention in 1788, Hamilton elaborated his views quite bluntly: "As riches increase and accumulate in few hands; as luxury prevails in society; virtue will be in a greater degree considered as only a graceful appendage of wealth, and *the tendency of things will be to depart from the republican standard*. This is the real disposition of human nature: It is what, neither the honorable member nor myself can correct. It is a common misfortune, that awaits our state constitution, as well as all others."[115]

A fundamental change of perspective emerges from Hamilton's social analysis. Virtue, or public-spiritedness, from Machiavelli to Montesquieu, Rousseau, and Mably, was believed to be possible only in conditions of individual poverty, or at any rate "mediocrity of fortunes."[116] And now Hamilton presented a radically different interpretation, according to which zeal for the public good would be "a graceful appendage of wealth"! Public-spiritedness as a by-product of private enrichment rather than as its substitute! I shall deal with Hamilton's striking views on the relationship between private and public good in Chapter III. Here, it needs to be stressed that his assault on a theory of republican government that bore the seal of the great Montesquieu and was glorified by America's epic struggle against England was no personal fancy. It was not the rationalization of a power-hungry man or of a spokesman for economic "interests," and it was not even the startling formulation of a new and original theory.

Hamilton's ideas show unmistakably the influence of Hume, though on this occasion it was not acknowledged.[117] Hume's *Essays* presented the most persuasive and comprehensive exposition of what was called "the modern policy." In the essay "Of Commerce" Hamilton could read:

Ancient policy was violent and contrary to the more natural and usual course of things. It is well known with what peculiar laws Sparta was governed and what a prodigy that republic is justly esteemed. . . . Were the testimony of history less positive and circumstantial, such a government would appear a mere philosophical whim or fiction and impossible ever to be reduced to practice. . . .

And the less natural any set of principles are which support a particular society, the more difficulty will a legislator meet with in raising and cultivating them. It is his best policy to comply with the common bent of mankind and give it all the improvements of which it is susceptible. . . . That policy is violent which aggrandizes the public by the poverty of individuals.[118]

Hume here expressed the final breakthrough of modernity in political thought. The first stage of modern political thought, from Machiavelli's *Discourses* to the early books of Montesquieu's *magnum opus*, to Mably, and to Rousseau (who in turn became the point of departure of developments altogether outside this inquiry), had been distinguished by the tenuous fusion of the ancient ideal of public-spiritedness with a view of human nature that denied genuine high-mindedness to man. A republic of men impelled by zeal for the public good could be contrived only by manipulating the passions; the private passions had to be put into the straitjacket of "virtue" and of social equality.

It was this principle which James Madison attacked vigorously in No. 10 of *The Federalist*: "Theoretic politicians, who have patronized this species of government, have erroneously supposed that by reducing mankind to a perfect equality in their political rights, they would, at the same time, be perfectly equalized and assimilated in their possessions, their opinions, and their passions."[119] Well might another, less well-known American critic of Montesquieu and Mably observe that if the principle of virtue were "of so delicate a nature, as to suffer extinction by the prevalence of those luxurious habits to which all national improvements lead—it certainly is a principle of too whimsical a nature to be relied on."[120]

Actually, the champions of virtuous republicanism in the eighteenth century were less liable to criticism than their opponents thought. Many of their readers, especially those in America, who were eager for ready-made recipes for good government, took at face value what was meant to be understood and applied with many qualifications. Mably refused to recognize in America the conditions essential for the reign of virtue. Rousseau (less significant in the American debates) distinguished sharply between the principles of virtuous citizenship sketched in the *Social Contract*, which apart from some Swiss cantons were applicable only in Corsica, and the principle of education for private enjoyment, appropriate only in corrupt nations, that is, most modern countries.[121] And in the later books of *The Spirit of the Laws*, Montesquieu noted the changed manners and temper of modern times. Instead of singing the praise of Sparta, or of Plato's *Republic*, he extolled that commercial and corrupt nation, England. For the liberty of the ancients, he substituted the liberty of the moderns. For virtue, the driving force of the former, he substituted self-interest, the principal motor of the latter.[122]

The second stage of modern political thought then asserted the primacy of the private passions for individual self-preservation, self-enrichment, and self-aggrandizement in three respects. First, on the level of psychology, these selfish passions were assumed to be fundamental to human nature; thus a political society could safely be built only upon an understanding of that fact. Second, on the level of morality, the self-interest of the individual was made the yardstick of the public good. This would have been inconceivable earlier; formerly the public good was regarded as something surpassing the sum total of individual interests in self-preservation, whether it was the virtuous commonwealth of the classical philosophers, the protection of the Christian Church in this world, or even worldly glory and greatness. The unorthodox Hobbes had stated the new position in its most uncompromising form, followed by the more cautious Locke.[123] Third, on the level of political and social theory, the private passions were believed to work to the advantage of the body politic. Hobbes, on the very first page of his *Leviathan* wrote that "the *wealth* and *riches* of all the particular members, are the *strength*" of the commonwealth[124]—an idea for which we search in vain in the blueprints for republican government from Machiavelli to

Montesquieu and Rousseau. More famous than Hobbes's statement is Bernard Mandeville's formula "private vices, public benefits." Hume agreed with both Hobbes and Mandeville when he said that "according to the most natural course of things, industry and arts and trade increase the power of the sovereign as well as the happiness of the subjects."[125]

Alexander Hamilton firmly rejoined this tradition when he told the New York Ratifying Convention: "Look through the rich and the poor of the community; the learned and the ignorant. Where does virtue predominate? The difference indeed consists, not in the quantity but kind of vices, which are incident to the various classes; and here the advantage of character belongs to the wealthy. Their vices are probably more favorable to the prosperity of the state, than those of the indigent; and partake less of moral depravity."[126]

The Founders' quest for the principles and the form of good government in America derives much of its poignancy from the fact that they were exposed to the conflicting claims of ancient and modern ways of thought and, even more baffling, to the ideas of those thinkers who made a last, desperate attempt to bridge the cleavage between antiquity and modernity. There was no agreement, and much groping in the dark among the Americans of the first generation of the Republic with respect to the substance of the liberty that was the object of their search. To the theoretical intricacies of the issue, there were added the problems of persuasion inherent in a democracy—the need for simplifying issues less than clear even to the most learned and brilliant. How incredibly complex are the ideas incorporated in Hamilton's statement in Washington's Farewell Address: "'Tis substantially true, that virtue or morality is a necessary spring of popular government.— The rule indeed extends with more or less force to every species of Free Government."[127] The statesman's prudence was compelled to do injustice to the political theorist's discrimination: Montesquieu's public or republican virtue, became, for general consumption, "morality" pure and simple.

Hamilton's exhortation shows that his commitment to the policy of the moderns by no means eased the task of his statesmanship. A nation had to be built upon the double premise of the actual selfishness of most, though perhaps not all, men and the principle that the sense of the majority ought to prevail. Human nature, as Hamilton saw it, and its implications for operating a republican government will consequently be the main issue of the next chapter.

III

THE SPRINGS OF
REPUBLICAN GOVERNMENT

PRIVATE PASSIONS, PUBLIC INTEREST, AND THE
LOVE OF FAME

The Age of Human Nature

The Age of Reason, puzzled observers have thought, might just as well be called the Age of Passion.[1] Indeed, the student of the eighteenth century is struck again and again by the extent to which the passions of mankind were the object of moral and political discourse, and by the extent to which these passions were regarded as the perennial and ubiquitous prime mover of human affairs. Reason, which is so monotonously extolled as the Enlightenment's hallmark, was not understood to have subdued Passion, but Superstition. The Age of Reason did not succeed the Age of Passion, but the Age of Superstition, or so the Enlightened ones thought. It would be more accurate, then, to regard the eighteenth century as the Age of Human Nature, or the Age of Psychology. Psychology, in fact, dominated the moral and political science of the eighteenth century as theology had dominated the seventeenth century. There is an immediacy of argument, of genuine debate, in our approach to the eighteenth century that transcends the respectful but somewhat historical curiosity with which we study the theological controversies of the preceding age.

Alexander Hamilton was by no means at odds with his age. "The science of policy," he is said to have remarked, "is the knowledge of human nature."[2] On another occasion, Hamilton spoke of "principles of human nature, that are as infallible as any mathematical calculations."[3] It is our task, then, to inquire into these principles as Hamilton perceived them.

There are many instances which suggest that Hamilton thought human nature fairly rotten. Often he deplored the "depravity of mankind."[4] In a less rhetorical tone, in truth in one of the most moving letters Hamilton ever wrote, the assurance of friendship—the deepest he ever felt—served to express his skepticism of human nature. To John Laurens, he wrote: "You know the opinion I entertain of mankind, and how much it is my desire to preserve myself free from particular attachments, and to keep my happiness independent on the caprice of others. You sh[ould] not have taken advantage of my sensibility to ste[al] into my affections without my consent."[5]

What was implied in the "depravity" of man? In general terms, it was self-seeking without regard for the good of a larger whole. In his pamphlet *The Farmer Refuted*, of 1775, there runs along his crusade for the "sacred rights of mankind" a profound awareness of the human limitations that provide the very stuff of politics. Hamilton, unlike John Adams, was not given to making long equotations, yet he inserted a lengthy excerpt from the *Essays* of the "ingenious" Hume, as Hamilton called him on several occasions:

"Political writers (say a celebrated author) have established it as a maxim, that, in contriving any system of government, and fixing the several checks and controuls of the constitution, *every man* ought to be supposed a *knave*; and to have no other end in all his actions, but *private interest*. By this interest, we must govern him, and by means of it, *make him co-operate to public good*, notwithstanding his insatiable avarice and ambition. Without this, we shall in vain boast of the advantages of *any constitution*, and shall find in the end, that we have no security for our liberties and possessions, except the *good will* of our rulers; that is, we should have no security at all.

"It is therefore a just *political* maxim, that *every man must be supposed a knave*. Though, at the same time, it appears somewhat strange, that a maxim should be true in politics, which is false in fact. But to satisfy us on this head, we may consider, that men are generally more honest in a private than in a public capacity; and will go greater lengths to serve a party, than when their own private interest is alone concerned. Honour is a great check upon mankind. But, where a considerable body of men act together, this check is in a great measure removed; since a man is sure to be approved by his own party, for what promotes the common interest, and he soon learns to despise the clamours of adversaries. To this we may add that every court, or senate is determined by the greater number of voices; so that if self-interest influences only the majority, (as it will always do) the whole senate follows the allurements of this separate interest, and acts as if it contained not one member, who had any regard to public interest and liberty."[6]

These reflections of Hume's illuminate in a flash the whole edifice of Hamilton's political science. In a way, what follows consists of mere elaborations of Hume's ideas. In this passage we perceive not only the basis of Hamilton's "pessimistic" conception of human nature; we also discern many of those distinctions, subtle but vital, that prepare us for the discovery that generalizations about the goodness or badness of human nature are among the most misleading and futile of the political theorist's pursuits.

Hume had postulated that most men are devoted to self-interest, and Hamilton followed him closely. "A vast majority of mankind is intirely biassed by motives of self-interest," he had written in his first political work, *A Full Vindication*. "Most men are glad to remove any burthens off themselves, and place them upon the necks of their neighbours."[7] In *The Farmer Refuted*, he called "self-interest" the "most powerful incentive of human actions"; Hume's phraseology can also be recognized in Hamilton's conclusion that the Lords and Commons of Britain had "a private and separate interest to pursue. They must be, wonderfully, disinterested, if they would not make us bear a very disproportional part of the public burthens."[8] Nevertheless, Hamilton was ready to admit, in a way that Hume would not have disapproved of, that the fervor of the American side in the conflict with England was productive of "a certain enthusiasm in liberty, that makes human nature rise above itself, in acts of bravery and heroism."[9] Three years later, when Hamilton was serving as George Washington's aide-de-camp, there was included in a report of the Commander in Chief to a Congressional committee, a discussion of the issue of interest *vs.* disinterestedness that bears Hamilton's mark. Washington's report pleaded for better pay for his officers:

A small knowledge of human nature will convince us, that, with far the greatest part of mankind, interest is the governing principle; and that almost every man is more or less, under its influence. Motives of public virtue may for a time, or in particular instances, actuate men to the observance of a conduct purely disinterested; but they are not of themselves sufficient to produce a persevering conformity to the refined dictates and obligations of social duty. Few men are capable of making a continual sacrifice of all views of private interest, or advantage, to the common good. It is vain to exclaim against the depravity of human nature on this account; the fact is so, the experience of every age and nation has proved it and we must in a great measure, change the constitution of man, before we can make it otherwise. No institution, not built on the presumptive truth of these maxims can succeed.[10]

Still later, in the Federal Convention, Hamilton's conviction was unchanged. As paraphrased by Yates, Hamilton said:

Take mankind in general, they are vicious—their passions may be operated upon. . . . Take mankind as they are, and what are they governed by? Their passions. There may be in every government a few choice spirits, who may act from more worthy motives. One great error is that we suppose mankind more honest than they are. Our prevailing passions are ambition and interest; and it will ever be the duty of a wise government to avail itself of those passions, in order to make them subservient to the public good—for these ever induce us to action.[11]

And in the New York Ratifying Convention, Hamilton again revealed his fundamental principles of constitution making: "I rely more on the interests and the opinions of men, than on any speculative parchment provisions whatever. I have found, that Constitutions are more or less excellent, as they are more or less agreeable to the natural operation of things." He added: "Men will pursue their interests. It is as easy to change human nature, as to oppose the strong current of the selfish passions."[12]

A number of provocative questions arise from these samples of Hamilton's reflections on the nature of man. What encourages selfishness and unselfishness in human nature? Is there actually such a thing as disinterestedness? How do the passionate and rational qualities of man's nature enter into the contradiction between interest and disinterestedness? Does reason make men less egoistic, or might the passion of benevolence alone redeem the enlightened pursuit of self-interest? Is it possible to coordinate private and public, individual and national, interest? What criterion, in the end, decides whether we call human nature good or bad? It is essential to transcend the approach that lumps these questions together in the fairly vague assumption that self-interest is bad, altruism good.

The Meaning of Interest and the Rise of Utilitarian Morality

First of all, an elucidation of the meaning of "interest" is called for. The most telling and satisfactory answer has come to us from the pen of James Madison. Madison, in 1786, distinguished between two meanings of "interest." If it were taken to be "synonymous with ultimate happiness," it was "qualified with every moral ingredient." Taken "in the popular sense," however, it referred "to the immediate augmentation of property and wealth."[13] This is, for instance, what Gouverneur Morris meant when he wrote to George Washington that "the great mass of the common people" had "no morals but their interest."[14] Madison's lead is most helpful for an appreciation of Hamilton's terminology. There, too, the notion of self-interest vacillates between a broad and a specific meaning. Self-interest in its more general application was one of the central ideas of the eighteenth century, though it was often called "self-love."[15] William Blackstone considered self-love the "universal principle of action."[16] Its significance is best illuminated if we join to it, as both Hume and Hamilton sometimes did, the adjective *private*. The furthering of one's private or individual pursuits regardless of the public good, was the almost universal principle of human conduct. This was the meaning of Hamilton's observation in *The Continentalist* of 1782, that societies, as well as individuals, preferred "partial to general interest." And Hamilton went on to stress those "personal concerns, by which the passions of the vulgar, if not of all men are most strongly affected."[17] In the New York Ratifying Convention, Hamilton analyzed "certain social principles in human nature," from which he drew "the most solid conclusions with respect to the conduct of individuals, and of communities." Self-love, indeed, reigned supreme, though Hamilton discreetly began with the love for one's family. "We love our families, more than our neighbours: We love our neighbours, more than our countrymen in general." After this perhaps questionable generalization Hamilton added imaginatively: "The human affections, like solar heat, lose their intensity, as they depart from the center; and become languid, in proportion to the expansion of the circle, on which they act."[18]

If one meaning of self-interest is an exclusive regard for private interests, it is only a small step to what Madison called the "popular meaning" of the term—the pursuit of material security and prosperity. In this sense, self-interest often was called "avarice," in one of the eighteenth century's favorite pairs of passions (also quoted by Hamilton from Hume), ambition and avarice. This was the significance of Hamilton's remark in the Federal Convention (as paraphrased by Yates) that "our prevailing passions are ambition and interest."[19] The quest for material goods starts with the search for mere shelter and food. Security is achieved by "avarice" rather than by "ambition." There is little glamor to this passion, since it is more common and usually less dangerous than the passion for power. Some great modern political thinkers who have earned a reputation as theoreticians of power, like Machiavelli and Montesquieu, actually felt that most men did not thirst for power, but for security—chiefly material security; they were impressed with the moderate and lowly nature of the average man's desires. Montesquieu put it most succinctly: "When virtue is banished, ambition invades the minds of those who are disposed to receive it, and avarice possesses the whole community."[20]

Americans like John Adams and Hamilton agreed. Adams, in

a profound observation, said that the people are "naturally of a peaceable temper, minding nothing but a free enjoyment; but if circumvented, misled, or squeezed by such as they have trusted, they swell like the sea, overrun the bounds of justice and honesty, ruining all before them."[21] Hamilton, we shall see presently, regarded the love of power as a strong passion. Yet he was very much aware of men's pettier quest for material safety and affluence. One of Hamilton's most serious reservations on political democracy, usually overlooked, was the people's lack of interest in important matters of policy. Political incompetence was not so much the result of inborn stupidity as of the lack of genuine concern. Democracy as a theory of the principles of political obligation, as expressed in the image of the social contract, presupposes political interest, talent, and training in everyone. Democracy as a political reality shows that the instinct for political leadership and the degree of concern for things political vary widely. In the New York Ratifying Convention Hamilton commented on a remark that "a numerous representation was necessary to obtain the confidence of the people. This is not generally true. The confidence of the people will easily be gained by a good administration. This is the true touchstone." Hamilton then selected historical examples, from Sparta's Ephori and Rome's tribunes of the people to the representative institutions of his own day, to illustrate the small number of active politicians in a democracy. He concluded: "The popular confidence depends on circumstances very distinct from considerations of number. Probably the public attachment is more strongly secured by a train of prosperous events, which are the result of wise deliberation and of vigorous execution, and to which large bodies are much less competent than small ones."[22]

Here emerges an important motive for Hamilton's view of the paramount importance of the executive in a sound system of government. Hamilton's lack of interest in the theory of checks and balances distinguishes his political thought from that of many of his contemporaries. He knew that he was opposed by the prevailing current of opinion, which was distressed by the abuses of "monarchy" in Great Britain and unwilling to face the problem of executive leadership with detachment. The conflict between the temper of the times and Hamilton's conviction accounts for a revealing twist of his argument in *The Federalist*: "Though we cannot acquiesce in the political heresy of the poet who says—

> 'For forms of government let fools contest—
> That which is best administered is best.'

—yet we may safely pronounce, that the true test of a good government is its aptitude and tendency to produce a good administration." It is a recurring theme of Hamilton's political writing.[23]

Men's almost ubiquitous pursuit of material security and prosperity, that is, their passion of "avarice," looms large in Hamilton's political design. "Men will naturally go to those who pay them best," he had argued as a young officer anxious to enlist men in his company.[24] The reverse side of the argument was brutally put by Hamilton in the Federal Convention: "It is a general remark that he who pays is the master."[25] And in *The Federalist*, he rephrased the thought again: "There are men who could neither be distressed nor won into a sacrifice of their duty; but this stern virtue is the growth of few soils; and in the main it will be found that a power over a man's support is a power over his will." In another essay, he repeated: "In the general course of human nature, *a power over a man's subsistence amounts to a power over his will*."[26]

The assumptions stated above provide the context for Hamilton's views on "influence" and his appreciation of the British political system of the eighteenth century, which to Jefferson seemed the height of perversity. Jefferson has recorded a dinner conversation in April 1791 in which John Adams advocated purging the British Constitution of its "corruption" to make it the most perfect government ever devised. Hamilton retorted that if purged of its corruption, the British system of government would become impracticable.[27] By corruption Hamilton meant the Crown's influence over a part of the House of Commons. Hamilton's seemingly shocking attitude was shared by his two most respected authorities—Blackstone and Hume! Blackstone pointed out that the balance between King, Lords, and Commons, legally weighted in favor of the Commons, had been redressed by the "instruments of power" available to the Crown, which were "not perhaps so open and avowed" as formerly. Increased revenue had vastly enlarged the number of offices at the disposal of the executive. Furthermore, there were now "frequent opportunities of conferring particular obligations" with a variety of "money-transactions," which would greatly increase the Crown's "influence; and that over those persons whose attachment, on account of their wealth, is frequently the most desirable."[28] It was Hume, however, whom Hamilton explicitly invoked in favor of executive "influence." Hume also pointed to the legal preponderance of the Commons in the British Constitution and asked how "this member of our constitution" was "confined within the proper limits." His answer pointed to the Crown's peculiar resources:

The crown has so many offices at its disposal that, when assisted by the honest and disinterested part of the House, it will always command the resolutions of the whole, so far, at least, as to preserve the ancient constitution from danger. We may therefore give to this influence what name we please; we may call it by the invidious appellations of *corruption* and *dependence*; but some degree and some kind of it are inseparable from the very nature of the constitution and necessary to the preservation of our mixed government.[29]

These considerations, an extension of the speculations on political conduct that Hamilton quoted in full in 1775, were in Hamilton's mind at the Convention, when he opposed too strict a rule on the ineligibility of representatives for civil offices under federal authority. "We must take man as we find him," Hamilton said, as paraphrased by Madison, "and if we expect him to serve the public must interest his passions in doing so." A "reliance on pure patriotism" was "the source of many of our errors." Hamilton then invoked Hume: "It was known that [one] of the ablest politicians (Mr. Hume) had pronounced all that influence on the side of the crown, which went under the name of corruption, an essential part of the weight which maintained the equilibrium of the Constitution."[30]

The insistence of Hamilton and his contemporaries on considering private interest in material terms must be seen in the context of an age that was supremely conscious of the novelty of "commerce," which as a way of life had supplanted the mores of agricultural societies. When Blackstone examined how "the stern commands of prerogative have yielded to the milder voice of influence," he referred to the social effects of commerce. "All this," he said, "is the natural, though perhaps the unforeseen, consequence of erecting our funds of credit, and to support them establishing our present perpetual taxes: the whole of which is entirely new since the restoration in 1660; and by far the greatest part since the revolution in 1688."[31]

The moral implications of the spirit of commerce were profound. Montesquieu had noted: "The spirit of trade produces in the mind of a man a certain sense of exact justice, opposite, on the one hand, to robbery, and on the other to those moral virtues which forbid our always adhering rigidly to the rules of private interest, and suffer us to neglect this for the advantage of others."[32] The "rules of private interest" obliged the merchant to exact his due, though it need not be a pound of flesh. The mores of a commercial society, then, explain the puzzling ambiguity of the word "interest." In such a society, Madison's "popular" notion of the word would approach universality. As both Montesquieu and Adam Smith showed, feudal rulers in primitive societies could afford to be generous or disinterested—in fact they might have to be, since conspicuous consumption was the only way of disposing of surplus production.[33] The standard-bearer of a commercial society, on the other hand, could hardly afford to be disinterested. "I have never known much good done," Adam Smith commented, "by those who affected to trade for the public good. It is an affectation, indeed, not very common among merchants, and very few words need be employed in dissuading them from it."[34]

To this analysis in material terms must be added, of course, the store that Christianity at all times has set on the virtue of disinterestedness; and there can be no question of reducing this Christian injunction to the economics of primitive autarchy. Yet all these considerations taken together help to explain the ambivalent way in which the eighteenth century looked upon interest. If seen from the vantage point of a Christian tradition that continued to provide a standard, even if honored in the breach more often than in the observance, "self-interest" was bad, and there are references to the virtue of disinterestedness in the writings of Hamilton and of other Founding Fathers.[35] However, as we have noted before, Hamilton did not hesitate to ridicule "disinterestedness in republics" to the utmost of his rhetorical power. He proclaimed instead the natural, and therefore moral primacy of self-interest, or self-love.[36]

The very interchangeability of these terms in eighteenth-century parlance suggests an additional difficulty. Even granted the psychological and moral primacy of self-interest or self-love, are we to understand its pursuit as an exercise of reason or of passion? Does reason or passion impel us to follow self-interested purposes? An observation of Hume's, startling to those who consider the Enlightenment as the Age of Reason, will be helpful. "We speak not strictly and philosophically, when we talk of the combat of passion and of reason. Reason is, and ought to be, the slave of the passions, and can never pretend to any other office than to serve and obey them."[37] The use of reason, in other words, is an instrumental one. This is the core of a utilitarian psychology and morality that was widespread before the rise of utilitarianism in its more technical sense.

How should this insight be applied to our concern with the Age of Commerce? It might be a man's passion to prosper, to accumulate wealth—in eighteenth-century terms, he would pursue the passion of "avarice," or simply his "interest" in the second sense used by Madison—yet we hardly doubt that an "enlightened" sense of his interest, a rational use of the means most appropriate to the end desired, would lead to more satisfactory results than unthinking lack of discipline or merely common-sense. "Interest" then might refer both to an end conceived as the satisfaction of a passion and to the informed, rational, "enlightened" way of attaining that end.

This relationship of ends desired and means employed might vary in different ways; not only would different people act differently, but the same people might act differently at different times. There was, for instance, the difference between the people drunk and the people sober. Hamilton was very much aware of it. Hamilton's famous justification of judicial review in No. 78 of *The Federalist* gave him the opportunity of guarding against those "ill humours which the arts of designing men, or the influence of particular conjunctures, sometimes disseminate among the people themselves, and which, though they speedily give place to better information and more deliberate reflection, have a tendency in the mean time to occasion dangerous innovations in the government, and serious oppressions of the minor party in the community."[38]

There were also, and perhaps even more importantly as far as the everyday business of government was concerned, differences of conduct among the various walks of life, marked by various degrees of education and of means. To these we must now turn.

Human Nature and Social Classes

Hamilton has devoted one paper of *The Federalist*, No. 35, to a sociological analysis that testifies to his powers of discrimination and his insight into the varieties of human conduct. It was occasioned by a criticism directed against the Federal Constitution to the effect that the House of Representatives might not be "sufficiently numerous for the reception of all the different classes of citizens, in order to combine the interests and feelings of every part of the community.[39] The representative body, Hamilton predicted, would be and should be made up of three classes: "landholders, merchants, and men of the learned professions."[40]

Hamilton argued that wealthy landowners no less than the "middling farmer" or the "poor tenant" had "a common interest to keep the taxes on land as low as possible; and common interest may always be reckoned upon as the surest bond of sympathy."[41] This three-part division of America's agricultural population qualifies one of Hamilton's most widely misunderstood views— his division of society into the "rich" and the "poor."[42] Although he stated this division in no uncertain terms in the Federal Convention,[43] it seems likely to have reflected less a faulty perception of American society as it then existed than Hamilton's conviction that America should become a commercial country. This view was part of Hamilton's preoccupation with those financiers who were in a position to erect a structure of national credit in the new nation. Hamilton's "rich" were the very wealthy, in real as well as personal property, whose possessions individually counted for much in the wealth of the nation and whose stake in its prosperity was accordingly great and personal.[44]

Hamilton's concept of private interest led to striking conclusions in his discussion of the learned professions.[45] Hamilton asserted that the learned professions "truly form no distinct interest in society, and according to their situation and talents, will be indiscriminately the objects of the confidence and choice of each other, and of other parts of the community." This confidence was earned, Hamilton contended, because the member of a learned profession "will feel a neutrality to the rivalships between the different branches of industry" and would be "likely to prove an impartial arbiter between them, ready to promote either, so far as it shall appear to him conducive to the general interests of the society."[46]

There remained, then, the "manufacturing classes." These were broken down, upon closer analysis, into mechanics, manufacturers, and merchants. Hamilton argued that mechanics and manufacturers would generally be inclined to give their votes to merchants in preference to persons of their own professions or trades. These "discerning citizens," he continued, were "well aware that the mechanic and manufacturing arts furnish the materials of mercantile enterprise and industry." The mechanics and manufacturers—that is, the artisans who then were virtually alone in operating industry—knew that "the merchant is their natural patron and friend."[47] Actually, Hamilton's argument in *The Federalist* was borne out insofar as the mechanics and laborers of New York voted for the Constitution.[48]

Hamilton's proposition that merchants—the big financiers of the period — would represent mechanics and manufacturers in Congress has an important implication. It will be recalled that Hamilton invited the New York Ratifying Convention to "look at the rich and poor of the community; the learned and the ignorant." There he had felt that not the quantity, but the kind of "vices," "incident to the various classes" favored the rich; that in this respect "the advantage of character" belonged to the wealthy. Hamilton's reference to "the learned and the ignorant" offers a cue for the direction of his argument in *The Federalist*, No. 35. We shall understand it better after an examination of another paper.

In the 71st paper of *The Federalist*, Hamilton paid an odd compliment to "the people." "It is a just observation," he said, "that the people commonly *intend* the PUBLIC GOOD. This often applies to their very errors. But their good sense would despise the adulator, who should pretend that they always *reason right* about the *means* of promoting it."[49] Hamilton's phrasing betrays a hitherto unsuspected source. His old master Blackstone had displayed this condescending attitude: "In a democracy, where the right of making laws resides in the people at large, public virtue, or goodness of intention, is more likely to be found, than either of the other qualities of government. Popular assemblies are frequently foolish in their contrivance, and weak in their execution; but generally mean to do the thing that is right and just, and have always a degree of patriotism or public spirit."[50] In this strangely diluted form, Montesquieu's political virtue again appears to feed the Founders' political debate!

Hamilton appealed to the people with rhetoric, but not demagoguery.[51] Taking up Blackstone's argument in the 35th *Federalist*, he allowed that the lowly and simple were endowed by "good sense." The mechanics and manufacturers, therefore, were aware that "however great the confidence they may justly feel in their own good sense, their interests can be more effectually promoted by the merchant than by themselves. They are sensible that their habits in life have not been such as to give them *those acquired endowments*, without which, in a deliberative assembly, the greatest natural abilities are for the most part useless."[52] That aristocratic reflection was tempered, in the subsequent paper, with the assurance that "there are strong minds in every walk of life that will rise superior to the disadvantages of situation, and will command the tribute due to their merit, not only from the classes to which they particularly belong, but from the society in general. The door ought to be equally open to all," Hamilton continued in terms that evoke his own extraordinary career, yet he concluded with the warning that "occasional instances of this sort" would not render his reasoning, "formed upon the general course of things," less conclusive.[53]

The Ambiguity of Self-Interest and the Hierarchy of Passions

Hamilton's theory of human nature cannot be explained by the notion of a crude and uniform self-interest alone. Louis Hartz has justly observed that "all pessimistic views of human nature are not alike." He distinguishes "a feudal bleakness about man which sees him fit only for external domination" and "a liberal bleakness about man which sees him working autonomously on the basis of his own self-interest." The latter view, a rationalist "Federalist Hobbesianism," is supposed to characterize Hamilton's political theory.[54] Yet Hamilton, under Hume's influence, rarely succumbed to the single-cause fallacy of positing a ubiquitous and uniform self-interest as the prime mover of human behavior. He distinguished between narrow and broad, benighted and reasonable, private and public conceptions of interest, as well as between interest in wealth, power, or fame.

It was Macaulay who said: "When we see the actions of a man, we know with certainty what he thinks his interest to be."[55] Quite apart from the fact that today we are inclined to consider man a more complicated and inscrutable being, Macaulay's assertion reduces itself to the truism that men govern themselves by what seems best to them. But this kind of interest may change many times a day; it may range from projects of world domination to suicide. The task of a leader of men is infinitely more complex than we might infer from Macaulay's statement. It requires him not only to understand the asserted interests and claims of private individuals and groups, but to fit these, whether enlightened or not, into his concept of the public good, or the national interest.[56] In a democracy, the task of persuasion adds another dimension of complexity.

It is a measure of Hamilton's statesmanship that he was to a large degree aware of these intricacies. Of course, like Montesquieu and Adam Smith, Hamilton thought that men of affairs were fairly rational, and that was one of the reasons why he wanted to place them close to the top of the political and social pyramid. "The men of property in America," he wrote early in his career, "are enlightened about their own interest."[57] This consideration was the main argument of his *First Report on Public Credit*: "Those who are most commonly creditors of a nation, are, generally speaking, enlightened men; and there are signal examples to warrant a conclusion, that when a candid and fair appeal is made to them, they will understand their true interest too well to refuse their concurrence in such modifications of their claims, as any real necessity may demand."[58] Yet businessmen were only a section of political society. Hamilton constantly feared, as he told the New York Ratifying Convention, "that some sinister prejudice, or some prevailing passion, may assume the form of a genuine interest. The influence of these is as powerful as the most permanent conviction of the public good; and against this influence we ought to provide."[59] "What Government," he exclaimed in his *Report on a National Bank*, "ever uniformly consulted its true interest, in opposition to the temptations of momentary exigencies? What nation was ever blessed with a constant succession of upright and wise Administrators?"[60] In his brilliant *Camillus* essays justifying Jay's Treaty, Hamilton defended the administration against the reproach that more might have been done than was done by arguing that governments—in this instance the British—by no means always acted according to the requirements of a situation. Any results depended

not on the real situation of the country, but on the opinion entertained of it by its own administration,—on the personal character of the prince and of his council,—on the degree in which they were influenced by pride and passion, or by reason. The hypothesis that the dispositions of a government are conformable with its situation, is as fallacious a one as can be entertained. It is to suppose, contrary to every day's experience, that Cabinets are always wise.[61]

Camillus elaborated this view in a way that incidentally refutes Macaulay's understanding of interests: "Though nations, in the main, are governed by what they suppose their interest," Hamilton said, "he must be imperfectly versed in human nature who thinks it indifferent whether the maxims of a State tend to excite kind or unkind dispositions in others, or who does not know that these dispositions may insensibly mould or bias the views of self-interest. This were to suppose that rulers only reason—do not feel; in other words, are not men."[62]

Hamilton formulated these qualifications of the theory of self-interest quite early in his career as a political writer. His concept of self-interest was tempered by insight into the power of opinion. When Hamilton began speculating about the raising of public credit, he wrote to Robert Morris: "A great source of error in disquisitions of this nature is the judging of events by abstract calculations, which—though geometrically true are false as they relate to the concerns of beings governed more by passion and prejudice than by an enlightened sense of their interests. A degree of illusion mixes itself in all the affairs of society. The opinion of objects has more influence than their real nature."[63]

It is here that Hume's influence on Hamilton is most clearly visible. Hume had said that "though men be much governed by interest, yet even interest itself and all human affairs are entirely governed by *opinion*"—an assertion frequently repeated in one form or another.[64] Hamilton faithfully mirrored the theory. In

1778 he wrote that "opinion, whether well or ill founded, is the governing principle of human affairs." This principle reappears in various of his subsequent writings.[65]

There are perhaps three major difficulties in any political theory of self-interest. First, there is the "degree of illusion" separating imaginary from real interest. But even if this degree of illusion is made infinitesimal, the very achievement of "enlightened self-interest"—a favorite notion of Americans as Tocqueville has noted and as we can confirm today—poses a second dilemma. Enlightened private interest may not coincide with an enlightened view of social harmony, or of mutual interest. It is this ambiguity of vantage point that more often than not befuddles those who fasten upon the idea of enlightened self-interest to suppress the tragedy of a conflict where justice may be on both sides.

There is yet a third difficulty in developing a theory of self-interest; we might call it the dilemma of the hierarchy of passions. If ambition and avarice, to take that favorite pair of the eighteenth century's moral discourse, were two important human passions, was it better, for example, to pursue wealth or to pursue power? Was there, in other words, a normative order of priority beyond and above the subjective prevalence of one or the other passion in a particular human being? The modern conception of man as a fundamentally passionate being faced, then, a predicament unknown both to classical and Christian ideas of human nature. Both the classics and Christianity saw man's progress toward fulfillment within the frame of a hierarchy of generally valid virtues. The modern theory of self-interest reduces itself, in the last analysis, to an ethics of authenticity. Once the classical or Christian hierarchy of perfection had been replaced by the modern idea of the normative as well as actual primacy of the selfish passions, modern man found himself in a ghastly void, which accounts for the gradual but inevitable degeneration of the morality of self-interest from the days of Thomas Hobbes to our own. Hobbes's identification of the good with the pleasant was still firmly, if illogically, placed in the frame of ancient tradition.

Hobbes stopped short of endorsing dishonorable passions such as cruelty, and he put suicide in the realm of insanity.[66] Montesquieu was perhaps the first great political and moral thinker of modernity to have allowed the possibility that suicide was ethically legitimate. Gradually the morality of self-interest expanded from the Hobbesian notion of self-preservation to the Romantic idea of self-expression. The Romantic morality of authenticity has finally reached its logical conclusion in our century. Its *reductio ad absurdum* is found in Ortega y Gasset's argument that it was immoral for a man destined to be a thief to refrain from theft, or in André Gide's idea that a gratuitous murder, done for the sake of affirming the murderer's freedom to act, was good.[67]

Alexander Hamilton found himself very much in the middle of the turmoil created by the irreducible conflict of three radically diverse moral systems that have gone into the making—and perhaps unmaking—of modern Western civilization.[68] To a psychological and political theory chiefly derived from the modern premise of the primacy of the selfish passions, he added a sense of honor and *noblesse oblige*, inherited ultimately from the aristocratic morality of ancient Greece, and, in his last years, an increasing devotion to Christianity. Incompatible values clashed most fiercely when Hamilton, having accepted Aaron Burr's challenge to a duel, also obeyed the injunctions of Christianity by throwing away his shot.[69] The conflict between the code of honor and the standards of Christianity was heightened by the political motivation that may have led Hamilton to accept the challenge at all. In earlier years, he had on various occasions offered challenges, and had thus conformed to an accepted code. By 1804, chastened by his eldest son's death in a duel and the ensuing insanity of his daughter Angelica, more and more devoted to Christianity, Hamilton might have sacrificed his earlier ideas of honor, had he not believed that "the ability to be in future useful ... in those crises of our public affairs which seem likely to happen, would probably be inseparable from a conformity to the prejudice in this particular."[70] There was, to properly employ a much abused word, tragic irony in the martyr's death of one of America's first great statesmen.

The Love of Power, Demagoguery, and "The Ruling Passion of the Noblest Minds"

The hierarchy of passions was the crucial problem of modern political theory after it had rejected the rational virtue of classical antiquity as well as Christian revelation. How did Hamilton, both psychologically and morally, face this challenge?

It is extraordinary to find more than a clue, the core of a mature outlook on politics in the letter of a lad of fourteen:

... to confess my weakness, Ned, my Ambition is prevalent that I contemn the grov'ling condition of a Clerk or the like, to which my Fortune &c. condemns me and would willingly risk my life tho' not my Character to exalt my Station. I am confident, Ned that my Youth excludes me from any hopes of immediate Preferment nor do I desire it, but I mean to prepare the way for futurity. Im no Philosopher you see and may be jusly said to Build Castles in the Air. My Folly makes me ashamd and beg youll Conceal it, yet Neddy we have seen such Schemes successfull when the Projector is Constant I shall Conclude saying I wish there was a War.[71]

If ambition was prevalent with Hamilton, and if he knew it, it was not difficult for him to detect it in others. The striving for power looms large in Hamilton's reflections on politics. "Men must cease to be as fond of power as they are," he wrote in *The Farmer Refuted*, before mere "force of intreaty" could frustrate England's design against America's liberties.[72] The "thirst of domination," the "love of power" are expressions that recur in Hamilton's utterances.[73] It is important to point out that, nevertheless, his own ambitions, his insight into the nature of politics are not alone responsible for this slant displayed in his work. It will soon appear that Hamilton's most significant contribution to the discussion of political power was a blow to the brand of thought that made lust for power and its corruptions the cornerstone of political speculation.

The desire for power and its alleged corrupting influence were at the center of Whig political ideas. "He that thinks absolute power purifies men's blood, and corrects the baseness of human nature," John Locke wrote, "need read but the history of this, or any other age, to be convinced to the contrary." To put one man into a position of absolute power, Locke continued, would but compound the troubles of the state of nature. "This is to think that men are so foolish that they take care to avoid what mischiefs may be done them by polecats or foxes, but are content, nay, think it safety, to be devoured by lions."[74] In the eighteenth century, the Whig tradition of limited government produced radical broadsides against political power that are among the most outspoken and radical to be found anywhere in modern political thought. Whiggism, a close study of only recently rediscovered literature informs us, found itself on the confines of anarchism on more than one occasion. The pessimism about political power of a Jacob Burckhardt or a Lord Acton looks like a pale imitation when compared with some of the eighteenth-century political classics. We think of *Cato's Letters* by Gordon and Trenchard; or the writings of that unfortunate Tory, Bolingbroke, whose perennial banishment into opposition led him to produce some of the most radical Whig doctrines on record; or the *Political Disquisitions* of James Burgh.[75] These English authors, all of them well known in Revolutionary America, were surpassed, perhaps, only by some of the Americans who set about to turn radical Whig doctrine against the Federal Constitution's grants of powers. "Men of Little Faith" these writers have been called by their perceptive student who tells us of the preposterous extremes of their imagination.[76] There were fears that the Pope might be elected President, that the ten miles square of the Federal Capital might give the central government power to "hang any man who shall act contrary to their commands . . . without benefits of the clergy." There were fears that the lack of a specified site for the ten miles square might empower Congress to seat itself and other government offices in Peking. As Professor Cecelia M. Kenyon has pointed out, "All in all, a terrible prospect: the Pope as President, operating from a base in Peking, superintending a series of hangings without benefit of clergy! Or worse."[77]

The Whig tradition of political pessimism found its most dignified American spokesman in that reputed optimist, Thomas

Jefferson. It was Jefferson who included in his first inaugural address one of the most damaging reflections ever made on the chances of trust and confidence among men: "Sometimes it is said that man cannot be trusted with the government of himself. Can, he, then, be trusted with the government of others? Or have we found angels in the forms of kings to govern him? Let history answer this question."[78] Jefferson turned this pessimistic outlook on himself; he had written, shortly before the Federal Convention, that if the people "become inattentive to the public affairs, you and I, and Congress and Assemblies, Judges and Governors, shall all become wolves."[79] The radical pessimism of liberal philosophy regarding the possibilities of trust was perhaps most sharply thrown into relief by Henry Clay, in 1840: "The pervading principles of our system of government—of all free government—is not merely the possibility, but the absolute certainty of infidelity and treachery, with even the highest functionary of the State."[80]

What did Hamilton think of the corrupting influence of power? His attitude was complex and not always consistent. His general references to the "love of power" are perhaps the least illuminating evidence of his ideas, since they are so much in tune with the radical Whig fashion of the times. Upon closer analysis, his implication of the ubiquity of lust for power is resolved into a number of specific and quite discriminating assertions about the varied effects of the love of power on different people in different circumstances. There is ample evidence of Hamilton's apprehensions about the baneful effects of political ambition—yet his arguments derive their force precisely from being related to specific circumstances. There runs persistently through Hamilton's writings the fear of demagoguery (etymologically so close to democracy), the fear that the gullible people would be exploited by selfish, ambitious men. This is where Hamilton's emphasis on the passion of ambition parts company with radical Whig doctrine. Democracy offered more rather than fewer opportunities for the corrupting tendencies of power. Not that the people themselves were corrupt; but the lack of interest in politics, with its concomitant, lack of training and competency, opened the door to men least resistant to the temptations of power. This concern of Hamilton's provided the framework of *The Federalist*. In the first paper, Hamilton observed that

a dangerous ambition more often lurks behind the specious mask of zeal for the rights of the people, than under the forbidding appearance of zeal for the firmness and efficiency of government. History will teach us, that the former has been found a much more certain road to the introduction of despotism, than the latter, and that of those men who have overturned the liberties of republics the greatest number have begun their carreer, by paying an obsequious court to the people, commencing Demagogues and ending Tyrants.[81]

In the last *Federalist*, Hamilton warned against the "military despotism of a victorious demagogue."[82]

Only a few years later, the specter of the demagogue depicted in the papers of "Publius" took on the flesh and blood of the man who eventually became the tool of Hamilton's end—Aaron Burr. "In a word, if we have an embryo-Caesar in the United States," Hamilton exclaimed in 1792, " 'tis Burr."[83] Political incidents that need not detain us led Hamilton to oppose Burr's political ambitions, and gave him opportunity to paint the demagogue's picture in colors infinitely more vivid than in the abstract anticipations of *The Federalist*. Hamilton denounced a "class of men, who in all the stages of our republican system, either from desperate circumstances, or irregular ambition, or a mixture of both, will labour incessantly to keep the government in a troubled and unsettled state, to sow disquietudes in the minds of the people and to promote confusion and change. Every republic at all times has its Catilines and its Caesars."[84]

In a Cabinet paper written for President Washington, Hamilton was more specific, though no name was mentioned:

When a man unprincipled in private life desperate in his fortune, bold in his temper, possessed of considerable talents, having the advantage of military habits—despotic in his ordinary demeanour—known to have scoffed in private at the principles of liberty—when such a man is seen to mount the hobby horse of popularity—to join in the cry of danger to liberty ... It may justly be suspected that his object is to throw things into confusion. . . .

It has aptly been observed that *Cato* was the Tory—*Caesar* the Whig of his day. The former frequently resisted—the latter always flattered the follies of the people. Yet the former perished with the Republic the latter destroyed it."[85]

Students of Hamilton have been struck by the similarity between Hamilton and Burr. In particular, it has been noted that "both were aflame with a similar thirst for power and glory."[86] Yet that comparison does injustice to a point that Hamilton took pains to stress—a point that, indeed, helps us understand Hamilton's solution of the dilemma of the hierarchy of human passions. "Let it be remembered," Hamilton wrote on the occasion of Burr's and Jefferson's contest for the presidency, "that Mr. Burr has never appeared solicitous for fame, and that great ambition, unchecked by principle or the love of glory, is an unruly tyrant, which never can keep long in a course which good men will approve. As to the last point, the proposition is against the experience of all times. Ambition without principle never was long under the guidance of good sense."[87]

The love of glory now emerges as a passion of prime significance in Hamilton's outlook. In this century, we are not inclined to make much of a distinction between love of power and love of fame. With modern sociological theories about ideological superstructures and "real" bases, whether of Marx's, Pareto's, or Mannheim's variety, with Freudian and Adlerian ventures into the subconscious, we hold that power rather than fame is the "real thing." Real, because tangible; real, because more expressive of "self-interest," which still provides the basis of our moral and political speculations; real, because more productive of material goods; real, because more conducive to enjoyment of superiority over others.

Yet beyond and before these recent trends, there were two important sources of the depreciation of glory in favor of power. One, already anticipated in Stoicism, was Christianity. For Christianity, there is no glory before God, or rather, glory in the eyes of God was obtained at the price of renouncing worldly fame, at the price of humbleness, or even at the price of martyrdom. *Gloria* was annexed to otherworldly pursuits.[88] As long, however, as an aristocratic structure of society persisted, as long as the noble and the lowly continued to follow—in spite of a common religion —distinct moral patterns, honor continued to mean more than honesty, greatness more than happiness, and fame more than vanity. The end of an epoch had indeed come when Thomas Jefferson, while minister of the United States to the Court of France, struck out "the care of one's honor" from Lafayette's draft of the Declaration of the Rights of Man and Citizen.[89] That end had come gradually with the decline of European aristocracy and the rise of an acquisitive bourgeois society. It had been anticipated by the founders of modern political psychology like Machiavelli and Hobbes. In particular, the psychological egalitarianism of Thomas Hobbes did much to divest honor—which Aristotle called the greatest of external goods—of its high rank.[90]

Yet even Hobbes did not quite escape the "undemocratic" distinction between men of worth and the rest of mankind, though he lifted this distinction out of the classical frame of a fixed hierarchy of values and placed it in a subjective, merely psychological setting. "Love of virtue from love of praise"—so Hobbes entitled a paragraph of the *Leviathan* in which he showed how "desire of praise, disposeth to laudable actions, such as please them whose judgment they value; for of those men whom we contemn, we contemn also the praises." Furthermore, the desire for immortality—particularly if devoid of a firm belief in another world—evokes the wish to be remembered, honorably, by posterity. "Desire of fame after death," Hobbes continued, "does the same." In terms in which it is difficult not to suspect irony, he added:

And though after death there be no sense of the praise given us on earth, as being joys, that are either swallowed up in the unspeakable joys of Heaven, or extinguished in the extreme torments of hell: yet is not such fame vain; because men have a present delight therein, from the foresight of it, and of the benefit that may redound thereby to their posterity; which though they now see not, yet they imagine; and any-thing that is pleasure to the sense, the same also is pleasure in the imagi-nation.[91]

Hobbes's theme was taken up in Hume's *Essays*, and it is more likely than not that we here touch the most direct source of Ham-ilton's own idea on the subject. It was only fitting that in the Age of Human Nature Hume should write an essay "Of the Dignity or Meanness of Human Nature." The foundation of man's na-ture in passion rather than in reason could hardly be put more emphatically than in Hume's meditations on the love of fame. He took issue with those philosophers who had "insisted so much on the selfishness of man."[92] That insistence, he thought, had partly been based on the observation that "the virtuous are far from being indifferent to praise; and therefore they have been represented as a set of vain-glorious men, who had nothing in view but the applause of others." Hume retorted that this was a fallacy. "It is very unjust," he said, when "any tincture of van-ity in a laudable action" is found, "to depreciate it upon that account, or ascribe it entirely to that motive. The case is not the same with vanity, as with other passions." Vanity was so closely allied with virtue, Hume continued, "and to love the fame of laudable actions approaches so near the love of laudable actions for their own sake, that these passions are more capable of mix-ture, than any other kinds of affection; and it is almost impossible to have the latter without some degree of the former." As proof of this contention, Hume mentioned that the passion for glory varied according to one's disposition. Nero "had the same vanity in driving a chariot, that Trajan had in governing the empire with justice and ability." Vanity, if we may elaborate Hume's argument, was so mortified by obscurity that it might even reach for infamy if true fame was beyond the pale of attainment. This seems to be expressed in Hume's conclusion: "To love the glory of virtuous deeds is a sure proof of the love of virtue."[93]

This certainly is the manner in which Alexander Hamilton regarded the subject. This appears from a crucial passage which in a single flash enlightens the whole edifice of his mind, in the

72nd *Federalist* paper. There Hamilton invoked *"the love of fame, the ruling passion of the noblest minds, which would prompt a man to plan and undertake extensive and arduous enterprises for the public benefit, requiring considerable time to mature and perfect them."*[94] Should there be any doubt that Hamilton thought of himself when he wrote these lines, there is the testimony of his autobiographical letter of 1797, in which he expostulated against the "jealousy of power and the spirit of faction" because they diminished the "power of doing good," and diminished the prospects "for gratifying in future the love of fame, if that passion was to be the spring of action."[95]

Once the paramount significance of this idea is seen, Hamilton's character and his design for greatness appear in a new light. We now perceive the consistency that links the boy's determination to sacrifice life, but not character, to ambition, with the aging man's denunciation of Aaron Burr as a person devoid of the "love of glory" and therefore less fit to be President of the United States than Jefferson!

The passion of fame or glory, as distinct from the passion of power, offers insights into some of the Founding Fathers' minds; it also greatly helps us to understand how they understood themselves. It illuminates in a new way, for instance, that remote person, George Washington. When Washington settled with his wife at Mount Vernon, he ordered from Europe the busts of Alexander the Great, Charles XII of Sweden, Julius Caesar, Frederick of Prussia, Marlborough, and Prince Eugene.[96] In what is perhaps the most vivid and memorable characterization of Washington, Samuel E. Morison has stressed the heritage of Stoicism, of Catonic virtue, with its contempt of worldly goods, its praise of self-sufficiency and discipline. While not denying the force of these ideas, we may suspect that the love of fame burned more brightly in Washington's soul than the Stoic spirit would have permitted—famous generals and statesmen rather than Cato or Marcus Aurelius were among the men whose statues he ordered for Mount Vernon.[97] Perhaps Hamilton revealed a knowledge of Washington's character as well as of his own when he pleaded with Washington to accept the presidency: "Permit me to say," he wrote, "it would be inglorious in such a situation not to hazard the glory however great, ... previously acquired." The facts of the situation, Hamilton argued, "if I mistake not my dear Sir will suggest to your mind greater hazard to that fame, which must be and ought to be dear to you, in refusing your future aid to the system than in affording it."[98]

A hint that Hamilton indeed touched a responsive chord in Washington by invoking a passion uppermost in himself is given in Washington's own appreciation of Hamilton. "By some he is considered as an ambitious man, and therefore a dangerous one," Washington wrote toward the end of his life. "That he is ambitious I shall readily grant, but it is of that laudable kind which prompts a man to excel in whatever he takes in hand."[99] Similar evaluations of the inspiration of Hamilton's ambitions were made by other contemporaries whose minds were attuned to a psychological and a moral value that has since been obscured. "In Hamilton," Secretary of State Timothy Pickering wrote, "ambition was united with patriotism—but it was an ambition which could be satisfied only by the performance of laudable acts, which should entitle him to a high rank in public estimation."[100] In another unpublished sketch, entitled "Hamilton—Ambition, or Love of Fame," Pickering actually copied from *The Federalist* No. 72 the passage cited above, and went on: "That was his own ruling passion; & he sought for it in the ability and fidelity displayed in the contriving & executing of his public plans."[101] The most colorful formulation of what Madison called "honorable love of fame,"[102] with respect to Hamilton's achievement, was made by Fisher Ames. If Ames, like Madison, though unlike Washington or Pickering, clearly distinguished between ambition and the love of fame, he threw into relief even more sharply a dimension virtually lost to our present Age of Psychology. Ames began by refuting the mistaken accusations against Hamilton's "ambition": such men "as have a painful consciousness that their station happens to be far more exalted than their talents, are generally the most ambitious." Hamilton, Ames argued, "on the contrary, though he had many competitors, had no rivals; for he did not thirst for power, nor would he, as it was well known, descend to office." Of what, then, was Hamilton ambitious?

Not of wealth; no man held it cheaper. Was it of popularity? That weed of the dunghill he knew, when rankest, was nearest to withering. There is no doubt that he desired glory, which to most men is too inaccessible to be an object of desire; but feeling his own force, and that he was tall enough to reach the top of Pindus or of Helicon, he longed to deck his brow with the wreath of immortality. A vulgar ambition could as little comprehend as satisfy his views; he thirsted only for that fame, which virtue would not blush to confer, nor time to convey to the end of his course.[103]

Let us try to discover what has obscured, in our age, a spontaneous awareness of what Edmund Burke has called "a passion which is the instinct of all great souls."[104] The answer is simple. The ideal of the magnanimous, or in literal translation (*magna anima*) "great-souled" man seems sinister both to Christianity and to democracy because of its aristocratic lack of humility. Even in the time of the Founders, when the heritage of classical antiquity was so much more vital than it is today, we recognize the conflict that tossed John Adams, a man much more exposed to Christian—specifically, Puritan—influences than either Washington or Hamilton, back and forth between negative and positive evaluations of fame and ambition.[105] But only the final victory of liberal democracy brought with it the triumph of that pessimistic philosophy of power, which is the very essence of Jeffersonianism. Greatness, glory? No, all of us will turn wolves, was Jefferson's reply.

The extremes of the liberal theory of human selfishness were balanced, it is true, by a spirit of public-mindedness; yet this spirit is quite different from the magnanimous man's pursuit of greatness. To some extent, the Christian injunctions of humility and brotherly love may have gone into this self-defense of liberal democracy against its theoretical assumptions. More significant, perhaps, are other considerations, which no one but Tocqueville has grasped in all their distinctness. "The Americans," Tocqueville observed, "have combated by free institutions the tendency of equality to keep men asunder, and they have subdued it."[106]

When the members of a community are forced to attend to public affairs, they are necessarily drawn from the circle of their own interests and snatched at times from self-observation. As soon as a man begins to treat of public affairs in public, he begins to perceive that he is not so independent of his fellow men as he had at first imagined, and that in order to obtain their support he must often lend them his co-operation.

When the public govern, there is no man who does not feel the value of public goodwill or who does not endeavor to court it by drawing to himself the esteem and affection of those among whom he is to live. . . . Men learn at such times to think of their fellow men from ambitious motives; and they frequently find it, in a manner, their interest to forget themselves.[107]

Tocqueville's argument—only adumbrated in these lines—strikes a familiar note. From it there lead many paths to negative as well as positive aspects of the politics of democracy as we know it; yet it was not an argument of the Founding Fathers of the Republic.

The traditions of Christianity as well as those aspects of democracy pointed to by Tocqueville have nourished in us a tendency—always supported by a deeply rooted disposition to see things in black and white—to apply to morals and politics a simplified scale of standards. One is either selfish or unselfish; either egoistic or altruistic; either interested or disinterested. For instance, it has been said that "Hamilton was personally ambitious, yet again and again he subordinated his own interests to those of his country. A patriot is selfless, single-minded, energetic."[108] Yet this characterization is mistaken; flattering as it appears to us, it would have seemed mistaken even to Hamilton and his admirers Washington, Pickering, or Ames. To be sure, Hamilton was single-minded and energetic. Yet selfless, in the true, Christian meaning of that word Hamilton was only once in his life—when he threw away his shot at Aaron Burr. During his career as a statesman, "selfishness" and public service merged in a single passion, in a way that has nothing to do with generosity or sacrifice, but with the love of fame, "the great spring to noble

& illustrious actions," as Gouverneur Morris called it in the Federal Convention of 1787.[109] Again, it makes no sense, in the way in which Hamilton understood himself, to say that he was personally ambitious but subordinated his own interests to those of his country. Hamilton's ambition would have lost its meaning and its dynamic, had it been divorced from the interests of his country. He did not subordinate his personal interests to those of his country; he subordinated his pecuniary interests to his life's ruling passion, the quest for glory.

This passion topped all others in the eighteenth-century hierarchy of passions, since it was the only one to comprehend private and public, individual and general interest. What did that eighteenth-century classic, *Cato's Letters*, have to say about the contrivance of virtue?

... When we call any Man disinterested, we should intend no more by it, than that the Turn of his Mind is toward the Publick, and that he has placed his own personal Glory and Pleasure in serving it. To serve his Country is his private Pleasure, Mankind is his Mistress, and he does good to them by gratifying himself.

Disinterestedness, in any other Sense than this, there is none. . . . When the Passions of Men do good to others, it is called Virtue and publick Spirit; and when they do hurt to others, it is called selfishness, Dishonesty, Lust, and other Names of Infamy.[110]

In such a view of the matter, one grave issue stood out. If the love of fame, as Hamilton affirmed, was the passion of the noblest minds, if it was the privilege of few, how was it possible at all to build and maintain a social fabric? How was it possible to contrive a unity of purpose, which the freest society needed in a world of sovereign nations?

Nation-Building Without Patriotism: The Danger of "Foreign Corruption in Republics"

The political theory of the absolute primacy of self-interest that distinguishes the second stage of modern political thought has since been supplemented or even supplanted by modern nationalism. Allegiance to the nation state and its implication of a readiness to die for one's country, has, since the French Revolution, become firmly entrenched in the consciousness of Western man; it has been the fiber of political and moral loyalty in our time. Also since the French Revolution, transnational ideologies have attached themselves to the expanding nation states in the guise of national missions; as in turn we find more than one ideology with the claim of universal validity, which at bottom is little more than nationalistic doctrine fitted to the urges of expansionist energy.[111]

National loyalty belongs so much to the categories of our thinking that it requires considerable imagination to visualize a nation without patriots; yet this is the picture of the American Union we encounter in *The Federalist*, with one solitary and striking exception in the essays of John Jay.[112] The true predecessor of modern nationalism, in the history of political theory, is the doctrine of public virtue as developed by Montesquieu and Rousseau.[113] Yet we have seen that Hamilton discounted "disinterestedness in republics." Instead he held that "the passions of the vulgar, if not of all men" were most strongly affected by "personal concerns," and that societies as well as individuals were inclined "to prefer partial to general interest."[114] The conclusions of this doctrine of self-interest concerning the respective merits and demerits of monarchical and republican government are startling; they offer a key to some of the more obsolete of Hamilton's ideas, which he began to revise only in the last years of his life.

One of Hamilton's reasons for favoring monarchy, it appears, was a rather primitive one. The king was simply the biggest proprietor of his nation; his stake or interest (in Madison's popular, materialistic meaning) in his country was therefore greater than anyone else's. It was not by any means, then, the assumption that kings were by nature among the noblest minds or among those whom Hamilton once called "a few choice spirits, who may act from more worthy motives" than ambition and interest.[115] As Madison paraphrased Hamilton's explanation in the Federal

Convention, "The Hereditary interest of the King was so inter-
woven with that of the Nation, and his personal emoluments so
great, that he was placed above the danger of being corrupted
from abroad—and at the same time was both sufficiently independent and sufficiently controuled, to answer the purpose of the
institution at home."[116] In *The Federalist*, Hamilton embroi-
dered this bald admission somewhat, paying heed to popular
prejudices on the subject of kings and their warlike tendencies:

An hereditary monarch, though often disposed to sacrifice his subjects
to his ambition, has so great a personal interest in the government, and
in the external glory of the nation, that it is not easy for a foreign power
to give him an equivalent for what he would sacrifice by treachery to
the State. The world has accordingly been witness to few examples of
this species of royal prostitution, though there have been abundant speci-
mens of every other kind.[117]

It is Hamilton's conception of monarchy—and its consequences
for his appraisal of republican regimes—that perhaps constitutes
the most direct heritage from Hobbes in his system of political
thought. Hobbes's virtually identical argument in favor of monarchy affords another opportunity to strike a blow at a misguided
understanding of Enlightenment "rationalism." His reasoning
reflects a theory first fully elaborated in the age of the Tudors
and Stuarts, the theory of "the king's two bodies"—natural and
politic—which are at the bottom of the well-known fictions that
the king never dies and never can do wrong. The theory, incidentally, throws into relief the distinction between private and
public, personal and national interest that was of such outstanding
significance for Hamilton. Hobbes observed:

Whosoever beareth the person of the people, or is one of that assembly
that bears it, beareth also his own natural person. And though he be
careful in his politic person to procure the common interest; yet he is
more, or no less careful to procure the private good of himself, his
family, kindred, and friends; and for the most part, if the public interest chance to cross the private, he prefers the private: for the passions of men, are commonly more potent than their reason. From

whence it follows, that where the public and private interest are most closely united, there is the public more advanced. Now in monarchy, the private interest is the same with the public. The riches, power, and honour of a monarch arise only from the riches, strength, and reputation of his subjects. For no king can be rich, nor glorious, nor secure, whose subjects are either poor, or contemptible, or too weak through want or dissention, to maintain a war against their enemies: whereas in a democracy, or aristocracy, the public prosperity confers not so much to the private fortune of one that is corrupt, or ambitious, as doth many times a perfidious advice, a treacherous action, or a civil war.[118]

This is the background of Hamilton's fear that foreign influence "is truly the GRECIAN HORSE to a republic," as he put it in his *Pacificus*. Hamilton's insistence on it recurs from his early work in the Confederation Congress to Washington's Farewell Address.[119] An elaborate statement of it appears in *The Federalist*. Hamilton's skepticism about the national loyalty of *citizens* as opposed to the loyalty of royal *subjects* seems strange to the modern observer steeped in a patriotic tradition that is no weaker in republics like France or the United States than in monarchies like Great Britain. In republics, with their dependence on elected officials, Hamilton argued "persons elevated from the mass of the community, by the suffrages of their fellow-citizens, to stations of great pre-eminence and power, may find compensations for betraying their trust, which, to any but minds animated and guided by superior virtue, may appear to exceed the proportion of interest they have in the common stock, and to overbalance the obligations of duty."[120]

The danger from abroad, in Hamilton's eyes, was compounded by the rivalry of states, parties, and factions.[121] It was one of Hamilton's strongest apprehensions that the Union, unless safeguarded by a strong central government, might break up into two or three rival confederacies that would become the prey of competing European alliance systems. His concern for foreign policy, stemming from his awareness of the way that international politics might impinge upon the young country, profoundly colored his approach to the subject of factions.

Factions, Parties, Sections, and the Extent of Territory:
Hamilton vs. Madison

An appreciation of Hamilton's approach to parties and factions is impossible outside the context of that problem in the political theory of the time. Prior to Edmund Burke, who is inevitably drawn into a discussion of political parties, the eighteenth century's explorations of that subject were far more searching and advanced than is generally supposed. Only recently has this problem begun to receive the attention it deserves.[122] Analytically, it may be helpful to distinguish five positions regarding political parties and factions. The terms were used interchangeably by most writers, including Madison and Hamilton, with the somewhat ambiguous exception of Bolingbroke and the more conspicuous one of Burke.

First, we detect a clash between an exalted notion of the public good, symbolized in the stewardship of the sovereign, and the perhaps seditious, certainly divisive, existence of parties or factions. This clash merely expresses the great dichotomy between public, national, general interest and private, partial, individual interest. It was this dichotomy that Francis Bacon had in mind when he exhorted kings to "beware how they side themselves, and make themselves as of a faction or party; for leagues within the State are ever pernicious to monarchies; for they raise an obligation paramount to obligation of sovereignty, and make the king 'tamquam unus ex nobis' [like one of us]."[123] It is this respect for the exalted function of the sovereign that explains and characterizes both Hobbes's and Rousseau's condemnation of parties.[124] Bacon's warning to kings not to deviate from the straight path of public function points to the view that the sovereign, as the Elizabethans put it, possessed not only a body politic, but a body natural, or in Hobbes's words, a private interest in addition to the public.

A second approach to the role of parties could emerge once royal absolutism had been finally checked. In the era ushered in by the Glorious Revolution, but more particularly in the time of the first Hanoverian kings, parties or factions came to be regarded as signposts of liberty. The doctrine of balanced, or limited government opened the arena of political discussion to the view that "party divisions, whether on the whole operating for good or evil," were "inseparable from free government," as Burke put it.[125] James Madison's statement of the price of freedom in the tenth *Federalist* merely summed up widely current opinion.

Yet from an approach which held that "in all free governments there ever were, and ever will be, parties," it was only a small step to a third position holding that parties were "not only the effect, but the support, of liberty."[126] That conviction, whose roots in the teachings of Machiavelli's *Discourses* are unmistakable, produced the rudiments of a theory of loyal opposition by the middle of the eighteenth century: the "heads of an opposing party" were considered as persons useful "to the public."[127] Whatever the motives (often personal) or even the success of the leaders of an opposing party, Edward Spelman, whose views I am reporting, held that "the public reaps great benefit from the opposition," since this opposition kept ministers upon their guard and often prevented them from pursuing measures which uncontrolled power might otherwise tempt them to engage in.[128]

From that exposition of the role of parties in free governments it was again only a small step to what we might consider a fourth position. If even the existence of admittedly less than public-minded groups was not merely the effect, "but the support," of liberty, groups of truly public-minded men might be an even greater boon to society. The discussion had now come full circle and approached the first issue—private *vs.* public interest—from the opposite direction. For Bacon, Hobbes, and Rousseau, parties were bad because they disturbed the public business with private designs. Bolingbroke, and Burke—who plagiarized him in a way hitherto unsuspected—introduced the notion of a public-minded opposition against the negligent or even corrupt wielders of power. A party, then, indeed became, as Burke said, "a body of men united, for promoting by their joint endeavours the national interest, upon some particular principle in which they are all agreed."[129]

However, this approach did not by any means coincide with

a fifth outlook on parties, which is the one closest to our experience and imagination today: party government in the sense that the reins of the executive as well as the legislative branches of government are in the hands of one political party. Party government, then, was truly established only when party leadership and the holding of the sovereign prerogative became identified. This was not the case in England when the American colonies broke away from the mother country, nor had it happened when Americans framed the Federal Constitution, patterned on the British model. Party government in England was established when "the prime minister replaced the sovereign as actual head of the executive" and "the choice of the prime minister no longer lay with the sovereign."[130] But this happened quite some time after Thomas Jefferson's election to the American presidency had offered the novel—and therefore frightening—spectacle of a party leader stepping into the exalted station of the holder of the sovereign prerogative.[131]

Hamilton was not ahead of his times in evaluating the function of party; indeed he appears somewhat behind. Utterances scattered through his career convey the impression that he wanted to abolish parties. In *The Farmer Refuted* of 1775, years before Washington's warning against party spirit in the Farewell Address, Hamilton indignantly defended himself against the reproach of serving the cause of a party. He could not conceive that "a zealous attachment to the general measures of America" could be "denominated the effect of a party spirit." He accused Dr. Samuel Seabury: "You Sir, and your adherents may be justly deemed a faction, because you compose a small number inimical to the common voice of your country."[132] In 1788, after weary years of contending with the States under the Confederation, Hamilton concluded that the factions in Congress had arisen "from attachment to state prejudices. We are attempting by this Constitution to abolish factions, and to unite all parties for the general welfare."[133]

This seemingly absolute assertion demands, however, a qualified interpretation. Of course Hamilton had set out to reduce the power and rivalries of the States to a minimum, to weld them into a new nation; and this effort was similar to the reduction of faction or party. Hamilton took up the familiar dichotomy of partial *vs.* national, individual *vs.* general interest: "The local interests of a state ought in every case to give way to the interests of the Union. For when a sacrifice of one or the other is necessary, the former becomes only an apparent, partial interest, and should yield, on the principle that the small good ought never to oppose the great one."[134] Yet all this was bound to be a matter of degree. A careful reading of Hamilton's contributions to *The Federalist* demonstrates that Hamilton envisaged the continued existence of parties or factions under the new Constituiton. The fame of Madison's *Federalist* No. 10 and Hamilton's violent threat in No. 9 to suppress, by force, factions on the road to sedition and insurrection have completely obscured Hamilton's anticipation that parties or factions would, *to some degree*, be involved in the normal course of the new government: "As the spirit of party, in different degrees, must be expected to infect all political bodies, there will be, no doubt, persons in the national legislature willing enough to arraign the measures and criminate the views of the majority."[135] Hamilton expected the propaganda of "the party in opposition." There is also a hint that Hamilton regarded parties and factions as more than fleeting combinations created for an *ad hoc* purpose. For instance, when he discussed impeachment, Hamilton predicted that such a prosecution would "seldom fail to agitate the passions of the whole community, and to divide it into parties more or less friendly or inimical to the accused. In many cases it will connect itself with the preexisting factions, and will enlist all their animosities, partialities, influence, and interest on one side or on the other."[136]

Since Hamilton regarded the British monarch as the model for the American executive, he considered the sphere of party activity to be limited to the legislature, and in particular to the lower branch. With regard to Congress, particularly the House of Representatives, Hamilton was, even while writing *The Federalist*, under no illusion about the existence of parties, though his evaluation of their negative and positive aspects is somewhat in the balance. On one occasion, he went so far as to join those who saw in parties "not only the effect, but the support of liberty."[137] Concerning the legislature, he observed: "The differences of opinion, and the jarrings of parties in that department of the government, though they may sometimes obstruct salutary plans, yet often promote deliberation and circumspection, and serve to check excesses in the majority."[138] On the other hand, there were gloomy allusions to "the natural propensity of such bodies to party divisions," to "the pestilential breath of faction." It was on this negative note that Hamilton concluded *The Federalist* with a warning against "an obstinate adherence to party."[139]

There is little reason to wonder at the pessimism in Hamilton's outlook on parties. Few people doubt today that the tolerance and liberality on which Western democracy prides itself is predicated on two assurances: first, the assurance of consensus on fundamentals, which allows a wide margin of disagreement on minor issues; second, the guarantee of the innocuousness of a minority, though it may express fundamental disagreements. Hamilton, however, was confronted with a situation far different from the comfortable assurance with which stable liberal democracies tolerate dissent. It was different even from the situation in eighteenth-century England, where only recently the faint beginnings of a loyal opposition had appeared. In America a unified society was yet to be formed, a nation yet to be built, a consensus yet to be created, and fundamentals yet to be accepted.

James Madison, facing the same predicament, contrived, with Hume's help, a tool for the neutralization of faction in his theory of the "extended sphere" of the Union. But the praise so lavishly heaped upon Madison's theory makes it imperative to point out its lack of realism in one decisive respect: its neglect, whether intended or not, of the sectional, rather than state-centered character of the major alignments of interest in America. Frederick Jackson Turner, in a celebrated paper, has outlined a development that already at the time of the framing of the Constitution opposed the Eastern to the Southern states and, in subsequent decades, set them at odds over the control of the West.[140] Like many other members of the Federal Convention, both Madison and Hamilton were deeply aware of the sectional conflict.[141] All the stranger, therefore, is Madison's either bookish or highly political avoidance of sectional conflict in his theory of party in the tenth and fifty-first *Federalist*. If Madison limited his discussion to the states and the Union—ignoring the intermediate level of sectional conflict—Hamilton was all the more emphatic on the problems posed by the clustering of states around different interests.

In the Federal Convention, Hamilton had disposed of the artificial conflict between the small and the large states and claimed that sectional interests were more significant: "There could not be any ground for combination among the States whose influence was most dreaded. The only considerable distinction of interests, lay between the carrying & non-carrying States, which divide instead of uniting the largest States."[142] In the New York Ratifying Convention, he repeated: "The natural situation of this country seems to divide its interests into different classes. There are navigating and non-navigating States."[143] In several numbers of *The Federalist*, he envisaged "partial confederacies" as an alternative to the Union.[144] He was most outspoken in No. 13: "The entire separation of the States into thirteen unconnected sovereignties is a project too extravagant and too replete with danger to have many advocates. The ideas of men who speculate upon the dismemberment of the empire, seem generally turned towards three confederacies; one consisting of the four northern, another of the four middle, and a third of the five southern States. There is little probability that there would be a greater number."[145] This awareness of conflict among larger entities than the single states gave the problem of parties an ominous twist, which was absent in Madison's great papers.[146] Hamilton, however, emphasized it on various occasions in 1787 and 1788, which places the apprehensions about party politics that he wrote into Washington's Farewell Address in a broader context than one supplied by the admittedly heated controversies of the mid-1790's. It is startling to discover in a section of the Farewell Address that was largely suppressed, apparently at the last moment, by Washington, a full-fledged anti-Madisonian interpretation of party politics in a large nation. At the beginning of that section, which was preserved in the published version, Hamilton repeated a warning made in a previous section on the dangers of "founding our parties on Geographical discriminations."[147] Hamilton, apparently to a greater extent than Washington, wanted "to enlarge the view of this point and caution . . . in the most solemn manner against the baneful effects of party spirit in general." This spirit, he went on, "unfortunately is inseperable from human nature and has its root in the strongest passions of the human heart— It exists under different shapes in all governments in different degrees stifled controuled or repressed but in those of the popular form it is always seen in its utmost vigour & rankness and it is their worst enemy."[148]

Up to this point Hamilton's injunctions were taken over almost literally into Washington's final draft of his address and appeared also in the published version. But now Hamilton entered into the more specific question of the significance of the extent of territory for party spirit, and though the paragraph quoted below was included in Washington's final manuscript, it was omitted in the published address. Hamilton resumed a subject that never ceased to provoke his anxious fascination:

In republics of narrow extent, it is not difficult for those who at any time possess the reins of administration, or even for partial combinations of men, who from birth riches and other sour[c]es of distinction have an extraordinary influence by possessing or acquir[in]g the direction of the military force or by sudden efforts of partisans & followers to overturn the established order of things and effect a usurpation—But in republics of large extent the one or the other is scarcely possible— The powers and opportunities of resistance of a numerous and wide extended nation defy the successful efforts of the ordinary military force or of any assemblages which wealth and patronage may call to their aid—especially if there be no city of overbearing forc[e] resources and influence—In such Republics it is perhaps safe to assert that the conflic[t]s of popular faction offer the only avenues to tyranny & usurpation.[149]

This is an extraordinarily tight and complex argument, more like a disquisition on political theory than a public magistrate's Farewell Address—though it reminds one of the great tradition of Political Testaments in Europe, in which context Felix Gilbert has put the Farewell Address.

There is, to my knowledge, only one discussion of that problem by the Founders that approaches Hamilton's in originality and subtlety—and that is, of course, the tenth *Federalist*. Since Madison's indebtedness to Hume's essay "Idea of a Perfect Commonwealth" is now well established, it is sensible to look for clues to Hamilton's argument in the same work; this procedure also suggests itself because of Hamilton's confessed admiration for Hume, and because Hume's essay is the only original treatment of that intricate subject after and beyond Montesquieu.[150]

Hamilton's argument is obviously correlated with the contemporary conflict between "the wise, and good, and rich" and the Jeffersonians.[151] It sounds like an appeasement of disaffected Jeffersonians when Hamilton gives the assurance that usurpation of power by the wealthy classes is less likely in a large nation than in a small one. In support of this assurance, there is Hamilton's odd reference to cities "of overbearing forc[e] resources and influence." A close look at Hume's essay yields an admittedly conjectural explanation, yet one that plausibly accounts for an otherwise untraceable idea. Hume's "Idea of a Perfect Commonwealth" owed most in theory to Harrington's *Oceana* and in practice to the United Netherlands. However, Hume enumerated a number of improvements of his own scheme of government—tedious and irrelevant for our purposes—on that of the United Provinces. Among them was a provincial organization that remedied the defects of the seven Dutch provinces, "where the jealousy and envy of the smaller provinces and towns against the greater, particularly Holland and Amsterdam, have frequently disturbed the government."[152] The ascendancy of the province of Holland and the city of Amsterdam was, of course, a generally known fact. The twentieth *Federalist* paper, Madison's handiwork, with the help of some material from Hamilton, mentioned "the great wealth and influence of the province of

Holland"—though not specifically the city of Amsterdam.[153] It is more likely than not, then, to suspect in Hume's mention of Amsterdam the example of Hamilton's strange reference to a "city of overbearing forc[e] resources and influence."

Yet more important than the slightly bookish argument with which Hamilton apparently hoped to accommodate Jeffersonian misgivings on the designs of the "monocrats" or "Anglomen," there is the assertion—in stark contrast to Madison's optimism in *Federalist* No. 10—that in large republics like America "the conflicts of popular faction offer the only avenue to tyranny & usurpation."[154] Washington deemed the idea important enough to include in the published Farewell Address. Hamilton's long-standing fears about sectional factions had received, by the mid-1790's, enough fuel to produce the expectation of a majority faction ruling the entire nation—the very expectation Madison had hoped to dispel by emphasizing the large extent of the Union. Hamilton in 1796 anticipated what was to be realized a few years later by Jefferson's elevation to the presidency—the coincidence of party leadership and assumption of sovereign prerogative, party government in its truly modern meaning:

The domination ["alternate domination," in Washington's final manuscript] of one faction over another stimulated by that spirit of Revenge which is apt to be gradually engendered and which in different ages and countries have produced the greatest enormities is itself a frightful despotism—But this leads at length to a more formal and permanent despotism—The disorders and miseries which result predispose the minds of men to seek repose & security in the absolute power of a single man. And some leader of a prevailing faction more able or more fortunate than his competitiors turns this disposition to the purpose of an ambitious and criminal self aggrandisement.[155]

Hamilton presented, then, in the Farewell Address a theory of faction that differed decisively from Madison's theory expounded in *The Federalist* and elsewhere. Yet, strange as it may appear at first sight, Hamilton's fears of the establishment of despotism or absolute monarchy by a successful demagogue also found support in the very paper of Hume's that had inspired

Madison. Hume made a distinction that Madison neglected, perhaps to let sleeping dogs lie: the distinction between the problems of *establishing* and of *maintaining* a republic. To create a republic and to keep it stable, according to Hume, were different tasks, and of different degrees of difficulty in small or large republics. Hume argued that small republics might be established easily since consensus among neighbors could be speedily achieved, though the very speed of engineering majority consent would lead to turbulence and insecurity in the long run. Large republics, on the other hand, offered the greater promise of durability precisely because of the variety of their local interests, remote from one another. This, of course, was Madison's theory. In the tenth *Federalist*, Madison fastened upon Hume's argument in support of large republics after they had been established; but by so doing, he put the cart before the horse; Madison omitted, in effect, the first part of Hume's considerations on large republics, namely the difficulties of founding them. "It is not easy for distant parts of a large state," Hume had observed, "to combine in any plan of free government; but they easily conspire in the esteem and reverence for a single person who, by means of this popular favor, may seize the power and, forcing the more obstinate to submit, may establish a monarchical government."[156]

These are words strongly reminiscent of Hamilton's many misgivings on the chances of republican government in America. They anticipate the vast and sinister role that Hamilton so frequently ascribed to ambitious demagogues; they forecast even more explicitly Hamilton's argument that the capture of the people by a Caesar or Catiline would be the only road to monarchy in America.[157] They also point, however, to the function of outstanding individuals in the establishment of states (discussed in Chapter V).

Hamilton's and Madison's approaches to factions and parties went separate ways, above all with respect to sectionalism in America; with these approaches went different attitudes toward the special problems involved in founding rather than in maintaining a nation both free and extensive. Yet the difference between Madison and Hamilton was one of degree. In an obscure little essay on "Parties," written in 1792, Madison suggested five methods of combating the "evil" of parties! He recommended measures to insure political, legal, and maximum economic equality and, so far as the existence of parties could not be prevented, to make one party a check on the other. Madison closed on a note of sober warning: "From the expediency, in politics, of making natural parties, mutual checks on each other, to infer the propriety of creating artificial parties, in order to form them into mutual checks, is no less absurd than it would be in ethics, to say, that new vices ought to be promoted, where they would counteract each other, because this use may be made to existing vices."[158] This is scarcely different from Hamilton's final word on the subject in the Farewell Address, which displays remarkable restraint and detachment:

There is an opinion that parties in free countries are salutary checks upon the administration of the Government & serve to invigorate the spirit of Liberty—This within certain limits is true and *in governments of a monarchical character or byass patriotism may look with some favour on the spirit of party*. But in those of the popular kind in those purely elective, it is a spirit not to be fostered or incouraged. From the natural tendency of such governments, it is certain there will always be enough of it for every salutary purpose and there being constant danger of excess the effort ought to be by force of public opinion to mitigate & correct it.[159]

Hamilton's Discovery of Collective Emotions

Hamilton's appeal to public opinion to correct the vices of factionalism indicates a new emphasis in his theory of political motivation. A party or a faction, Hamilton's earlier writings had made clear, was but one aspect of the ever-present friction and fusion of private passions or interests that directed the lives of all men, save those filled with the most exalted thirst for fame. In the 1780's, and in the years when he produced his great economic reports, Hamilton would no doubt have endorsed literally, as he did in substance, the idea that his collaborator in the *Camil-*

lus letters, Rufus King, lifted wholly out of Adam Smith: that the "private interests" of individuals were much more unconquerable than "public opinion."[160] Even in the Farewell Address, traces of this idea can be found. In it the evocation of patriotism, of the common struggle for Liberty and Independence, of the affections owed by the children of a common country, is followed by the observation that "the considerations which address themselves to your sensibility are even outweighed by those which apply to your interest—Here every portion of our Country will find the most urgent and commanding motives for guarding and preserving the Union of the whole."[161] Though the appeal to the "interested passions" still prevails it does not weigh as heavily in the balance as in Hamilton's earlier writings. The direction was plainly toward reestablishing the importance of those intangibles of collective and national consciousness which, in *The Federalist*, had been taken care of by Jay and even Madison, rather than Hamilton.[162]

With the progress of the French Revolution and the enthusiasm and excitement it produced in America, Hamilton was bound to be impressed with a phenomenon that had little place in his early system of political things: men's devotion and abandonment to abstract causes—to ideologies, as we would say today. Not that such a thing would have been unimaginable to informed and thoughtful men in the eighteenth century. David Hume had conceived of ideological parties, in his analysis "Parties in General," in a way that strikes us as startlingly modern. "Parties from *principle*," Hume said, "especially abstract speculative principle, are known only to modern times and are, perhaps, the most extraordinary and unaccountable phenomenon that has yet appeared in human affairs." Unaccountable as it might seem, Hume was not at a loss to provide a psychological explanation that again astonishes the reader by its ring of contemporaneity. "Such is the nature of the human mind," according to Hume, "that it always lays hold on every mind that approaches it, and as it is wonderfully fortified by a unanimity of sentiments, so it is shocked and disturbed by any contrariety."[163] These comments were addressed to the religious controversies of the preceding centuries.

The French Revolution renewed the contest for principle that the philosophers of the Enlightenment had hoped to replace with the milder contests of interest well understood. This trend was strongest in its Girondist phase of worldwide proselytizing, carried to America by the notorious Citizen Genêt. The ideological fervor of Jeffersonian propaganda, kindled by the fire of the French Revolution itself, had a profound impact on Hamilton. "Federalists and Republicans alike," Samuel Eliot Morison has said, "believed that their country's fate depended on the issue of events across the Atlantic."[164] The early divisions on Hamilton's economic policies, notwithstanding, Jefferson was quite correct when he wrote that only the great war between France and the European powers "brought forward the two parties [in America] with an ardour which our own interests merely, could never excite."[165] The wars of the French Revolution exerted a deeply corroding influence on Hamilton's earlier theories of self-interest.

The internationalist ideology of the French Revolution, when backed up by the bayonets of Napoleon's armies, aroused European nationalism. Similarly, the infusion of ideological enthusiasm into American politics prompted Hamilton to counter internationalist ideology with nationalist ideology. Traces of an appreciation of nationalism in Hamilton's thought can be seen in *Pacificus* or in the Farewell Address, and by 1798, Hamilton clearly articulated "that the prominent original feature of her [France's] revolution is the spirit of proselytism, or the desire of new modelling the political institutions of the rest of the world according to her standard." His reaction was to stress those "venerable pillars that support the edifice of civilized society"—religious opinion, in particular the teachings of Christianity.[166] Hamilton now paid heed to the potent, if often submerged, influence of ideas. He stressed that "ideas which have once taken deep root in a community, and have enlisted its passions against one object and in favor of another, cannot suddenly be changed."[167] In 1802,

Hamilton spoke about the conditions of national unity in republican regimes in a manner for which one would have looked in vain one or two decades earlier: "The safety of a republic depends essentially on the energy of a common national sentiment; on a uniformity of principles and habits; on the exemption of the citizens from foreign bias, and prejudice; and on that love of country which will almost invariably be found to be closely connected with birth, education, and family."[168]

It was a sign of the times that Hamilton now abandoned his earlier liberal views on immigration as expressed in the *Report on Manufactures*[169] and pleaded for the homogeneity of Americans. By 1802, he paid Jefferson the surprising compliment that the "opinion advanced in the Notes on Virginia is undoubtedly correct" that foreigners would generally bring with them attachments to their native country; even if they were led to America from a preference to its government, how extremely unlikely was it "that they will bring with them that *temperate love of liberty*, so essential to real republicanism." The influx of foreigners would tend "to produce a heterogeneous compound; to change and corrupt the national spirit." If a decade earlier immigration had been for Hamilton a vehicle of industrial growth for America, he now feared the introduction of "foreign propensities."[170] In the same year, Hamilton searched his conscience for the mistakes that had caused the downfall of the Federalist party. The results of this self-examination mirrored the bitterness of a man who feels that he has been duped:

Men are rather reasoning than reasonable animals, for the most part governed by the impulse of passion. This is a truth well understood by our adversaries, who have practised upon it with no small benefit to their cause; for at the very moment they are eulogizing the reason of men, and professing to appeal only to the faculty, they are courting the strongest and most active passion in the human heart, *vanity*! It is no less true, that the Federalists seem not to have attended to the fact sufficiently; and that they erred in relying so much on the rectitude and utility of their measures as to have neglected the cultivation of popular favor, by fair and justifiable expedients.[171]

The twist in this self-criticism is strange because Hamilton had, of course, appealed in his great speech in the Federal Convention to the management of the passions: "... The government must be so constituted as to offer strong motives. In short, to interest all the *passions* of individuals.[172]

Hamilton was deceiving himself when the despair of defeat inspired him with the idea that the "noble" appeal to reason distinguished him and his fellow Federalists from the passion-manipulating Jeffersonians. What Hamilton had done was not to appeal to reason instead of passion, but to limit too severely the sphere of human passions by concentrating on "self-interest" or "selfishness." The ideological fervor of the French Revolution triggered off, both within France and without, the demonic potentialities of a passion that the eighteenth century had limited to the world of personal relations, remote from politics and business—benevolence. The mild passion of benevolence or altruism underwent a terrifying metamorphosis when brought into contact with politics. Nationalism has demonstrated what modern psychology, from Dostoevski, Nietzsche, and Freud to Erich Fromm and Eric Hoffer, has proclaimed—the amazing degree to which individuals may be willing to divest themselves of their self-interests, and the eagerness with which they may espouse a cause that demands self-sacrifice. The ability of modern man to identify himself with larger entities, of which the most conspicuous has been the nation state, was beyond the ken of Hamilton's theory of passions. This defect explains his amazing theory of "foreign influence in republics," which plays such a large role in *The Federalist* and in other writings of Hamilton. It was the great failure of the political psychology born in the seventeenth and eighteenth centuries that it ignored a whole dimension of human potentialities—perhaps because it paid little attention to the great mass of the people. In Hamilton's day, the essence of sin was *hybris*, pride. The direction in which man, like Milton's Satan, was seen to transgress his measure was that of rebellion, emancipation. The almost monotonous repetition of the "power theme" in the political literature of the late-seventeenth and eighteenth centuries

—the lust for power and corruption through power—is eloquent. Today, we seem to have become aware that our worst temptation may be idolatry, rather than pride.

Our experience of mass emotions makes Hamilton's somewhat labored theory of the individual interest appear in a pale and remote light. Hamilton, often called a despiser of human nature, actually looked upon the individual with his private passions as a much more solid entity than we can admit today. It was only toward the end of his life that he dimly perceived the flaws of his earlier theory and detected the strength of ideological sentiment —regardless of the form of government. It is surely a matter of regret that his discovery of nationalism as a potent factor in politics should have had such a questionable result as his suggestion of a Christian Constitutional Society, which was a fairly crude attempt to enlist the benevolent and altruistic traditions of Christianity for the purpose of bolstering, or rather breeding, nationalism. Hamilton paid his respects to the dawning Age of the True Believer reluctantly. He did not hold back, privately, his deep distaste for what no doubt he considered the essence of demagoguery. The clubs of the proposed Christian Constitutional Society, obviously patterned upon the Democratic-Republican Societies of the 1790's, though lacking their spontaneity, were regarded by Hamilton as a necessary evil. The "imitation" of Jeffersonian devices to which he admitted, was not meant to include "things intrinsically unworthy, but only ... such as may be denominated irregular; such as, in a sound and stable order of things, ought not to exist."[178] As we know, nothing came of the project.

These were hesitant, indeed clumsy, steps in a direction which plainly was that of the age to come. Brilliant in reasoned argument, Hamilton failed in the task of mass persuasion, thus reflecting not merely his peculiar talents, but his views of human nature as well. He grasped instinctively, as well as intellectually, the way men might transform their natural temptations by the quest for fame, yet he was unable to tackle the politics of incipient mass society. In all these respects Hamilton very much remained a man and statesman of his century.

IV

THE FOREIGN POLICY OF
REPUBLICAN GOVERNMENT

The Peacefulness of Republics: Charles Pinckney vs.
Alexander Hamilton

An exchange in the Federal Convention between Charles Pinckney of South Carolina and Alexander Hamilton contained the
seed of the great debates between "Idealists" and "Realists" that
have recurred at turning points of American history. Pinckney's
argument in the Convention, Louis Hartz has justly observed,
surpassed on a number of points what is now widely considered
the masterpiece of the Founding Fathers' political thought, Madison's *Federalist* No. 10.[1] Neither the virtues of the ancients nor
the vices of the moderns prevailed in America, Pinckney told the
august assembly. The people of this country were "not only very
different from the inhabitants of any State we are acquainted with
in the modern world," but their situation was "distinct from either
the people of Greece or Rome, or of any State we are acquainted
with among the ancients." Could the "orders introduced by the
institution of Solon" be found in the United States? Could the
"military habits & manners of Sparta be resembled to our habits
& manners?"[2]

Pinckney put forward a social and political analysis that anticipated in many respects Alexis de Tocqueville's comments. Among
the people of the United States there were "fewer distinctions of
fortune & less of rank, than among the inhabitants of any other
nation." Every freeman had "a right to the same protection &
security"; and "a very moderate share of property" entitled him
"to the possession of all the honors and privileges the public can

bestow." Hence arose "a greater equality, than is to be found among the people of any other country"—an equality that was likely to continue, because "in a new Country, possessing immense tracts of uncultivated lands, where every temptation is offered to emigration & where industry must be rewarded with competency, there will be few poor, and few dependent." Under these circumstances, the respects so widely paid to the British Constitution were of little help to the predicament of the Americans. Pinckney admitted that the British Constitution was "the best constitution in existence"; but, he said, "at the same time I am confident it is one that will not or can not be introduced into this Country, for many centuries."[3]

The peculiarity of the American situation was not without consequence for the conduct of foreign affairs. The social context, the constitutional fabric, and international relations were for Pinckney inseparable:

Our true situation appears to me to be this.—a new extensive Country containing within itself the materials for forming a Government capable of extending to its citizens all the blessings of civil & religious liberty—capable of making them happy at home. *This is the great end of Republican Establishments.* We mistake the object of our government, if we hope or wish that it is to make us respectable abroad. Conquest or superiority among other powers is not or ought not ever to be the object of republican systems. If they are sufficiently active & energetic to rescue us from contempt & preserve our domestic happiness & security, it is all we can expect from them,—it is more than almost any other Government ensures to its citizens.[4]

A few days later, Alexander Hamilton retorted sharply: "It has been said that respectability in the eyes of foreign nations was not the object at which we aimed; that the proper object of republican Government was domestic tranquillity & happiness. This was an ideal distinction. No Governmt. could give us tranquillity & happiness at home, which did not possess sufficient stability and strength to make us respectable abroad."[5]

This exchange deserves careful examination.[6] For a century and a half, the study of political theory and the study of international relations have been divorced from one another. Foreign affairs have been the domain of the diplomatic historian, of the international lawyer, and of the economist. The political theorist's quest for the good society has proceeded within the walls of the city. Principles of political obligation and organization have been sought and studied within the confines of a given society. Foreign affairs, when they figure at all, have been seldom more than a kind of afterthought, a consequence, an implication of the proper ordering of domestic society.

The divorce of political theory and international relations has left its imprint on our approach to the study of the Founders' intent and procedure while framing new forms of government. Alexander Hamilton's thought, in particular, cannot be properly understood unless one grasps the interrelationship of the foreign and domestic halves of his political theory as much as of his statesmanship. There is a need, then, to scrutinize the background of the issue that found Pinckney and Hamilton on different sides. We shall fail to understand the purpose as well as the form of Hamilton's struggle for America's respectability abroad unless we first come to grips with the notions he opposed.

Was Charles Pinckney, boldly cutting through all kinds of prejudices, an innovator of theories of foreign policy? There is every reason to think that he was not. Pinckney's originality lay in his unconventional and ingenious application of ideas and principles already in existence, and not in sketching new political theories. With slight variations, the clash between Pinckney and Hamilton was duplicated elsewhere. Its most striking recurrence was perhaps in the Ratifying Convention of Virginia, where James Madison opposed Patrick Henry. The old orator Henry, with less moderation and perspicacity than Pinckney, expatiated on the changing times with their trend toward absolutism, monarchism, and imperialism. His rhetoric struck a surprisingly modern note:

The American spirit has fled from hence: it has gone to regions where it has never been expected; it has gone to the people of France, in search of a splendid government—a strong, energetic government.

Shall we imitate the example of those nations who have gone from a simple to a splendid government? Are those nations more worthy of our imitation? What can make an adequate satisfaction to them for the loss they have suffered in attaining such a government—for the loss of their liberty? If we admit this consolidated government, it will be because we like a great, splendid one. Some way or other we must be a great and mighty empire; we must have an army, and a navy, and a number of things. When the American spirit was in its youth, the language of America was different: liberty, sir, was then the primary object.[7]

Patrick Henry, of course, by 1788 had become a living monument to his earlier fame, and he spoke accordingly. In actual debate, he proved inferior to his opponents, among them James Madison, who refused to be drawn into Henry's alternatives. Less emotionally, Madison said: "I agree with the honorable gentleman [Mr. Henry] that national splendor and glory are not our objects; but does he distinguish between what will render us secure and happy at home, and what will render us respectable abroad? If we be free and happy at home we shall be respectable abroad."[8] Madison and Henry obviously differed about the conditions for domestic security and happiness, but they certainly agreed on the evil of expansionism for republics. Other voices with the same intent were heard. John Dickinson of "Pennsylvania Farmer" fame, anxiously watching for signs of decaying virtue, pointed out that the imitation of foreign fashions might destroy republican simplicity and continued, with a logic that seems strange to our times: "The other fault, of which, as yet, there are no symptoms among us, is the *thirst of empire*. This is a vice, that ever has been, and from the nature of things, ever must be, fatal to republican forms of government."[9]

Foreign policy, it appears, played a far from negligible role in the Founders' debates on a proper frame of government. We again find Tom Paine's *Common Sense* the most appropriate point of departure. This pamphlet has long been recognized as one of the earliest authentic voices of American isolationism,[10] but the peculiar interdependence of constitutional arguments and those drawn from foreign policy deserves special attention. Paine's indictment of monarchy, starting with Biblical times, was phrased so as to prove royal responsibility for bloodshed and war: "In the early ages of the world, according to the Scripture chronology there were no kings; the consequence of which was there were no wars; it is the pride of kings which throws mankind into confusion. Holland without a king hath enjoyed more peace for this last century than any of the monarchical governments in Europe. Antiquity favors the same remark; for the quiet and rural lives of the first patriarchs have a happy something in them, which vanishes when we come to the history of Jewish royalty."[11] After a series of no less doubtful historical assertions Paine satisfied himself that "in short, monarchy and succession have laid (not this or that kingdom only) but the world in blood and ashes. 'Tis a form of government which the word of God bears testimony against, and blood will attend it."[12] The opposite qualities of republican government were now easy to deduce.

How did the generation of the Founding Fathers come to think, as Hamilton put it in the outline to his great speech of June 18, 1787, that the "Genius of republics" was "pacific"? Tom Paine, after all, was a born popularizer, an eclectic and synthetic writer who intuitively knew how to turn ideas picked up almost at random into the right argument at the right time. Yet the ancestry of the notion that peacefulness characterizes republican foreign policy is intricate indeed. It is largely uncharted territory that we now enter, and extensive exploration is called for.

Peace and the Good Society in Classical Political Thought

A number of distinct, though interrelated sources went into the making of a thesis that provoked Hamilton's criticism. Basically, there were two complexes of ideas that confronted the Founders with impressive evidence about the predetermined character of republican foreign policy. There was, first, the classical ideal of the good life in a perfect commonwealth, tied to a state of radically limited size and, by implication, to a defensive rather than an aggressive foreign policy. There was, second, the distinctly *modern* idea of the effects of free international trade on the conduct of international affairs.

The time-spanning impact of classical political philosophy was conveyed to the Founders through Montesquieu's statement that "the spirit of monarchy is war and enlargement of dominion: peace and moderation are the spirit of a republic."[13] When Plato and Aristotle regarded peace as a more truly human condition than war, when they considered perfection as a more dignified quest than the ambition to rule, they expressed a theory of politics that has aptly been described by Leo Strauss as "the primacy of internal policy."[14] Strauss summed up Plato's theory of justice as

the unconditional primacy of internal policy. . . . For this theory says: there is no happiness for men without justice; justice means attending to one's own business, bringing oneself into the right disposition with regard to the transcendent unchanging norm, to which the soul is akin, and not meddling into other people's affairs; and justice in the State is not different from justice in the individual, except that the State is self-sufficient and can thus practice justice—attending to his own business—incomparably more perfectly than can the individual who is not self-sufficient. Accordingly for the properly constituted State its self-assertion against other States is an accidental result of its proper constitution and not its main object.[15]

In Aristotle's *Politics* too, the primacy of conquest and domination in a state's scale of aims is condemned. It is perfectly possible "to imagine a solitary state which is happy in itself and in isolation. Assume such a state, living somewhere or other all by itself, and living under a good system of law. It will obviously have a good constitution; but the scheme of its constitution will have no regard to war, or to the conquest of enemies, who, upon our hypothesis, will not exist."[16] Aristotle, of course, took great pains to point out that virtually all existing states gave priority to conquest and domination, and he produced an impressive list of the customs and practices of many peoples, Greek and non-Greek, that reflected the primacy of military pursuits: "It is true that, in most states, most of the laws are only a promiscuous heap of legislation; but we have to confess that where they are directed, in any degree, to a single object, that object is always conquest."[17] Of course there was need for military preparedness. If a state had neighbors, it was the duty of a lawgiver to "provide the modes of military training suited to their different characters, and, generally, to take the proper measures for meeting the challenge offered by each."[18] Yet the needs of defense should be strictly subordinated to the true goal of legislation:

In support of the view that the legislator should make leisure and peace the cardinal aims of all legislation bearing on war—or indeed, for that matter, on anything else—we may cite the evidence of actual fact. Most of the states which make war their aim are safe only while they are fighting. They collapse as soon as they have established an empire, and lose the edge of their temper, like an unused sword, in time of peace. The legislator is to blame for having provided no training for the proper use of leisure.[19]

Early Modern Thought on Foreign Policy: Empirical Study and Natural Law

The founder of modern political thought, Machiavelli, found his inspiration in the practice of antiquity rather than in its philosophy. What Aristotle had deplored as an unhappy reality, Machiavelli made the cornerstone of his new approach to politics. The classical philosophers had proclaimed the normative primacy of internal policy, while admitting the actual primacy of foreign policy. Machiavelli elevated the primacy of foreign policy to a normative level. And yet the classical philosophers' distinction between the actual and the desirable was not entirely extinguished, even in Machiavelli: "If any one therefore wishes to establish an entirely new republic," Machiavelli said in the *Discourses*, "he will have to consider whether he wishes to have her expand in power and dominion like Rome, or whether he intends to confine her within narrow limits."[20] Machiavelli admitted—or perhaps paid lip-service to—the ethical priority of a life of peace when he said that a republic designed for self-preservation rather than aggrandizement "would be the best political existence, and would insure to any state real tranquillity."[21] At any rate, there seemed room for choice even in the "realistic" universe in which foreign policy was of primary importance, beyond and above the grim Hobbesian predicament of *homo homini lupus*. If a republic aimed at aggrandizement, it would be necessary "to organize her as Rome was." If not, a legislator might

organize her like Sparta and Venice; but as expansion is the poison of such republics, he must by every means in his power prevent her from making conquests, for such acquisitions by a feeble republic always prove their ruin, as happened to both Sparta and Venice.

I think, then, that to found a republic which should endure a long time it would be best to organize her internally like Sparta, or to locate her, like Venice, in some strong place; and to make her sufficiently powerful, so that no one could hope to overcome her readily, and yet on the other hand not so powerful as to make her formidable to her neighbors. In this wise she might long enjoy her independence. For there are but two motives for making war against a republic: one, the desire to subjugate her; the other, the apprehension of being subjugated by her. The two means which we have indicated remove, as it were, both these pretexts for war; for if the republic is difficult to be conquered, her defences being well organized, as I presuppose, then it will seldom or never happen that any one will venture upon the project of conquering her. If she remains quiet within her limits, and experience shows that she entertains no ambitious projects, the fear of her power will never prompt any one to attack her; and this would even be more certainly the case if her constitution and laws prohibited all aggrandizement.[22]

It is not difficult to recognize in this passage the nucleus of the American Founders' debates on the proper relationship of foreign policy and constitutional structure in the new republic. Their concern was prompted less by the perusal of Machiavelli himself, than by the impact of widely known writers such as Francis Bacon, James Harrington, Algernon Sidney, and Montesquieu.

The unfortunate tendency in recent times to regard the seventeenth- and eigtheenth-century philosophers of natural rights as the representative political theorists of that time is responsible for our neglect of a tradition in political thought that applied the most subtle and discriminating insights to the relationship between social and political structure and the conduct of foreign policy. When Hobbes equated the state of nature, in which every individual was endowed with the same rights, with the state of international society, he created the conditions for a simplistic and one-sided approach to foreign affairs that he no doubt did not intend and that he probably did not anticipate; he, like Locke and others, was well aware of the peculiarly moral and juridical limits of his task. It was a juridical line of reasoning that endowed every independent "sovereign" entity with "equal" rights. Hobbes thus became the founder of the doctrine of the sovereign equality of states, received by John Locke, Samuel Pufendorf, and virtually the whole body of subsequent international law.[23] Significantly, we encounter it in Hamilton's writings at a place devoted to the "opinion of jurists" in a work that contained his most extensive examination of international law, the *Camillus* essays. Hamilton closely paraphrased Vattel when he defined the voluntary law of nations as "a system of rules resulting from the equality and independence of nations, and which, in the administration of their affairs, and the pursuit of their pretensions, proceeding on the principle of their having no common judge upon earth, attributes equal validity, as to external effects, to the measures or conduct of one as of another, without regard to the intrinsic justice of those measures or that conduct."[24] Vattel had gone even further in explaining the juridical, nonpolitical aspect of the equality of states in a famous phrase: "Strength or weakness, in this case, counts for nothing. A dwarf is as much a man as a giant is; a small Republic is no less a sovereign State than the most powerful Kingdom."[25]

The doctrine of the equality of states has fulfilled and fulfills a valid function as a brake on too blatant efforts of great power imperialism.[26] Its incompatibility with the doctrine of just war, with the punitive idea of war, has served and serves to check attempts to submerge national boundaries in transnational, ideological "civil" wars of potentially worldwide character.[27] Yet the emphasis that a legalistic approach to foreign policy has put on this doctrine has kept the analysis of international relations from ever reaching the level of empirical investigation that alone points the way to fruitful generalizations in an area wider than international law. When recognized within its legal limits, the notion of the equality of states was eminently useful; yet extending it to the field of political analysis was apt to breed illusions—the characteristic illusions of Wilsonianism.[28]

Both the Wilsonian approach to foreign affairs and the reaction it caused—the "pure power politics" school of international relations—have obscured the great subtlety of an empirical science of international politics that flourished in the epoch between Machiavelli and the French Revolution. The analytical concern of that science with the manifold nuances and distinctions in the international behavior of nations, the discriminating discernment of varied motivations and goals in foreign affairs beyond the ubiquitous and formal aim of "self-preservation," is best shown by Montesquieu:

Though all governments have the same general end, which is that of preservation, yet each has another particular object. Increase of dominion was the object of Rome; war, that of Sparta; religion, that of the Jewish laws; commerce, that of Marseilles; public tranquillity, that of the laws of China; navigation, that of the laws of Rhodes; natural liberty, that of the policy of the Savages; in general, the pleasure of the prince, that of despotic states; that of monarchies, the prince's and the kingdom's glory; the independence of individuals is the end aimed at by the laws of Poland, thence results the oppression of the whole.

One nation [England] there is also in the world that has for the direct end of its constitution political liberty.[29]

The more we become aware of this empirical tradition, of a science of politics that considered internal and external policy merely as the two sides of one coin, the more our realization of its impact on the American Founders grows.[30] James Harrington, whom John Adams read and admired, knew of Machiavelli's division of commonwealths "into such as are for *preservation* ... and such as are for *encrease*."[31] Algernon Sidney was more outspoken: he believed that the primacy of foreign policy should be a factor in constitution making. Sidney alluded to Machiavelli's classification in a section entitled "Commonwealths seek peace or war, according to the variety of their constitutions." Sidney's analysis was enriched by a vastly significant element in the maritime power politics of an expanding Britain: commerce, or the pursuit of private wealth in international trade. "Many have doubted whether it were better to constitute a commonwealth for war, or for trade; and of such as intend for war, whether those are most to be praised who prepare for defence only, or those who design by conquest to enlarge their dominions. Or, if they admit of trade, whether they should propose the acquisition of riches for their ultimate end, and depend upon foreign or mercenary forces to defend them; or to be as helps to enable their own people to carry on those wars, in which they may frequently be engaged."[32] Sidney's answer was unequivocal. Not only were those forms of government better which were designed for war, but conquest was better than defense!

But experience teaching us, that those only can be safe who are strong, and that no people was ever well defended, but those who fought for themselves, the best judges of these matters have always given the preference to those constitutions that principally intend war, and make use of trade as assisting to that end; and think it better to aim at conquest, than simply to stand upon their own defence: since he that loses all, if he be overcome, fights upon very unequal terms; and if he obtain the victory, gains no other advantage, than for the present to repel the danger that threatened him.[33]

Sidney's examples were those also set forth by Machiavelli: Rome and Carthage; Sparta and Venice. In another section, entitled "That is the best government which best provides for war," Sidney pointed out that the division of governments according to their fitness for a vigorous conduct of foreign policy overshadowed all other distinctions. "This does not less concern monarchies than commonwealths; not the absolute less than the mixed: all of them have been prosperous or miserable; glorious or contemptible, as they were better or worse armed, disciplined, or conducted."[34]

Sidney's reference to "the best judges in these matters" is most likely to have meant Machiavelli. Machiavelli's acknowledgment that states built for preservation and tranquillity might, in theory, be best, gave way to the practical consideration that the uncertainty made the risk hardly worth taking. In other words, Machiavelli's freedom of choice in foreign policy was severely limited. All things being in perpetual movement, states were compelled "to many acts to which reason will not influence them." Heedless of Aristotle's exhortations, Machiavelli argued that continued tranquillity was likely to enervate a republic, or to provoke internal dissensions, both things that were apt to bring it to ruin. It was "proper," then, "in the organization of a republic to select the most honorable course, and to constitute her so that, even if necessity should oblige her to expand, she may yet be able to preserve her acquisitions." It was therefore "necessary rather to take the constitution of Rome as a model than that of any other republic."[35]

Machiavelli proclaimed the primacy of foreign policy in terms hardly different from its most brutally candid formulation in Hobbes's *Leviathan*: "And as for very little commonwealths, be they popular, or monarchical, there is no human wisdom can uphold them, longer than the jealousy lasteth of their potent neighbours."[36]

We find ourselves amidst the beginning of a political tradition that included Alexander Hamilton among its most forceful defenders, as appears from No. 8 of *The Federalist*:

Safety from external danger is the most powerful director of national conduct. Even the ardent love of liberty will, after a time, give way to its dictates. The violent destruction of life and property incident to war—the continual effort and alarm attendant on a state of continual danger, will compel nations the most attached to liberty, to resort for repose and security, to institutions, which have a tendency to destroy their civil and political rights. To be more safe they, at length, become willing to run the risk of being less free.[37]

If we disregard, for the time being, Hamilton's predispositions, it is surely striking to see both the absolutist Hobbes and the republican Sidney assert the primacy of war over peace. As regards the thesis of the peacefulness of republican governments, the belligerent attitudes of republicans like Machiavelli and Sidney surely must raise grave doubts. To the experience of history the recommendations of respected theoreticians were added, creating a predisposition not only against the rhetoric of Tom Paine, but against a much greater authority, Montesquieu himself.

Montesquieu's Concept of International Relations

If it seems that early modern thinkers were virtually unanimous in asserting the primacy of foreign policy, Montesquieu—and Rousseau, who followed him in this respect—appear to hark back to classical political philosophy. We now have to recall our previous investigations, in Chapter II, of the early modern republican efforts to join ideals of antiquity with a modern conception of human nature. But in contrast to this earlier instance, the differences between Machiavelli and Montesquieu are now striking and significant. Montesquieu was concerned with the philosophy of antiquity in addition to its history, whereas Machiavelli was not. Montesquieu's effort to attain with the contrivance of the passions what the classics upheld as the highest achievement of reason was also reflected in his preferences in the realm of foreign policy. Aristotle contrasted the desirable pursuit of peace and leisure with the actual pursuit of war and conquest. Machiavelli juxtaposed the quest for stable and merely defensive government with the practical need for glorious expansion. Montesquieu took yet a third stand. He abandoned the Aristotelian concern for leisure and peace, since his virtuous republic lacked the slave class whose manual labor made leisure possible, and ignored the perfection of reason that made it worthwhile. The end of his ideal republic was the passionate love of the public good contrived by individual austerity—the ideal of a contemplative life had definitely sunk beneath the horizon. On the other hand, Montesquieu rejected Machiavelli's preference for Roman expansion in favor of Spartan stability. Sparta, that touchstone of centuries of political theorizing, received strikingly different treatment by these three giants of political science. Aristotle condemned it in no uncertain terms as a warlike state.[38] Machiavelli judged it an ultimate failure and proof of the unreliability of republics designed merely for preservation.[39] But Montesquieu praised Sparta in a way that would have shocked Aristotle and might have met the skeptical smile of Machiavelli: "The long duration of the republic of Sparta was owing to her having continued in the same extent of territory after all her wars. The sole aim of Sparta was liberty; and the sole advantage of her liberty, glory." Montesquieu added that it "was the spirit of the Greek republics to be as contented with their territories as with their laws." All was lost only "upon the starting up of monarchy—a government whose spirit is more turned to increase of dominion."[40]

Montesquieu, then, presented noteworthy modifications of both ancient and early modern trends of thought. For the reasons just indicated, the Aristotelian ideal of leisure and peace was replaced by Machiavelli's "Spartan" alternative of defensive war, of stability and longevity with liberty and virtue, which meant zeal for the public good. In other words, a close reading of Montesquieu's prescriptions for *virtuous* republics—there exist other kinds as well—shows us that "peace" as a principle of these republics only means the absence of wars of expansion!

Montesquieu's peculiar slant on the different proclivities of republican and monarchical governments toward expansion stands in contrast to both Machiavelli and Sidney. Those two republicans were not afraid of large territories for republics, for free and virtuous states—even though classical political philosophy had held that large states could only be despotisms, where fear and coercion took the place of friendship and trust. Machiavelli thought that he had found the remedy in a rigorous enforcement of private austerity and frugality—the lack of which he regarded as responsible for the decline of Rome.[41] Sidney felt that representative government solved the difficulties that otherwise might exist.[42] Montesquieu, however, was more pessimistic than Machiavelli about the possibility of avoiding the evils that led to the downfall of Rome.[43] The very expansion and overextension of Rome, Montesquieu believed, had brought about the decay of republican virtue, for "in an extensive republic there are men of large fortunes, and consequently of less moderation. . . . In an extensive republic the public good is sacrificed to a thousand private views."[44]

There is yet another reason for Montesquieu's vindication of peace and moderation as safeguards of virtue. During the sixteenth, seventeenth, and eighteenth centuries, France was the scene of one of the most famous political debates of early modern times—the debate on the pursuit of "universal monarchy." In the time of the emperor Charles V (whom Alexander Hamilton regarded as "a sovereign who bid fair to realize the project of universal monarchy"),[45] the French were the foremost enemies of that concept.[46] In the seventeenth-century, Louis XIV attracted the international hostility of all enemies of "universal monarchy," and the opposition was not limited to foreigners, as is shown by the example of Fénelon, who supposedly influenced Montesquieu's own *Reflections on Universal Monarchy*. Yet soon French envy was to raise the damning accusation against the efforts of Great Britain to conquer universal empire at sea. Montesquieu, most concerned with the effects of Louis XIV's absolute government on the liberties and laws of France, pointed out in the *Reflections* that the "mediocre size" of a state alone was apt to guarantee a "government of laws."[47]

Montesquieu's Second Contribution: The Political Theory of International Commerce

However, the significance of Montesquieu's principles so far discussed for the constitutional debates of the young American Republic might have been far less, had they not been reinforced by another complex of ideas. Evidence to be presented, both by Alexander Hamilton and his American contemporaries suggests that a quite different preoccupation of Montesquieu's injected the urgency and force into the Americans' concern with the "peacefulness" of republics that we discover in their records. This urgency was supplied by the political theory of international commerce.

Montesquieu, aware of the fundamentally changed conditions of modern times, had taken the greatest care—unheeded by many Americans—to circumscribe the competence of *virtuous* republics:

The laws of Minos, of Lycurgus, and of Plato suppose a particular attention and care, which the citizens ought to have over one another's conduct. But an attention of this kind cannot be expected in the confusion and multitude of affairs in which a large nation is entangled.

In institutions of this kind, money ... must be banished. But in great societies, the multiplicity, variety, embarrassment, and importance of affairs, as well as the facility of purchasing, and the slowness of exchange, require a common measure. In order to support or extend our power, we must be possessed of the means to which, by the unanimous consent of mankind, this power is annexed.[48]

The revolution in the composition of national power, which made money the measure of all things, was above all due to maritime expansion. Machiavelli, at the beginning of modern times, had not been impressed with the importance of finances; and Francis Bacon, though Lord Chancellor of a budding maritime empire, was also anxious to refute the idea that money provided "the sinews of war."[49] But Thomas Hobbes regarded money as "the blood of the commonwealth"—it "goes round about, nourishing, as it passeth, every part thereof."[50] Alexander Hamilton, on two occasions, certainly appeared to have been inspired by *Leviathan* himself: "In the present system of things the health of a state *particularly a commercial one* depends on a due quantity and regular circulation of Cash, as much as the health of an animal body depends upon the due quantity and regular circulation of the blood."[51] This image, expressed by Hamilton in 1781 in connection with plans to set up a national bank for the Confederation, was echoed several years later in *The Federalist*: Money is with propriety considered as the vital principle of the body politic; as that which sustains its life and motion, and enables it to perform its most essential functions."[52]

The eighteenth century, even more than the previous one, was profoundly aware that the center of gravity of international politics had shifted from the possession of raw military force to the disposition of wealth. In the past, the young Montesquieu had speculated in his *Reflections on Universal Monarchy*, a poor people might have been formidable merely because of its ferocity and sudden striking force; but now, wealth created power—*"ce sont les richesses qui font la puissance."*[53] In a treatise on international politics employed by Hamilton while writing *The Federalist* the Abbé Mably threw into relief "two memorable events" that had produced political revolutions—the conquest of America by Spain and the Portuguese exploration of the East Indies:

Princes were in a hurry to favor luxury and commerce which might render their courts more brilliant and might augment the revenues of their customs. Navigation spread to all the seas; trading posts were established in all parts of the world; colonies were founded. It was necessary to devote to manufactures and commerce a prodigious number of men who would have been soldiers. . . . Money became the sinews of war and of politics; and a nation that desired to be a conquering one, had to become a commercial one in order to entertain armies.[54]

Hamilton took account of these developments in *The Federalist*. The militia-type citizen armies envisaged by both Machiavelli and Bacon, which aroused the enthusiasm of so many of the American revolutionaries, did not conform to the requirements of the times:

The industrious habits of the people of the present day, absorbed in the pursuits of gain, and devoted to the improvements of agriculture and commerce are incompatible with the condition of a nation of soldiers, which was the true condition of the people of those [ancient] republics. The means of revenue, which have been so greatly multiplied by the increase of gold and silver, and of the arts of industry, and the science of finance, which is the offspring of modern times, concurring with the habits of nations, have produced an intire revolution in the system of war, and have rendered disciplined armies, distinct from the body of the citizens, the inseparable companion of frequent hostility.[55]

The "commercial" character of modern international politics recurs in Hamilton's writings with undeviating insistence. "The prosperity of commerce," he wrote, "is now perceived and acknowledged by all enlightened statesmen to be the most useful as well as the most productive source of national wealth; and has accordingly become a primary object of their political cares."[56] "Power without revenue," he earlier had observed, "in political society is a name."[57] "In the modern system of war," he pointed out on another occasion, "nations the most wealthy are obliged to have recourse to large loans."[58] And if Hamilton thought that for the time being the United States was still predominantly an agricultural country,[59] he felt a change both inevitable and desirable. The program detailed in his great economic papers is foreshadowed in *The Federalist*: "If we mean to be a commercial people, it must form a part of our policy, to be able one day to defend that commerce."[60]

The eighteenth-century thinkers' analysis of the impact of "commerce" upon foreign policy was by no means exhausted with these considerations. It was not sufficient to distinguish "ancient" and "modern" policies. The genius of the political philosopher impelled Montesquieu, like Hume, to describe the "ideal type" of the modern commercial policy, to carefully separate extraneous factors like princely love of splendor or the need to finance wars of expansion from the natural laws of commercial intercourse, to distinguish between the impeded and the unimpeded operation of the modern policy. At this stage of analysis, "forms of government" again loom large; the investigation partakes of political philosophy as much as of purely economic analysis or of the observation of diplomatic history.

Montesquieu's early writings expressed views on the commercial interdependence of nations that we usually associate with David Hume or Adam Smith. Fifty years before Smith spoke of the "great mercantile republic" uniting the merchants of all nations, Montesquieu had suggested that all trading nations really were members of a "grand Republic."[61] In *The Spirit of the Laws*, these views had matured. If wealth consisted in land, then it belonged "to every state in particular"; movable effects, on the other hand, belonged as it were to the world in general, and in this respect the world was indeed "composed of but one single state, of which all the societies upon earth are members."[62] Since within a society of free and equal members, or a "republic," peace and the absence of arbitrariness constituted the normal state of affairs, it followed that peace was the natural effect of trade. "Two nations who traffic with each other become reciprocally dependent; for if one has an interest in buying, the other has an interest in selling; and thus their union is founded on their mutual necessities."[63]

Trade, Montesquieu continued, "has some relation to forms of government"! In monarchies, trade would chiefly serve to satisfy "the pride, the pleasure, and the capricious whims of the nation." In republics, on the other hand, trade was "commonly founded on economy. Their merchants, having an eye to all the nations of the earth, bring from one what is wanted by another. . . . Besides, the grand enterprises of merchants are always necessarily connected with the affairs of the public. But, in monarchies, these public affairs give as much distrust to the merchants as in free states they appear to give safety. Great enterprises, therefore, in commerce are not for monarchical, but for republican, governments."[64]

Montesquieu, it appears, was most concerned with the distinction between rational and irrational policies of commerce. Republics were more likely to pursue a rational policy, since they were not sidetracked by dynastic interests. Montesquieu's prescriptions for a rational commercial policy included international division of labor and free competition among nations, though he respected, as the *Camillus* essays were to note, the right of nations to control the trade of their colonies.[65] Despite colonial monopolies, rational commercial policies with due regard to mutual interests were bound to reduce arbitrariness and violence among nations. The somewhat misplaced stress of later generations on "mercantilism" as a cause of the American Revolution— combatted as early as 1795 in the *Camillus* essays[66]—has veiled from our view the joy with which men like Montesquieu and some of the American Founders greeted the increasing importance of commerce as a check on princely arbitrariness. "We begin to be cured of Machiavelism," rejoiced Montesquieu in a chapter describing "How Commerce broke through the Barbarism of Europe." "More moderation has become necessary in the councils of princes. What would formerly have been called a masterstroke in politics would be now, independent of the horror it might occasion, the greatest imprudence. . . . Happy it is for men that they are in a situation in which, though their passions prompt them to be wicked, it is, nevertheless, to their interest to be humane and virtuous."[67] Continental Europe showed still many vestiges of less rational times, and this is what Montesquieu, with his apprehensions about French expansionism, had in mind when he compared England with the rest of Europe: "Other nations have made the interests of commerce yield to those of politics; the English, on the contrary, have ever made their political interests give way to those of commerce."[68]

Free Trade, Sea Power, and American Independence

Mutatis mutandis, it was this line of reasoning that advised Americans after independence to stay away from European alliances concluded for dynastic wars. This was the message of *Common Sense*, and it was to be found in many places of American political debate. A revealing example occurs in the "Letters of 'Cato' " of 1787.[69] The author, a New York opponent of the Federal Constitution, inveighed against its proposed treaty-making power. That power, remote from state and popular control, might involve Americans in engagements that would require them to raise armies and send them to Europe to fight the wars of ambitious princes."[70] Another opponent of the Federal Constitution, "Agrippa" of Massachusetts, extolled the principle of "commerce" as a substitute for closer union of the States. The impact of Montesquieu, revealed in numerous instances throughout "Agrippa's" letters, shines through his exposition of the interdependence of peace, trade, and republican government.

The argument against republicks, as it is derived from the Greek and Roman states, is unfair. . . . We find, however, in practice, that limited monarchy is more friendly to commerce, because more friendly to the rights of the subject, than an absolute government; and that it is more liable to be disturbed than a republick, because less friendly to trade and the rights of individuals. . . .

In a republick, we ought to guard, as much as possible, against the predominance of any particular interest. It is the object of government to protect them all. When commerce is left to take its own course, the advantage of every class will be nearly equal.[71]

These theories were tested in the crucible of America's foreign relations. In the year of independence, hopes in America ran high for a new beginning at home and abroad. Above all, it was John Adams who was determined to place America's future relations with Europe on the footing of "commerce" rather than "politics." In March 1776, Adams excluded any future "political connection" that involved submission, as much as any "military connection" involving the sending of troops, from the projected understanding with France. "Only a commercial connection" was called for, and it has been suggested that this formula, repeatedly used by Adams, was influenced by Paine's *Common Sense*;[72] perhaps James Burgh's writings should be added.[73] Yet it seems also possible that in addition to the radical Whig tradition of Burgh and Paine, Montesquieu—whose ideas permeate all of Adams's political speculations during that crucial year—shared this influence on Adams's commercial approach to a liberal, peaceful foreign policy.[74] The intransigent anti-monopoly slant of America's first important diplomatic document, the draft treaty with France prepared in 1776, is a remarkable example of a "free nation's" foreign policy.[75]

By the mid-1780's, Adams's expectations had been keenly disappointed. "The increasing liberality of sentiment among philosophers and men of letters, in various nations," he wrote to Secretary of Foreign Affairs John Jay, "has for some time given reason to hope for a *reformation*, a kind of *protestantism*, in the commercial system of the world." Adams then referred to a decree of Louis XVI which proclaimed that the principle of free trade was apt to "make of all nations, as it were, but one, in point of trade," but which in practice took away what it granted in theory: as long as liberty of trade could not be "universally admitted, and everywhere reciprocally, the interest of the kingdom requires of his Majesty's wisdom, that he should exclude from it, or suffer to be imported by the nation only, those foreign goods, the free importation of which would be hurtful to his kingdom and manufactories, and might make the balance of trade to be against him." Mindful of his own efforts and hopes of 1776, Adams commented with bitterness that "the United States of America have done more than all the economists in France towards propagating in the world" the "magnanimous sentiment" of free trade; but, he concluded, "as the French Court has condescended to adopt our principle in theory, I am very much afraid we shall be obliged to imitate their wisdom in practice, and exclude from the United States, or suffer to be imported by our nation only, and in their own ships, those foreign goods which would be hurtful to the United States and their manufactories, make the balance of trade to be against them, or annihilate or diminish their shipping or mariners."[76]

Adams's reasoning, which reflected the experience of the young nation, effectively removed the question of the merits or demerits of unshackled commerce among nations from the level of political and constitutional theory to an altogether different one. Whether commerce was served better, and in turn served the cause of peace better, in monarchies or republics, had become irrelevant. What Adams did was to state a Gresham's Law of foreign policy: bad policy drove out good policy. There was no choice for the high-minded but to meet their opponents on the low level chosen by the latter.

It is here that the primacy of foreign policy is seen in its most absolute and uncompromising form. The necessity of self-preservation put a gigantic questionmark after the "peacefulness of republics." Issues so important to Montesquieu and Americans like Paine, the young John Adams, Charles Pinckney, and Patrick

Henry—the unreason of absolute monarchs *vs.* the reasonableness of republics, the evils of monopoly *vs.* the merits of free trade—were replaced by an altogether different perspective. This new perspective focused on the alternative of defense *vs.* opulence. Montesquieu as well as the physiocrats had adumbrated a system of free trade that Adam Smith brought to theoretical perfection. Yet Adam Smith himself respected the all-important conditional clause: "As defense, however, is of much more importance than opulence, the act of navigation is, perhaps, the wisest of all the commercial regulations of England."[77] In other words, the political theorists' hope that they had found in the natural laws of commerce among nations an engine of peaceful government gave way to the altogether different calculus of seapower—a calculus, as will appear, of the utmost importance to Alexander Hamilton's system of politics. "Politics," which Montesquieu had hoped to subordinate to "commerce," reasserted itself in a new guise. In fact, the laws of sea power, pursued persistently, might well lead to a dominion more secure and greater than any conquest of land, which was subject to the vagaries both of dynastic changes and weak economics.

Alexander Hamilton and the Primacy of Foreign Policy

It is only now that the context and meaning of Hamilton's retort to Pinckney, given at the beginning of this chapter, fully emerges. We have recorded Hamilton's observation that the distinction between the pursuit of happiness at home and respectability abroad was "an ideal one"—that is, it was unrealistic. His arguments can be drawn from many of his writings. In fact, his statesmanship was carried by the conviction expressed in his reply to Pinckney in the Convention. His lifework was devoted to the effort of transforming conviction into policy and of thus saving America from imminent as well as remote disaster.

To the multi-barrelled argument in favor of the peaceful nature of republican government, Hamilton opposed an equally diversified reasoning designed to level off the alleged differences between the motivations of monarchies and republics. This Hamilton did most concisely in Nos. 6, 7, 8, 9, and 11 of *The Federalist*. These papers remain the very core of Hamilton's theory of the primacy of foreign policy. Later writings, like *Pacificus*, *Americanus*, and *Camillus*, present applications to specific cases, they refine and shed additional light on points of detail, yet they never surpassed the sustained force of the foreign policy analysis in *The Federalist*.

It was the experience of human nature as revealed in history that provided Hamilton with the needed ammunition. "To look for a continuation of harmony between a number of independent unconnected sovereignties, situated in the same neighbourhood," his general argument began, "would be to disregard the uniform course of human events, and to set at defiance the accumulated experience of ages." He proceeded to look into the innumerable causes of hostility among nations: "There are some which have a general and almost constant operation upon the collective bodies of society: Of this description are the love of power or the desire of preeminence and dominion—the jealousy of power, or the desire of equality and safety. There are others which have a more circumscribed, though an equally operative influence, within their spheres: Such are the rivalships and competitions of commerce between commercial nations."[78] The significance of the latter point for the American scene was taken into account in Hamilton's polemic against the opposing school of thought. In spite of the testimony of experience, there were

still to be found visionary, or designing men, who stand ready to advocate the paradox of perpetual peace between the States, though dismembered and alienated from each other. The genius of republics (they say) is pacific; the spirit of commerce has a tendency to soften the manners of men and to extinguish those inflammable humours which have so often kindled into wars. Commercial republics, like ours, will never be disposed to waste themselves in ruinous contentions with each other. They will be governed by mutual interest, and will cultivate a spirit of mutual amity and concord.[79]

It should not be difficult now to recognize how Hamilton's polemic mirrors not merely the relevance of Montesquieu's ideas but also the great hopes of the early years of independence spread in public by Tom Paine's *Common Sense* and advocated in actual diplomacy by men like John Adams. Hamilton asked "these projectors in politics" if it were not "the true interest of all nations to cultivate the same benevolent and philosophic spirit? If this be their true interest, have they in fact pursued it? Has it not, on the contrary, invariably been found, that momentary passions and immediate interests have a more active and imperious controul over human conduct than general or remote considerations of policy, utility or justice? Have republics in practice been less addicted to war than monarchies?"[80] He went on to attack the supposed peacefulness of commerce. Had commerce "done any thing more than change the objects of war?" Was not the love of wealth "as domineering and enterprising a passion" as that of power and glory? "Have there not been as many wars founded upon commercial motives, since that has become the prevailing system of nations, as were before occasioned b[y] the cupidity of territory or dominion? Has not the spirit of commerce in many instances administered new incentives to the appetite both for the one and for the other? Let experience the least fallible guide of human opinions be appealed to for an answer to these inquiries."[81] Hamilton above cited examples of warlike commercial republics in antiquity and modernity—Athens, Carthage, Venice, and the Netherlands. Above all, there was England, and Hamilton's interpretation of English foreign policy surely was miles apart from Montesquieu's: "In the government of Britain the representatives of the people compose one branch of the national legislature. Commerce has been for ages the predominant pursuit of that country. Few nations, nevertheless, have been more frequently engaged in war; and the wars in which that kingdom has been engaged have, in numerous instances, proceeded from the people."[82]

If Hamilton was intent upon destroying the illusion of the peaceful effects of commerce, he did not by any means stop there. He launched another attack upon the general notion, so widely accepted in America as a consequence of Thomas Paine's creation of "the royal brute of Great Britain," that the selfish ambition for aggrandizement was a monopoly of princely blood. To the causes of hostility among nations first enumerated he added others, "not less numerous than either of the former, which take their origin intirely in private passions; in the attachments, enmities, interests, hopes and fears of leading individuals in the communities of which they are members."[83] Again, Hamilton offered examples, from Pericles, who "in compliance with the resentments of a prostitute" attacked and destroyed the city of the Samnites, to Cardinal Wolsey, who aspired to the "Tripple-Crown" of the Pope.[84] In a final thrust at the doctrine that free governments reduced arbitrariness and created a "government of laws," Hamilton ruthlessly appealed to the evidence of history:

Have republics in practice been less addicted to war than monarchies? Are not the former administered by *men* as well as the latter? Are there not aversions, predilections, rivalships, and desires of unjust acquisitions, that affect nations as well as kings? Are not popular assemblies frequently subject to the impulses of rage, resentment, jealousy, avarice, and of other irregular and violent propensities? Is it not well known that their determinations are often governed by a few individuals in whom they place confidence, and are, of course, liable to be tinctured by the passions and views of those individuals?[85]

Hamilton, with polemic genius, confounded democratic majority rule with a "government of laws" attained through mixed or balanced government; the prevailing habit of applying the term "republic" to both made it an easy task. "There have been, if I may so express it, almost as many popular as royal wars." Hamilton pointed toward the conclusion of his argument. "The cries of the nation and the importunities of their representatives have, upon various occasions, dragged their monarchs into war, or continued them in it, contrary to their inclinations, and sometimes contrary to the real interests of the state."[86] The strength of the opinion Hamilton had set out to attack is strikingly illustrated by the fact that it was shared by one of Hamilton's coauthors, John Jay. Perhaps Hamilton's slight qualification that there have been "almost" as many popular as royal wars was a feeble attempt to maintain a consistent argument between Nos. 4 and 6 of "Publius's" *Federalist* papers. John Jay's emphasis in No. 4 certainly differed noticeably from Hamilton's intense effort to disabuse republicans of any illusions that they were exempted from the vices of princes. "It is true, however disgraceful it may be to human nature," Jay had complained, that

nations in general will make war whenever they have a prospect of getting any thing by it, nay that absolute monarchs will often make war when their nations are to get nothing by it, but for purposes and objects merely personal, such as, a thirst for military glory, revenge for personal affronts; ambition or private compacts to aggrandize or support their particular families, or partizans. These and a variety of motives, which affect only the mind of the Sovereign, often lead him to engage in wars not sanctified by justice, or the voice and interests of his people. But independent of these inducements to war, which are more prevalent in absolute monarchies, but which well deserve our attention, there are others which affect nations as often as Kings.[87]

Hamilton, on the other hand, concluded the sixth paper with a stern warning against "the fallacy and extravagance of those idle theories which have amused us with promises of an exemption from the imperfections, weaknesses, and evils incident to society in every shape." The philosophical ideal of the "primacy of internal policy"—the ideal of human perfection set forth in classical philosophy—emerges as the ultimate target of Hamilton's polemic, beyond and above the merits and demerits of "commerce" or other merely accessory factors: "Is it not time to awake from the deceitful dream of a golden age, and to adopt as a practical maxim for the direction of our political conduct that we, as well as the other inhabitants of the globe, are yet remote from the happy empire of perfect wisdom and perfect virtue?"[88] Hamilton ended where he began. With Hobbesian thoroughness he regarded the existence of states in a state of nature as the alpha and omega of a theory of foreign policy. Nuances and qualifications introduced by various forms of government disappeared: "So far is the general sense of mankind from corresponding with the tenets of those who endeavor to lull asleep our apprehensions

of discord and hostility between the States, in the event of disunion, that it has from long observation of the progress of society
become a sort of axiom in politics, that vicinity, or nearness of
situation, constitutes nations natural enemies."[89] Hamilton supported his claim with a quotation from Mably's celebrated work
on foreign policy — though his use of it out of context did injustice to Mably's conviction of the diversifying role of "principles" such as preservation, expansion, or commerce in foreign
affairs.[90] "An intelligent writer expresses himself on this subject
to this effect," Hamilton said in introducing Mably: " 'NEIGH-
BOURING NATIONS (says he) are naturally ENEMIES of each other,
unless their common weakness forces them to league in a CONFED-
ERATE REPUBLIC, and their constitution prevents the differences
that neighbourhood occasions, extinguishing that secret jealousy,
which disposes all States, to aggrandise themselves at the expence
of their neighbours.' This passage, at the same time points out
the EVIL and suggests the REMEDY."[91]

The Optimum Size of Nations: Montesquieu, Hamilton, and the Meaning of "Confederation"

We thus reach the last great domain of the Founders' political
speculations, in which the interdependence of forms of government and types of conducting foreign policies, of constitution-
making and international environment, is at the very center of
concern. The text for this section, as it were, is again taken from
Montesquieu. "If a republic be small," Montesquieu said, "it is
destroyed by a foreign force; if it be large, it is ruined by an
internal imperfection."[92] Montesquieu's solution, as Hamilton
put it in *The Federalist*, was to suggest "a CONFEDERATE REPUB-
LIC as the expedient for extending the sphere of popular government and reconciling the advantages of monarchy with those of
republicanism."[93] Hamilton proceeded to quote *verbatim* about
half of a chapter of *The Spirit of the Laws*, the crucial part of
which goes as follows: " 'It is very probable' (says he) 'that mankind would have been obliged, at length, to live constantly under
the government of a SINGLE PERSON, had they not contrived a

kind of constitution, that has all the internal advantages of a republican, together with the external force of a monarchical government. I mean a CONFEDERATE REPUBLIC.' "[94] This task of blending, as Hamilton put it, as early as 1780, "the advantages of a monarchy and republic in our constitution," was properly the core of his political lifework.[95]

An empirical fact and a thoroughly misinterpreted principle of classical political philosophy united to make the Founders' debate on the "extent of territory" one of the subjectively most important, most frustrating, and also most disingenuous battles of words. The empirical fact was the existence of thirteen colonies and their joint Declaration of Independence as the United States of America in Congress Assembled. The principle of political theory was Plato's and Aristotle's emphasis on the optimum size of the political community. The eighteenth century produced the last great champions of the classical ideal of smallness— Montesquieu, Mably, and Rousseau. The debate as to the proper size of the best state was born in Aristotle's criticism of Plato's constitutional plans—though the two differed only in detail.[96] The classical ideal that the best state required mutual trust and mutual acquaintance as its intrinsic condition was countered, in the course of centuries, by three opposing theories. First, there was the idea of universal monarchy as the engine of *homonoia*, or universal harmony, first consciously striven for, it seems, by Alexander the Great and later rationalized in the idea of *pax Romana* and of the Christian *imperium*.[97] Second, there was the Machiavellian theory of Roman greatness, arguing for expansion both on grounds of greatest safety and greatest worldly glory. Third, there was the theory of commerce as a way of life, tied up with the rise of individualism and anonymity, which dominated the breakthrough of the "policy of the moderns" as expressed by Hobbes, by Montesquieu in the later books, by Hume, and by Adam Smith.[98]

In the year of independence, Americans anxiously sought prescriptions for republican government. They turned to a book that prescribed two sharply divergent policies—one prescribing a coun-

terfeit of ancient virtue, the other the private passions of a trading society. The first extolled "ancient liberty," the other, "modern liberty." For both kinds of republics, whether on the ancient
or the modern model, Montesquieu posited "peace" as the fundamental tendency, though its causes, in each instance, were radically diverse. The peace of republics on the ancient model was
merely a tendency toward moderation, stability, self-preservation,
and tranquillity; the peace of modern republics was a result of
the natural laws of commerce. It cannot be a matter of surprise
that Americans, detecting the same word—"peace"—in so many
of the book's passages on republican government, were unable
to perceive the gulf that, in Montesquieu's intention, separated
the two worlds of ancient and modern liberty. In addition, no
one was likely to admit that he was *not* looking for a virtuous
form of government, and Montesquieu's explicit caution concerning the peculiar character of his principle of "political virtue" remained largely unheeded. Thus it came about that Montesquieu's
imitation of the ancients in requiring a small territory for the
virtuous republic was widely held to apply to the thirteen colonies.

It was a handy argument with which to oppose the Federal
Constitution, if one recognized in the Constitution the blueprint
for a continental empire—as many people did. The opponents of
the Constitution accepted without much questioning the assumption that the size of the thirteen colonies *severally* corresponded to
Montesquieu's prescription, and that a confederation of thirteen
sovereign states akin to a league for defensive and offensive alliance took care of the problems of foreign policy outlined by
Montesquieu.[99]

There were others, not numerous, whose study both of *The
Spirit of the Laws* and of the situation of the thirteen states went
deeper. One of these was James Bowdoin, Jr., of Dorchester,
Massachusetts, an advocate of the Federal Constitution whose
confrontation of theory with fact was more honest as well as more
perceptive than most others on record. Bowdoin proposed to his
fellow-delegates that it might not be improper "to examine

whether the federal Constitution proposed has a likeness to the different state constitutions, and such alone as to give the spirit and features of the particular governments; for Baron Montesquieu observes, that all governments ought to be relative to their particular principles."[100] Bowdoin soon turned to foreign policy. He quoted Montesquieu's statement of the dilemma of a republican government threatened by annihilation from abroad or corruption from within, and his proposal of confederation as the only expedient to shake off despotic government. Admitting this principle of Baron Montesquieu's, Bowdoin went on, "the several states are either too small to be defended against a foreign enemy, or too large for republican constitutions of government. If we apply the first position to the different states, which reason and the experience of the late war point out to be true, a confederate government is necessary. But if we admit the latter position, then the several governments, being in their own nature imperfect, will be necessarily destroyed, from their being too extensive for republican governments." Bowdoin was one of the few people to openly doubt whether the states individually did not already exceed the optimum size prescribed by Montesquieu. Bowdoin's argument in favor of the Federal Constitution, predicated on the choice of continental despotism as the lesser evil when compared with rival despotisms and mutual annihilation, stands out in its boldness: "From whence it follows, if the foregoing principles are true . . . that we ought to adopt a confederation, presuming the different states well calculated for republican governments; for, if they are not, their corruption will work their destruction separately; and if they are destined for destruction, from their natural imperfection, it will certainly be more advantageous to have them destroyed collectively than separately, as, in that case, we should fall under one great national government."

Even more outspoken than Bowdoin was Alexander Hamilton. Hamilton's criticism of the anti-Federalists' use of Montesquieu correctly appraises the latter's conception of optimum size, though Hamilton's contempt for republicanism on the model of antiquity comes out into the open. Hamilton felt that the opponents of the Constitution who "with great assiduity cited and circulated" Montesquieu's observations "on the necessity of a contracted territory for a republican government" did not seem to heed the consequences of the principle to which they so readily subscribed.

When Montesquieu recommends a small extent for republics, the standards he had in view were of dimensions, far short of the limits of almost every one of these States. Neither Virginia, Massachusetts, Pennsylvania, New-York, North-Carolina, nor Georgia, can by any means be compared with the models, from which he reasoned and to which the terms of his description apply. If we therefore take his ideas on this point, as the criterion of truth, we shall be driven to the alternative, either of taking refuge at once in the arms of monarchy, or of splitting ourselves into an infinity of little jealous, clashing, tumultuous commonwealths, the wretched nurseries of unceasing discord and the miserable objects of universal pity or contempt.[101]

The alternative depicted was a grim one; it impelled some of the most creative minds of the eighteenth century to look for a way out. David Hume, for instance, combatted "the falsehood of the common opinion that no large state such as France or Great Britain could ever be modeled into a commonwealth, but that such a form of government can only take place in a city or small territory." The contrary seemed more likely to Hume. The turbulence of democracy would be much more felt in the "near habitation of a city," whereas in a large government, not only might there be more room for complicated gradations of the electoral machinery, but the very distance and remoteness of the different parts of a country would make the combination of intrigues, prejudices, and passions against the public interest difficult.[102] It is known, of course, that James Madison presented similar views in *The Federalist* No. 10, and Madison's very great indebtedness to Hume was pointed out some time ago.[103]

The theory of republican government in a large territory is one significant aspect in which Hamilton differed from his admired Hume. Madison accepted both parts of Hume's theory: the first was the greater reasonableness and integrity to be expected from a representative system that allowed both for a larger choice of good men and for a more satisfactory ratio of population and representatives; the second was the greater variety of interests to be encountered in a larger sphere.[104] Hamilton, it has never been properly noticed, actually accepted the first part of the Hume-Madison theory; it reappears unexpectedly in the 27th *Federalist*. The general government, Hamilton argued, was likely to be superior to the state governments, chiefly because "the extension of the spheres of election will present a greater option, or latitude of choice, to the people."[105] The national councils might be "less apt to be tainted by the spirit of faction, and more out of the reach of those occasional ill-humors, or temporary prejudices and propensities, which, in smaller societies, frequently contaminate the public councils."[106]

If there might be "more extensive information in the national councils," we look in vain for an endorsement of the second part of the Hume-Madison theory, the mutual checks provided by a greater variety of interests in a large society. In this respect, Hamilton was too obsessed with the dangers of dissolution and anarchy to appreciate the "checking" effects of a balance of interests. Hamilton, therefore, was unable to escape the dilemma that Montesquieu had so forcefully drawn. There is a good deal of irony in Hamilton's gloomy description of the republican predicament according to Montesquieu. Hamilton, however, was willing to choose and to look for refuge in the arms of monarchy or a near monarchical government with more equanimity than Montesquieu. In truth, Hamilton found a virtue in necessity. The huge size of the American empire, following Montesquieu's logic, required a strong executive, and Hamilton was perfectly ready to accept Montesquieu's reasoning. Unlike Hume and Madison, who hoped that the inherent fragmentation of interests in a large and checkered country would prevent majority factions, Montesquieu and Hamilton looked for salvation in the increased possibility of armed repression. Hamilton quoted from *The Spirit of the Laws*: "Should a popular insurrection happen in one of the confederate states, the others are able to quell it. Should abuses creep into one part, they are reformed by those that re-main sound."[107] In Hamilton's words, this consideration took the form of the observation that "the utility of a confederacy, as well to suppress faction and to guard the internal tranquillity of States, as to increase their external force and security, is in reality not a new idea."[108] The stress was not on prevention of a majority faction, but, as is obvious from the very choice of words, on sup-pression, on "the tendency of the Union to repress domestic faction and insurrection."[109]

The need to suppress domestic faction as well as to defend against external danger called for a twofold emphasis in the plan of government: the strengthening of the executive as compared with the legislative power, as well as the strengthening of the central at the expense of the state government. The latter need drove Hamilton to some cloudy and unconvincing rhetorical stratagems. It will be recalled that his comment on Mably's ex-pedient of a "confederative republic" extolled the "remedy" offered to the evil of warring neighbors. Yet Hamilton omitted, without indicating it, the very specific remedy to which Mably had alluded. The "constitution" of a "confederative republic," according to Mably, should be "similar or equivalent to that of the Swiss."[110] The Swiss, however, had a confederative arrange-ment that did not by any stretch of the imagination fit into Ham-ilton's constitutional plans. Hamilton had warned as early as 1780,

The Swiss-cantons . . . have had wars with each other which would have been fatal to them, had not the different powers in their neighbour-hood been too jealous of one-another and too equally matched to suffer either to take advantage of their quarrels. That they have remained so long united at all is to be attributed to their weakness, to their poverty, and to the cause just mentioned. These ties will not exist in America; a little time hence, some of the states will be powerful empires, and we are so remote from other nations that we shall have all the leisure and opportunity we can wish to cut each others throats.[111]

With a few embellishments added, the same indictment appeared in the precursor to the *Federalist*, the *Continentalist* essays of

1781–82.[112] The expectation of foreign quarrels in Hamilton's scheme of things is striking. If not involved in the conflicts of Europe, the American states would immediately create their own "international" system with all the dire concomitants of a Hobbesian state of nature.

The result, of course, was the unitary state as the ideal of Hamilton's statesmanship. Even in 1780, Hamilton looked at the thirteen colonies as a unit. At that time he wanted Congress vested with full power *"to preserve the republic from harm"*—a striking instance of a verbal image anticipating rather than merely codifying, reality; it was bold and unusual to refer to the thirteen states under the Articles of Confederation as "the republic"—and it is proof of Hamilton's wishful thinking.[113] In 1787, in the Federal Convention, Hamilton frankly reduced the states to hardly more than administrative units by proposing that the state governors be appointed by the central government and be endowed with an absolute veto on any state legislation.[114] The very principle of confederation in Montesquieu's or Mably's sense, then, was against the grain of Hamilton's political concept. This state of affairs had two consequences. The first was the complete absence of interest on Hamilton's part in theories of confederation and in the truly "federal" aspects of the proposed Constitution. One of the most striking and most easily discernible differences between Hamilton's and Madison's writings in *The Federalist* is their contributions on that subject. The analysis of historical confederations in Essays 18, 19, and 20 was Madison's work—indeed, it can be appreciated only in the context of his elaborate prior studies on that subject.[115] Similarly, the theory of American federalism as expounded in Essays 39 to 46 of *The Federalist* by Madison could never have been written by Hamilton.[116] The second consequence was that Hamilton's lack of commitment to the theory of federalism led him to rather ambiguous and tortuous references about the confederative character of the new American government. There was the probably deliberate attempt to call the proposed new government a "confederacy" as much as the old system about to be discarded.[117] The rationale of this effort to blur rather than clarify the essential difference in the character of the old and new government was provided by Hamilton in No. 9 of *The Federalist*:

The definition of a *Confederate Republic* seems simply to be, an "assemblage of societies" or an association of two or more states into one state. The extent, modification and objects of the Fœderal authority are mere matters of discretion. So long as the separate organisation of the members be not abolished, *so long as it exists by a constitutional necessity for local purposes, though it should be in perfect subordination to the general authority of the Union*, it would still be, in fact and in theory, an association of States, or a confederacy. The proposed Constitution, so far from implying an abolition of the State Governments, makes them constituent parts of the national sovereignty by allowing them a direct representation in the Senate, and leaves in their possession certain exclusive and very important portions of sovereign power. This fully corresponds, in every rational import of the terms, with the idea of a Fœderal Government.[118]

This definition was so elastic as hardly to deserve the name. Its irrelevance for Hamilton's true purpose and design became apparent wherever he vindicated the limitless supremacy of the national government in the name of the primacy of foreign policy, of defense, of a "respectable" stature abroad.

Foreign Policy, Military Policy, and the Concept of Unitary Government

Numbers 23 to 35 of *The Federalist*, all written by Hamilton, are among the earliest, and remain among the most impressive statements of what has become known as the doctrine of implied powers. Its connection with Hamilton's approach to foreign policy has perhaps been somewhat obscured because attention has been focused in his paper on the constitutionality of the Bank of the United States as a precursor of John Marshall's doctrines. Thus the context of the powerful statement of implied powers in the pages of "Publius" needs to be recalled. "The circumstances that endanger the safety of nations are infinite," Hamilton observed in No. 23, "and for this reason no constitutional shackles can wisely be imposed on the power to which the care of it is committed. This power ought to be co-extensive with all the possible combinations of such circumstances; and ought to be under the direction of the same councils, which are appointed to preside over the common defence.[119] The same urgent concern was displayed in the effort to prove the need for the central government's unlimited taxing power: "There ought to be CAPACITY to provide for future contingencies, as they may happen; and, as these are illimitable in their nature, it is impossible safely to limit that capacity."[120]

The logic of implied powers pushed Hamilton far beyond the principles of a confederation along the lines of Montesquieu. If Hamilton, in *Federalist* No. 9, had given the appearance of following the "remedy" suggested by both Mably and Montesquieu, he revealed the unitary character of his concept of America in Nos. 13 and 23. Yet actually, Hamilton proved to be a more faithful follower of Montesquieu than Madison. It was a basic assumption of Montsequieu's that increase in size produced an increase in the firmness of government: if monarchy was appropriate to larger territory than republics, very large territories could be held together only by despotisms. Hamilton proved to be more old-fashioned than either Hume or Madison when he wrote to Lafayette: "I hold with *Montesquieu*, that a government must be fitted to a nation, as much as a coat to the individual; and consequently, that what may be good at Philadelphia may be bad at Paris, and ridiculous at Petersburgh."[121] Hamilton thus paralleled one of the most famous conservative reactions against the leveling ideas of the French Revolution, that of Joseph de Maistre: "I have seen, in my time, Frenchmen, Italians, Russians, etc.; I even know, thanks to Montesquieu, that one may be a Persian: but as for *Man*, I declare I never met him in my life; if he exists, it is without my knowledge."[122]

The implications of this concept for Hamilton's design for America were far-reaching. In 1780, Hamilton had written privately that for him it was "an axiom that in our constitution an army is essential to the American union."[123] In the Federal Convention, his conviction was unchanged that "a certain portion of military force is absolutely necessary in large communities."[124] In *The Federalist*, the need for a standing national army in peacetime was related to the danger of internal convulsions or insurrections as well as external attacks. Hamilton's call for national powers "without limitation" for the care of the common defense culminated in the blunt admission that the difficulty inherent in "the extent of country, is the strongest argument in favour of an energetic government; for any other can certainly never preserve the Union of so large an empire."[125] Hamilton did, however, attempt to limit the insidious implications of the doctrine of optimum size for a nation of America's extent. If taken literally, the specter of despotism arose. Hamilton hastened, then, to dispel it, yet he did so at the price of divulging his predilection for the British Constitution as the "model" to be approached:

When the dimensions of a State attain to a certain magnitude, it requires the same energy of government and the same forms of administration which are requisite in one of much greater extent. This idea admits not of precise demonstration, because there is no rule by which we can measure the momentum of civil power necessary to the government of any given number of individuals; but when we consider that the island of Britain . . . contains about eight millions of people, and when we reflect upon the degree of authority required to direct the passions of so large a society to the public good, we shall see no reason to doubt that the like portion of power would be sufficient to perform the same task in a society far more numerous.

"Civil power," Hamilton concluded, "if properly organized and exerted, is capable of diffusing its force to a very great extent; and can, in a manner, reproduce itself in every part of a great empire by a judicious arrangement of subordinate institutions."[126] The very uncertainty with which Hamilton ventured to put forward his argument reveals his deep anxiety about the feasibility of the American experiment. That anxiety had by no means abated when the time of Washington's Farewell Address came. For once, the Hamiltonian origin of an argument revealed itself by its hesitancy rather than its forceful conviction: "Is there a doubt, whether a common government can embrace so large a sphere?— Let experience solve it.—To listen to mere speculation in such a case were criminal.—We are authorized to hope that a proper organization of the whole, with the auxiliary agency of governments for the respective Subdivisions, will afford a happy issue to the experiment.—'Tis well worth a fair and full experiment."[127]

There was no question, however, that foreign danger was a more appealing argument for energetic government and a strong military force than anticipated insurrections, and Hamilton's crusade in *The Federalist* for the unshackled preparation of defense proceeded mainly, though not exclusively, according to that consideration: "Let us recollect, that peace or war, will not always be left to our option; ... To judge from the history of mankind, we shall be compelled to conclude, that the fiery and destructive passions of war, reign in the human breast, with much more powerful sway, than the mild and beneficent sentiments of peace; and, that to model our political systems upon speculations of lasting tranquility, is to calculate on the weaker springs of the human character."[128]

This admonition reflected the sober appraisal of America's foreign relations that Hamilton had first made in 1783 in a letter to Governor Clinton of New York:

It is true our situation secures us from conquest, if internal dissensions do not open the way; but when Nations now make war upon each other the object seldom is total conquest—partial acquisitions, the jealousy of power, the rivalship of dominion or of commerce, sometimes national emulation and antipathy are the motives. Nothing shelters us from the operation of either of these causes. The fisheries, the fur trade, the navigation of the lakes and of the Mississippi—the Western territory—the Island[s] in the West Indies with the referrence to traffic, *in short the passions of human nature* are abundant sources of contention and hostility.[129]

When Hamilton enlarged upon this theme four years later with the pen of "Publius," he carried his insistence too far. Overanxious to make a point very dear to him, he found himself adducing contradictory arguments in support of it. On the one hand, Hamilton predicted that the very remoteness of European powers might release the animosities of the American states and turn them against one another.[130] In fact, Hamilton had embellished this idea by remarking, "if we are wise enough to preserve the Union, we may for ages enjoy an advantage similar to that of an insulated situation. Europe is at a great distance from us. Her colonies in our vicinity, will be likely to continue too much disproportioned in strength, to be able to give us any dangerous annoyance. Extensive military establishments cannot, in this position, be necessary to our security."[131] On the other hand, Hamilton bolstered his plea for unlimited power of taxation with much less optimistic thoughts: "Though a wide ocean separates the United States from Europe; yet there are various considerations that warn us against an excess of confidence or security. On one side of us and stretching far into our rear are growing settlements subject to the dominion of Britain. On the other side and extending to meet the British settlements are colonies and establishments subject to the dominion of Spain."[132] These two powers, which also shared possession of the West Indies, were bound to have, with regard to the United States, a common interest. The Indians ought to be considered "our natural enemies[,] their natural allies; because they have most to fear from us and most to hope from them." Having rehabilitated the significance of the colonies, which he had earlier depreciated, Hamilton proceeded to devaluate his previous argument on the remoteness of the European powers as well: "The improvements in the art of navigation have, as to the facility of communication, rendered distant nations in a great measure neighbours. Britain and Spain are among the principal maritime powers of Europe."[133] "In proportion to our increase in strength," Hamilton now concluded, it was probable or even certain that Britain and Spain would "augment their military establishments in our neighbourhood."[134]

The vicious circle of what Herbert Butterfield has so aptly called the "Hobbesian fear" was reestablished.[135] To his own satisfaction, though perhaps not quite to ours, Hamilton had refuted Charles Pinckney's idea that there was a difference between the pursuit of happiness at home and of respectability abroad.

The End of an Age-Old Debate:
Once More the Victory of the Moderns

The partisans of smallness, in the age-old debate on the optimum size of nations, had defended their position by pointing to
the intrinsic superiority of seeking human perfection over destruction, whether offensive or defensive.[136] If the Hobbesian
scramble for *more* of everything was accepted as the premise for
the analysis of foreign affairs, the pursuit of bigness appeared in
a different light. Confederation strictly following the lines suggested by Montesquieu was hardly a realistic alternative. The
logic of implied powers impressively disposed of expedients that
in the period of Confederation had been tried and found wanting.
Yet another element made the optimum size of a nation appear in
a new light. In an age that was universally admitted to have
adopted a "commercial system" of relations among nations, strategic and economic analysis suggested that diversity in the domestic economy was indispensable to national preparedness. If free
trade were a reality, if the international division of labor urged
by its advocates were unhampered, concentration and specializa-
tion on a single product or mode of production—agriculture for
instance—might be possible. Limited modes of production might
allow smallness and uniformity of occupation; diverse modes of
production might not. Diversification, however, was called for,
if for no other reason, by the imperious needs of preparedness.

The national government had been operating less than a year
when the House of Representatives ordered the Secretary of the
Treasury to prepare a report on a plan, or plans "for the encouragement and promotion of such manufactories as will tend to
render the United States independent of other nations for essential, particularly for military supplies."[137] In the actual *Report on
Manufactures*, Hamilton observed:

Not only the wealth; but the independence and security of a Country,
appear to be materially connected with the prosperity of manufacturers.
Every nation, with a view to those great objects, ought to endeavour to

possess within itself all the essentials of national supply. These comprise the means of *Subsistence habitation clothing* and *defence.*

The possession of these is necessary to the perfection of the body politic, to the safety as well as to the welfare of the society; the want of either, is the want of an important organ of political life and Motion; and in the various crises which await a state, it must severely feel the effects of any such deficiency.[138]

The troubles experienced during the War of Independence, Hamilton continued, were a warning to remedy the defects still existing: "To effect this change as fast as shall be prudent, merits all the attention and all the Zeal of our Public Councils; 'tis the next great work to be accomplished."[139]

The primacy of foreign policy in the guise of the calculus of sea power, which impinged so heavily upon the reasoning of theoretical free traders like Adam Smith or John Adams, was likely to be expressed even more forcefully by Hamilton. And yet, as one of the most perceptive students of Hamilton's political concepts has observed, "it is doubtful if even Adam Smith could have written a fairer or more eloquent summary of the case for free trade than that which appears in Hamilton's Report on Manufactures."[140] Let us listen to Hamilton's summary:

If the system of perfect liberty to industry and commerce were the prevailing system of nations—the arguments which dissuade a country in the predicament of the United States, from the zealous pursuits of manufactures would doubtless have great force. It will not be affirmed, that they might not be permitted, with few exceptions, to serve as a rule of national conduct. . . .

But the system which has been mentioned, is far from characterising the general policy of Nations. [The prevalent one has been regulated by an opposite spirit.]

The consequence of it is, that the United States are to a certain extent in the situation of a country precluded from foreign Commerce. They can indeed, without difficulty obtain from abroad the manufactured supplies, of which they are in want; but they experience numerous and very injurious impediments to the emission and vent of their own commodities. Nor is this the case in reference to a single foreign nation only. The regulations of several countries, with which we have the most extensive intercourse, throw serious obstructions in the way of the principal staples of the United States.

In such a position of things, the United States cannot exchange with Europe on equal terms; and the want of reciprocity would render them the victim of a system, which should induce them to confine their views to Agriculture and refrain from Manufactures. . . .

Hamilton pointedly concluded that it was "for the United States to consider by what means they can render themselves least dependent, on the combinations, right or wrong, of foreign policy."[141] What emerges from these reflections is Hamilton's determination to make of America a modern country in the sense in which England, in the eighteenth century, was considered to be the most modern of nations. Yet nation-building according to the precepts of modern policy was altogether different from the construction of virtuous republics. America, under the guidance of the Founding Fathers, set out to pursue modern liberty rather than ancient virtue. It set out to prove, and proved, that a free state in the modern sense could live and prosper regardless of its size. The irony, of course, is that Montesquieu would have endorsed the proposition that modern republics are independent of the restrictions imposed on republics following the example of antiquity.

America quickly became a large, prospering republic, and by this fact alone helped to expedite into oblivion the political philosophers' insistence on the smallness of the good society. It was not the least achievement of the successful American experiment that it deeply impressed those French reformers and latent revolutionaries who despaired of reforming France because Montesquieu, Mably, and Rousseau had told them that France was too big a nation ever to become virtuous or to become a republic. It was America that caused the change of mind of a man like Brissot and helped other Frenchmen to discard a teaching which they came to regard as obsolete, though it would have been more correct to say that they misunderstood it in the first place. America set an example of a large republic soon enough to help eliminate the scruples of those who wanted to make a revolution in France. France became a republic with the very help of those who only a short while before would have sadly denied that France could ever become such a thing.[142] In due course, France proved not only that republics might exist in a large territory, but that they were capable of war and conquest. And only a few years later, at the dawn of the nineteenth century, one of the most eminent political publicists of Europe, Friedrich von Gentz, could hold a rather scornful—and quite misleading—postmortem of a view that seemed to him the height of futility, as much as it had at one time held the promise of salvation or the sentence of damnation for many of the American Founders. "Time was," Gentz said,

and as late as the middle of this century, when a fairly widespread opinion existed that true social happiness could be found only in small states. This strange folly—one is now fairly entitled to call it such— had its unmistakable origin in the dark and desperate barbarism which after the destruction of the Roman Empire covered the most beautiful countries of the world. . . . While the anarchy of feudalism tore apart great empires, and while following this, perennial wars for predominance prevented any speedy progress in the arts of society, all that could elevate men and make them happy had taken refuge in those smaller states. . . . [But] it may be proven from the present state of society that large states are necessary for the development of humanity. With increasing civilization, the relationships of men have become so infinitely intricate and varied that only a general legislation which encompasses a large mass of these relationships may order them and direct them to the general good.[143]

The contrast with the policy of the ancients was complete when Gentz added that "the tendency to build great States is not only a tendency of ambition and lust of dominion of the ruler; it is an inevitable consequence, a natural and beneficent tendency of the higher civilization of nations."[144]

Gentz, with all his incipient Romantic conservatism, was quite close in his last words to the spirit of Hume. "The greatness of a state," Hume had said, "and the happiness of its subjects, how independent soever they may be supposed in some respects, are commonly allowed to be inseparable with regard to commerce; and as private men receive greater security in the possession of their trade and riches from the power of the public, so the public becomes powerful in proportion to the opulence and extensive commerce of private men."[145] The nation that above all others carried out these precepts, of course, was England, a free nation, though a large and powerful one. Thus Hamilton, in 1787, anticipated the time "when others as well as himself would join in the praise bestowed by Mr. Neckar on the British Constitution, namely, that it is the only Govt. in the world 'which unites public strength with individual security.' "[146] It was indeed on the basis of that example that Alexander Hamilton planned to rear the fabric of the new nation.

V

THE PURSUIT OF GREATNESS

Liberty and Greatness

In June 1792, James Madison honored George Washington's request that he prepare the draft for the president's valedictory address. Madison's draft concluded with expressing the "extreme solicitude" that the president could never cease to feel for his fellow citizens' "liberty, their prosperity and their happiness."[1] Washington, of course, stayed on for a second term. When it was drawing to a close, he incorporated most of Madison's draft in a new version of his own, which he sent to Hamilton for comments and help. Hamilton succeeded in imposing the imprint of his mind on the Madisonian trinity of "liberty, prosperity, and happiness," which repeated the credo of the Declaration of Independence. His preliminary "Abstract of Points to Form an Address" combined an outline of the points in the Madison-Washington draft with his own ideas. In it, the Madisonian trinity is split up in a way that immediately reveals Hamilton's characteristic preoccupation with foreign policy and with America's place in a world of nations. This syllabus repeated the president's "solicitude for the happiness of his Country," but went into more detail concerning liberty and prosperity. Four points stood in the place of these two: safety, peace, liberty, and commerce. Under these four points Hamilton enumerated the following problems: first, "The strength & greater security from external danger"; second, "Internal peace & avoiding the necessity of establishments dangerous to liberty"; third, "Avoidi[n]g the effects of foreign intrigue";

fourth, "Bre[a]k the force of faction by rendering combination more difficult." These four points reappeared in Hamilton's "Original Major Draft," the main basis of Washington's final version. The major draft also expressed the president's solicitude for the "welfare" and the "felicity" of Americans; it presented the unity of their government as "a main pillar of your real independence of your peace safety freedom and happiness." In Washington's final manuscript, this unity became "a main Pillar in the edifice of you[r] real independence, the support of your tranquility at home; your peace abroad; of your safety; —of your prosperity; —of that very Liberty which you so highly prize."

The concern with the international context of American society emerges clearly from this metamorphosis of the original Madisonian phrasing with its Jeffersonian overtones. More subtle, but significant, is Hamilton's distinction between securing safety or tranquillity, in other words providing for defense, and aiming at ascendancy and greatness. In the Farewell Address, we find a revealing phrase that can be traced to Hamilton's "Original Major Draft." It would be worthy of "a free, enlightened, and, at no distant period, *a great Nation*, to give to mankind the magnanimous and too novel example of a People always guided by an exalted justice & benevolence."[2]

What was the meaning of national greatness as Hamilton envisaged it and as Washington endorsed it? Was it just another word for power? It does not seem so. If one recalls ancient Rome, the prime example of "greatness" for the historical understanding of centuries, including the century of Montesquieu and Gibbon, her greatness certainly included the notion of power; power, as it were, in space and time, extended over vast territories and stretched over vast tracts of time. Yet there is also an ingredient of positive moral valuation, which is absent from the "scientific" as well as morally derogatory concepts of power that loom large in our time. This positive moral valuation might reflect rather different criteria. As Howard White has pointed out in a searching analysis, the greatness of republican Rome evoked a different kind of admiration than that of imperial Rome.[3] For the founders of a new republic, the greatness of the former surely was a more

relevant point of reference than the latter, linked with the oppro-
brium of absolute rule. It was the Roman republic that in Hamilton's words "attained to the utmost heights of human greatness."
It was the Roman republic that Hamilton had in mind when in
1798 he condemned revolutionary France for playing the "*great
nation*"—"aping ancient Rome, except in her virtues."[4] Yet it
was also with reference to the Roman republic that Hamilton exhorted his fellow New Yorkers, in 1787: "[N]either the manners nor the genius of Rome are suited to the republic or the age
we live in. All her maxims and habits were military, her government was constituted for war. Ours is unfit for it, and our situation still less than our constitution, invites us to emulate the
conduct of Rome, or to attempt a display of unprofitable heroism."[5]

Indeed, the notion of greatness evoked by ancient Rome was
coming to be appreciated, or even recognized, less and less with
the victory of the moderns, the advent of liberalism and democracy. This lack of appreciation derived from two quite distinct
sources. The first was the Christian, particularly the Protestant,
belief in original sin. Its consequence was an injunction of humility to all men alike: there is no greatness but sanctity, no honor
but the arduous path of the imitation of Christ. Shakespeare's
Henry V, full of desire for worldly glory, reflects on that difficulty: "But if it be a sin to covet honour / I am the most offending
soul alive." The second source was the individualistic and egali-
tarian tradition of modern liberal utilitarianism. Its emphasis on
the rights, or merely the interests, of the individual set it apart
from the stress on the duties of men that had united the aristocratic tradition of classical antiquity with Christianity.

Though the psychological and moral premises of liberal utilitarian society were established in the sixteenth, seventeenth, and
eighteenth centuries, older and indeed classical traditions of political morality were preserved until the sweeping victory of the
Industrial Revolution in the nineteenth century. For understanding the political outlook of Alexander Hamilton, who was caught
in the cross fire of ancient and modern ways of thought, it is
essential to grasp the import of this older tradition.

The Scale of Greatness

At the beginning of the seventeenth century, Francis Bacon set forth a scale of political honor and greatness that evokes images almost beyond our comprehension. There were two different scales of honor for sovereigns and subjects; in this discussion, it is Bacon's scale of the "degrees of sovereign honor" that is most significant. In the first place were *"conditores imperiorum,* founders of States and commonwealths." Among them were Romulus, Cyrus, and Caesar. In the second place were *"legislatores,* lawgivers; which are also called second founders, or *perpetui principes,* because they govern by their ordinances after they are gone." Among them we find Lycurgus, Solon, Numa, and Justinian. The third place belongs to *"liberatores,* or *salvatores;* such as compound the long miseries of civil wars or deliver their countries from servitude of strangers or tyrants." Here we find Augustus, Henry VII of England, and Henry IV of France. Fourth, there were *"propagatores,* or *propugnatores imperii,* such as in honourable wars enlarge their territories, or make noble defence against invaders." And fifth were *"patres patriae,* which reign justly, and make the times good wherein they live." Both of the last kinds, Bacon added, "need no examples, they are in such number."[6]

Bacon's scale of political honor and greatness is only the most elaborate exposition of an idea that linked classical antiquity with early modern thought. Some of Bacon's categories were blurred, yet the substance of his values was retained in the observations of men like Hume and Adam Smith. "Of all men that distinguish themselves by memorable achievements," Hume wrote in one of his *Essays,* "the first place of honor seems due to legislators and founders of states who transmit a system of laws and institutions to secure the peace, happiness, and liberty of future generations."[7] Adam Smith likewise expressed his admiration for "the greatest and noblest of all characters, that of the reformer and legislator of a great state."[8]

Does this tradition have any relevance for the moral and political ideas of the American Founders? One of the few students to have taken notice of that tradition at all, Louis Hartz, has commented that "a hero is missing from the revolutionary literature of America. He is the legislator, the classical giant who almost invariably turns up at revolutionary moments to be given authority to lay the foundations of the free society." Professor Hartz further suggests that this hero is "not missing because the Americans were unfamiliar with images of ancient history, or because they had not read the Harringtons or the Machiavellis and Rousseaus of the modern period. . . . The legislator is missing because, in truth, the Americans had no need for his services."[9] The Founders were assuredly acquainted with the great authors of political science, whom Montesquieu regarded as the real legislators of mankind.[10] The figure of the founder or legislator was not, however, absent from the revolutionary literature of America. At the very beginning of the fateful year of 1776, John Adams sketched a "politician," in the exalted and now obsolete meaning of the word. It was "the Part of a great Politician to make the Character of his People, to extinguish among them the Follies and Vices that he sees, and to create in them the Virtues and Abilities which he sees wanting. I wish I was sure that America has one such Politician but I fear she has not."[11]

Alexander Hamilton spoke of the same subject two and a half years later, in his first series of papers attacking the weakness of Congress. His commitment to the goals that Bacon had so impressively described was even more obvious than Adams's. A member of Congress occupied a station "the most illustrious and important of any I am able to conceive. He is to be regarded not only as a legislator, but as the founder of an empire. A man of virtue and ability, dignified with so precious a trust, would rejoice that fortune had given him birth at a time, and placed him in circumstances so favourable for promoting human happiness. He would esteem it not more the duty, than the privilege and ornament of his office, to do good to mankind; from this commanding eminence, he would look down with contempt upon every mean or interested pursuit."[12]

How can we account for the fact that this avowal of the very purpose of Hamilton's lifework, delineated here even more clearly than in the seventy-second *Federalist*, has elicited so little comment? An answer is suggested if we look at another document that, though widely known, has rarely been placed in this context—James Madison's *Federalist* No. 38. Madison felt it "not a little remarkable" that in ancient history's examples of the establishment of governments "with deliberation and consent," the task was not "committed to an assembly of men," but was "performed by some individual citizen of pre-eminent wisdom and approved integrity."[13]

Madison's own discussion reveals at least two of the factors that account for the neglect of this issue during the last century and a half: the liberal theory of human nature, and the liberal democratic theory of the principles of political obligation. Both are obviously incongruous with the image of the great nation-builder. Madison alluded to the Whig or liberal conception of human nature when he asked how a people as jealous of their liberty as the Greeks "should so far abandon the rules of caution as to place their destiny in the hands of a single citizen." Indeed, the liberal obsession with the abuse of power must preclude such a procedure, and Madison voiced this preoccupation when he wondered why the Greeks should have preferred "one illustrious citizen" to "a select body of citizens, from whose common deliberations more wisdom, as well as more safety, might have been expected."[14] As to the second factor mentioned, there was the liberal principle of political obligation which has remained, in spite of all subsequent utilitarian, positivist, or historicist theories, the moral basis of American democracy—the social contract of free individuals possessing equal natural rights. Madison did not fail to mention the objection that the legislator theory would immediately provoke on that count. "What degree of agency these reputed lawgivers might have in their respective establishments," Madison speculated, "or how far they might be clothed with the legitimate authority of the people, cannot in every instance be ascertained."[15]

To these factors we must add a third that has contributed to obscuring the tradition of the individual lawgiver. This is the rise of the outlook peculiar to the social sciences in the last two hundred years. It is an outlook that denies the Aristotelian unity of political and social things and substitutes for it the separation of state and society, replacing the primacy of politics with the primacy of "society." This outlook has informed, over the last few generations, not only sociology in a narrow sense, but more recent liberal political theory and the whole edifice of socialist thought as well. The sweep of majestic forces of social evolution, moving slowly and gradually, even if interrupted by occasional cataclysms, has prevailed over the dignity as well as the effectiveness of the great individual. This approach has been in ascendancy ever since Adam Ferguson, the Scottish "father of sociology," asserted that "Mankind are to be taken in groups, as they have always subsisted. The history of the individual is but a detail of the sentiments and thoughts he has entertained in the view of his species: and every experiment relative to this subject [the history of the human species] should be made with entire societies, not with single men."[16] This approach was by no means irrelevant in the America of the Founders. Ferguson's substitution of a natural history of societies for moral and political science (which had prevailed even with his master Montesquieu) helped dissolve the traditional dichotomy between the state of nature and the state of society; that dichotomy became purely formal, if it was not rejected altogether. It was this approach, furthermore, that profoundly colored Jefferson's belief in the overwhelming impact of impersonal forces on human nature. There is no suggestion in Jefferson that an outstanding individual might overcome the limitations of his society; social forces, whether for good, like the healthy impact of the farmer's life, or for bad, like the corrupting interdependence of luxury and misery in urban society, were stronger.

The time-honored, but in so many respects mistaken, dichotomy between Hamiltonian and Jeffersonian principles may assume new relevance, I suggest, in the context of the role of the great individual in founding political institutions. In this light, the contrast between Hamilton's and Jefferson's outlook becomes one of the last great debates between ancients and moderns. Hamilton, to be sure, shared the psychological premises of modernity to a very great extent. Yet, when confronted with a new dimension of modern thought, the science of society as distinguished from the science of politics, he sided with the ancients and the early moderns who joined them.[17]

Interestingly enough, after an eclipse of over a century and a half the figures of the great individuals associated with the beginnings of political societies seem to have reentered political science, whence the united forces of democratic and sociological theories had exiled them. Not long ago, Bertrand de Jouvenel introduced the concept of *vis politica*. It is analyzed under three aspects, rarely found together in the same person: "the capacity to bring into being a stream of wills, the capacity to canalize the stream, and the capacity to regularize and institutionalize the resulting cooperation." The first two aspects, it seems, combine more readily in one type of person: "The man who leads into action a stream of wills, whether he found it or made it, is *dux*, the conductor or leader." The man who institutionalizes cooperation is "*rex*, the man who regularizes or rules."[18]

These types of political authority may be discerned in all social aggregates, de Jouvenel has pointed out, not only in states. Yet there can be no question that they assume enhanced significance if applied to the founding of political societies. De Jouvenel has explicitly made a distinction of considerable heuristic value for an understanding of founders or legislators in drawing our attention to the fact that Rousseau (perhaps the last great political theorist to have asserted the need for a lawgiver at the origin of societies) was struck by the different functions of the first two Roman kings: the name of *Romulus*, allegedly the actual founder of Rome, means *force*; the name of his successor, *Numa*, means *law*.[19] This hint, which de Jouvenel has supported with additional evidence from the Biblical tradition (David and Solomon) and research in cultural anthropology, is all the more interesting if we recall Bacon's distinction, between *conditores* and *legis-latores*; Bacon, too, put Romulus into the former class, Numa into the latter. In this context, Hamilton's exuberant exclamation that an American leader in A.D. 1778 was to be regarded "not only as a legislator, but as a founder of an empire" reveals his more than superficial acquaintance with this tradition of political thought.

It is noteworthy that among the few bits of evidence testifying to Hamilton's reading there should be excerpts from the first two pairs of Plutarch's *Lives*. In an order we are not wont to appreciate, Plutarch put first a pair of true *conditores*, Theseus and Romulus; second, a pair of *legislatores*, Lycurgus and Numa Pompilius. We should not draw too far-reaching conclusions from this fact. Hamilton's acquaintance with Plutarch exceeds those four biographies, and his notes reveal a wide, not visibly organized curiosity.[20] It is, however, worth observing that he was struck by a comment in Plutarch's comparison of the two *conditores*, which indeed touches the core of Hamilton's statesmanship. Plutarch blamed Theseus for having given in to popularity, Romulus for having erred in the opposite direction of tyranny: "For a Prince's first concern ought to be the preservation of the government itself; and in order to do this he should neither claim more authority than is his due, nor on the other hand give up any part of his prerogative."[21] Hamilton copied this in his notebook, though owing to a missing page (or missing pages) only the end of the sentence—"give up any part of his prerogative"—remains.[22] Hamilton continued to quote: "Whoever gives up his right, or extends his claim too far, is no more a king, but either a slave to the people or a tyrant, and so becomes odious or contemptible to his subjects. The one seems to be the fault of easiness and good nature, the other of pride and severity."[23] We know how frequently the alternatives of demagoguery and tyranny, both to be avoided like the plague, recur in Hamilton's later writings.[24] In later years, his emphasis was on the danger "from the left," as it were; but in 1777, when these notes most likely were written, the final break with George III was too immediate a memory and too important an issue.[25] It may be recalled that the most democratic of Hamilton's utterances were made at about the same time.[26] It is not surprising, then, to find Hamilton criticizing Plutarch's injunction against popular sympathies: "A false sentiment," he jotted down; "it would often be praiseworthy in a prince to relinquish a part of an excessive prerogative to establish a more moderate government, better adapted to the happiness or temper of his people."[27]

Whatever his feelings in 1777, we know Hamilton's growing disillusionment with the affairs of the Union, which was first publicly expressed late in 1778 in those very "Publius" letters that reveal him to have been fascinated by the great task of founding an empire. It is wasteful to indulge in lengthy speculations on whether Hamilton himself distinguished sharply between the different realms of greatness as they were sketched by Bacon, whether he considered his own tasks and predispositions akin to those of a founder, a legislator, a liberator, or a conqueror. We may say, perhaps, that Hamilton's talents as well as the tasks that confronted him in different periods of his life cut across that "scale of greatness." In the New York Ratifying Convention, an interesting comment escaped him that brightly illuminates his own conception of the task in 1787 and 1788: "Men will pursue their interests. It is as easy to change human nature, as to oppose the strong current of the selfish passions. *A wise legislator will gently divert the channel, and direct it, if possible, to the public good.*"[28] Yet in the "Publius" letters a decade earlier, clearly the founder of an empire ranks even higher than a legislator.

Power and Responsibility:
Hamiltonianism vs. Jeffersonianism

Hamilton believed in both the possibility and the desirability of personal leadership even beyond the admittedly extraordinary tasks of founding a nation and providing initial legislation. This belief was grounded in a theory of political conduct that opposed to the corrupting tendencies of power the sobering influence of responsibility. It is a notable contrast to the Jeffersonian tradition in American political thought.

The Jeffersonian conception of human nature predicated the possibility of human goodness on the equality not of legal rights only, but of material conditions and social status as well. Jeffersonian political theory had no remedy for a stratified society except the advice to do away with stratification.[29] Benjamin Rush, an ardent Jeffersonian, put this theory very concisely when he proclaimed that the wealth of the rich would "administer fuel to the love of arbitrary power that is common to all men"; the "lust for dominion" was "always connected with opulence."[30] If human goodness or virtue depended on material, social, and political equality that could only be achieved in a society of frugal, independent, and self-sufficient farmers, the prospects for a more complicated society were grim indeed. Jeffersonianism, bent on equality, would have liked to suspend the cleavage not only between the rich and the poor, but also between the strong and the weak. Yet for a society in which the powerful and the powerless continued to live side by side, the Jeffersonian diagnosis of "corruption" was devastating on two counts. Not only did it deny magnanimity to the strong, it also implied the meanness of the weak, as the very fruit of their subservience.[31] Since the original revolt against monarchy and aristocracy, Jeffersonianism has kept its function as the political theory of the underdog. This accounts for the relative obscurity of Jeffersonian loathing of "the mob of the cities" as well as for the prominence given to the polemics against exploitation and abuse by the great.

The threat of corruption through power has been answered, in the theory of constitutionalism, by the diffusion of power. Emphasis on the diffusion of power united the political theory of Jefferson's *Notes on Virginia* with that of the Federal Constitution.[32] Yet a political theory that predicates the diffusion of power as the very condition of human goodness or virtue, a theory that bets everything on this single factor, avoids the real issue of responsibility and justice. "Justice," Bertrand de Jouvenel has said, "is a quality, not of social arrangements, but of the human will."[33] He has indicted what is perhaps the most questionable implication of the theory of diffusion of power, the illusion of replacing moral qualities by institutional arrangements.

Whereas it used to be thought that social relationships are improved by justice in men, it is now thought, contrariwise, that the installation in institutions of a state of things called just promotes the improvement of men. This reversal is in the fashion of thought today, *which makes morality the creature of circumstance.*

We see then that justice today is not a habit of mind which each of us can acquire in proportion to his virtue and should acquire in proportion to his power; rather it is an organization or arrangement of things. . . . The justice now recommended is a quality not of a man and a man's actions, but of a certain configuration of things in social geometry, no matter by what means it is brought about. Justice is now something which exists independently of just men.[34]

Hamilton's political theory retained, amidst his undoubtedly "modern" psychological assumptions, certain elements of pre-modern thought, which combined with his common sense served as corrective to some of the radical implications of liberal political theory. Hamilton's theory of political responsibility opposed the Whig-Jeffersonian pessimism of the "Men of Little Faith" with compelling force: "We are told," he addressed the New York Legislature early in 1787,

it is dangerous to trust power any where; that *power* is liable to *abuse*, with a variety of trite maxims of the same kind. General propositions of this nature are easily framed, the truth of which cannot be denied, but they rarely convey any precise idea. To these we might oppose other propositions equally true and equally indefinite. It might be said that too little power is as dangerous as too much, that it leads to anarchy, and from anarchy to despotism. But the question still recurs, what is this *too much or too little*? where is the measure or standard to ascertain the happy mean?

Powers must be granted, or civil Society cannot exist; the possibility of abuse is no argument against the *thing*.[35]

In the New York Ratifying Convention in the following year, Hamilton reached great heights of oratorical power, supported by deep conviction, in defense of the same argument. "That responsibility which is so important in republican governments"

was perhaps the central theme of his exertions.[36] Hamilton combatted the opinion that no powers should be entrusted to any body
of men merely because they might be abused: "This is an argument of possibility and chance; one that would render useless all
reasonings upon the probable operation of things, and defeat the
established principles of natural and moral causes." This kind of
argument "would lead us to withdraw all confidence from our
fellow-citizens, and discard the chimerical idea of government."[37]
In another speech to that Convention, Hamilton appealed with
almost desperate intensity to the common sense of his audience,
taking care to pay homage to the current checks-and-balances
obsession of the "Men of Little Faith." "When you have divided
and nicely balanced the departments of government; When you
have strongly connected the virtue of your rulers with their interest; when, in short, you have rendered your system as perfect
as human forms can be; you must place confidence; you must
give power."[38]

We encounter a similar emphasis, of course, in *The Federalist*.
There Hamilton repeatedly pointed out the absurdity of establishing any government by delegation unless the responsibility
of the delegates were presumed: The "supposition of universal
venality in human nature," Hamilton observed, "is little less an
error in political reasoning, than the supposition of universal
rectitude. The institution of delegated power implies, that there
is a portion of virtue and honor among mankind, which may be
a reasonable foundation of confidence." Experience, he thought,
justified the theory. "It has been found to exist," Hamilton added
(in direct opposition to Jeffersonianism), "in the most corrupt
periods of the most corrupt governments," witness the contemporary British House of Commons.[39]

Cecelia M. Kenyon has pointed out the incongruity of the
Founders' black misgivings about the corrupting tendencies of
power with their own unimpeachable and public-spirited conduct.[40] John Adams is a case in point, but so is Jefferson or even
Madison. This incongruity of common sense with political theory
has an historical explanation. Whig theory was born in the seven-

teenth-century revolt against the absolute power of the Stuart kings; after the Glorious Revolution, a radical Whig tradition continued to polemicize against the government in power; crossing the Atlantic Ocean, Whiggism was revitalized by the Americans' resentments against George III. It entered American constitutional thought and practice after 1776 with its characteristic and extreme distrust of individual executive power and its overestimation of plural, collective bodies. This was the background of Hamilton's warning in 1782 that it was "certainly pernicious to leave any government in a situation of responsibility, disproportioned to its power."[41]

England's radical Whigs and America's anti-Federalist "Men of Little Faith" and their intellectual heirs, the Jeffersonians, produced two diverse—indeed contradictory—notions of public office. On one hand, the public official was considered as the mere mouthpiece of the people's sovereign will.[42] Regardless of the branch of government he actually belonged to, he was looked upon as the executor of the people's instructions, unselfishly identifying his will and judgment with that of the people.[43] On the other hand was the image of the purely self-seeking politician who cheated the public whenever he could get away with it, wallowing in the spoils of office. Actually, these two images had one common source: the conviction that the people's delegation of power is an evil in itself, that consequently the abuse of power mounts in proportion with the power delegated. The radical Whigs and their followers in America believed, then, in what we may be permitted to call Acton's law, namely that power tends to corrupt, and that absolute power corrupts absolutely. Yet the presumption, or, as Henry Clay put it in a passage mentioned before, even the certainty of abuse of delegated power made little or no provision for the common experience that it had to be discounted by the varying degrees of trustworthiness in men.[44] The doctrine of the universal law of human corruption through power pushed distrust in human nature to extreme dimensions.

Hamilton, profoundly influenced by Hume, would seem to have been a better psychologist than the "Men of Little Faith."

He refused to be blinded by the historical contingencies of the revolt against George III, which, superimposed on memories of the Glorious Revolution against James II, had produced in the American States the popularity of "that maxim of republican jealousy which considers power as safer in the hands of a number of men than of a single man."[45] To this simplification of the principle of Acton's law, Hamilton opposed different insights:

Has it been found that bodies of men act with more rectitude or greater disinterestedness than individuals? The contrary of this has been inferred by all accurate observers of the conduct of mankind; and the inference is founded upon obvious reasons. Regard to reputation has a less active influence, when the infamy of a bad action is to be divided among a number, than when it is to fall singly upon one. A spirit of faction, which is apt to mingle its poison in the deliberations of all bodies of men, will often hurry the persons of whom they are composed into improprieties and excesses, for which they would blush in a private capacity.[46]

"Regard to reputation" was a consideration neglected by the radical Whigs in England and the Anti-Federalists and Jeffersonians in America, who lowered their sights to take aim at the pursuers of power and wealth for their own sakes; they had dropped "regard to reputation" or honor from the implements of their political theory. Directing all their guns on the "abuse of power," on "corruption through power," they had lost sight of the psychology of responsibility. Hamilton trenchantly laid bare that deficiency. He was convinced that "the sense of responsibility is always strongest, in proportion as it is undivided."[47] Thus one of the weightiest objections against a plural executive was "that it tends to conceal faults, and destroy responsibility. Responsibility is of two kinds, to censure and to punishment. The first is the most important of the two; especially in an elective office. Man, in public trust, will much oftener act in such a manner as to render him unworthy of being any longer trusted, than in such a manner as to make him obnoxious to legal punishment."[48] Carelessness and abdication of individual judgment were perhaps as perilous violations of trust as the more lurid "corrup-

tions" of "enjoying" power that Jefferson aimed at in his fear
that "you and I, Congress and Assemblies, Judges and Governors, shall all become wolves" if not kept in check by the people.[49]
Yet if there was any device to prevent or restrain abuse of trust,
it was engaging that irreducible moral entity, individual man,
rather than diffusing responsibility beyond the point of recognition. The principle of "regard to reputation" as a standard of individual conduct, with its implications of self-discipline and self-
respect, ran counter to the radical Whig assumption that regarded
all men as "good" if power was taken away from them, all men
as "bad" if power was given them. That assumption divided men
into two kinds, the harmless and the harmful. But even the same
person might be considered harmless or "good" without power,
harmful or "bad" with it. It stands to reason that a conception of
human nature based on such criteria was bound to have difficulties
with the meaning of integrity and responsibility.

One of the most serious distortions in contemporary moral,
political, and psychological discourse may be found in the combination of contradictory qualities in the notion of *pride*. Pride has
come to mean opposite things: magnanimity as well as hybris,
self-respect as well as arrogance, honor as well as vainglory, a
sense of measure and proportion as well as its lack by excess. Winston Churchill reminded us that honor "is often influenced by
that element of pride which plays so large a part in its inspiration."[50] In other words, to act for the sake of self-esteem is the
next best thing to acting for the sake of virtue itself. This is what
Hamilton had in mind when he counted upon men's "pride, if
not upon their virtue" to exact political responsibility.[51]

The Scope of Responsibility: Public Interest and Reasons of State

The point has been reached where we should look beyond the
optimum conditions of responsibility and inquire into its scope.
D. W. Brogan once advised us to get away from the notion that
democracy means "whatever Lola wants, Lola gets." That pic-
turesque phrase adequately expresses a political theory that has
abolished the older distinction of public and private interest by re-

ducing the former to a mere concoction of the latter. "The national interest," an adept of this school of thought has said, "in actual practice is that which remains after mutual cancellation by opposing groups of interests too narrow and particular to be acceptable to a majority of representatives."[52]

An outstanding trait of Hamilton's political thought, as evidenced by his numerous references to it, was his belief in a genuine public good or national interest apart from and above the bargaining processes of conflicting private interests. Hamilton felt strongly *both* about the prevalence of considerations of private or partial interest in people's minds *and* about the prevalence of opinion of interest over real interest in the transactions of society.[53] But he did not therefore neutralize the dimension of *public* interest to a mere market place for the realization of private interests.

The autonomy of the sphere of public interest is strikingly apparent in Hamilton's claim that government should be "free from every other control but a regard to the public good *and* to the sense of the people."[54] These two, in other words, were not necessarily identical. At issue was the much-debated problem of representation *vs.* delegation. The significance of this distinction emerges from Hamilton's ideas on the senatorial office. Hamilton espoused a Burkean theory of representation when he set off the character of public trustees from that of private agents: "That a man should have the power, in private life, of recalling his agent, is proper; because in the business in which he is engaged, he has no other object but to gain the approbation of his principal. Is this the case with the senator? Is he simply the agent of the state? No: He is an agent for the union, and he is bound to perform services necessary to the good of the whole, though his state should condemn them."[55]

Once the genuineness of the public interest is granted, the further question arises: how to define its sphere in an age that expelled the concern for moral betterment from the competence of the *res publica*? It is surely revealing, though it will not come as a surprise, that Hamilton's most emphatic invocation of the public interest occurred in the context of his claim for full im-

plied powers of national defense and taxation. Government needed the means to fulfill "the purposes of its institution"; it needed
to "provide for the security, advance the prosperity, or support
the reputation of the commonwealth."[56] The first and third of
these propositions point without ambiguity to the sphere of foreign relations; yet if we are mindful of Hamilton's belief that
"commerce" was the great engine of the wealth of nations, it appears even more clearly that the clue to Hamilton's concept of
what he more often called the "public good," but sometimes
called "national interests," must be comprehended from a perspective encompassing the nation as one among many.

The context of foreign policy is an intrinsic ingredient of the
Hamiltonian concept of the public good; further evidence is furnished by another expression which Hamilton used on occasion
to set off the realm of public concern from private pursuits:
"reasons of state." Hamilton once argued on the problems of
raising national credit that individuals will "neither be actuated
by generosity nor reasons of state. 'Tis to their interest alone we
must appeal."[57] Yet with all regard to the subjective force of
private interests, it was clear that reasons of state formed an ob-
jective factor quite independent from the consensus or the compromises of individual interests. The concept of *raison d'état*, as
Friedrich Meinecke and (more recently) Felix Gilbert have
shown, dominated the discourse on the foreign policies of European nations from the sixteenth century to the eighteenth. Reasons of state were peculiarly expressive of the *external* pursuits
of nations. This is supported by Hamilton's understanding of the
term (which recalls our earlier discussion of Hamilton's disagreement with Charles Pinckney on the principles of republican
foreign policy). Even in the pages of *The Federalist*, Hamilton
did not refrain from bitterly complaining of America's commitment to "the novel and absurd experiment in politics of tying up
the hands of government from offensive war founded upon
reasons of state."[58]

It becomes our task, then, to inquire into Hamilton's understanding of the reasons of state that conditioned the life of the

United States as a nation among nations, and to place that understanding within the framework of his political morality.

The Meaning of Empire

Among the outstanding characteristics of the young American Republic was its consciousness of *empire*. From the lowly to the great, it pervaded the atmosphere of the emerging nation. For instance, the Postmaster of New York, one Sebastian Bauman, reported to his superior in 1792 on the advances he contemplated in the postal service of that city. He planned to hire a small shop near the coffee house, and to "fix a small oil lamp within and place the arms of the United states without to show Foreigners the greatness of our Rising Empior."[59] George Washington, about a decade earlier, had rejoiced that the "foundation of our Empire" was laid at a time when the "researches of the human mind, after social happiness" had been carried further than ever, at a time when "the Treasures of Knowledge, acquired by the labours of Philosophers, Sages and Legislators, through a long succession of years, are laid open for our use."[60] It was not by any means Hamilton alone, then, who looked upon the United States as an "empire," though there can be no doubt that Hamilton clung with particular intensity to that conception. It is a theme that leads from his exuberance on the opportunities of founding an empire in 1778, through his hope in 1787 of rescuing "the American empire from disunion, anarchy, and misery," to the cautious though proud remark of *Camillus* that "we are the embryo of a great empire," and finally to the political testament written on the eve of the mortal duel, warning of "the dismemberment of our empire" as the greatest of all dangers.[61]

The meaning of "empire" is full of puzzling ambiguities. For a century now, it has been linked with the liberal and undemocratic implications of the term "imperialism."[62] Yet even before the rise of "imperialism," even during the first generation of the Republic, "empire" was not always devoid of sinister undertones. From the times of the Roman republic, *imperium* had a double meaning; it might simply be synonymous with political rule or

government, but it might also mean *imperium Romanum* —
Rome's sway over other peoples.[63] It was the last conception, of
course, that lived on in the idea of universal empire, and in
the Holy Roman Empire up to its demise in 1806. The double
meaning of the Latin *imperium* was well understood by James
Harrington, who said that "Empire is of two kinds, *Domestick*
and *National*, or *Forrain* and *Provinciall*."[64] The first variety was
a nation's government of itself; the second variety was clearly
external rule—a rule that by Francis Bacon's time comprehended
the rule of the seas.[65] The ambiguity of empire was compounded
when it came to assume a meaning not to be found in antiquity,
namely, a large country. "A nation extended over vast tracts of
land, and numbers of people," William Temple said in 1672,
"arrives in time at the ancient name of kingdom, or modern of
empire."[66]

It was only natural that the intricate structure of the kingdoms
and possessions of the British crown—including colonies with a
considerable degree of self-government—should blur the boundaries between empire as external dominion and empire as a vast
nation. This somewhat cloudy connotation of the term "British
Empire," while by no means unknown prior to 1763, speedily
gained ground in the aftermath of the glorious victory over
France in the "Great War for Empire" as the Franco-British contest has so aptly been called. In 1760, after Canada had been
wrested from the French, one American colonist, Benjamin
Franklin, proudly paid homage to the "future grandeur and
stability of the British empire"—whose foundations he saw in
America.[67] But pride in the magnitude of "the empire," as it was
more and more often called after 1763, soon turned sour in the
thirteen colonies.[68]

As the troubles of America grew, so grew the Americans' concern with the science of politics. Yet those who consulted Montesquieu—and who didn't?—found a stern message for all admirers of the grandeur of empire. Vast extent of territory, according to Montesquieu, was the natural soil for despotism. Montesquieu was responsible, then, for the sinister identification of em-

pire, in the sense of vastness, with despotism—an identification that we encounter in John Adams's great *Novanglus* essays of 1775. There is considerable irony in Adams's defending the British Constitution as a government of laws, rather than an "empire," against the arguments of a Loyalist devoted to the British Empire and to the proposition that the colonies were part of it. Adams argued that the colonies were "not a part of the British empire; because the British government is not an empire. . . . An empire is a despotism, and an emperor a despot, bound by no law or limitation but his own will; it is a stretch of tyranny beyond absolute monarchy." Adams did admit that there was a sense in which the term empire could be applied "to the government of Geneva, or any other republic, as well as to monarchy or despotism. In this sense it is synonymous with *government, rule,* or *dominion.*"[69]

The ambiguity of the concept of empire, as the Americans approached independence, was considerable. Yet it is easy enough to see the conflict that was most likely to develop in the young republic: it was the conflict between the republican character of the new nation, i.e., its commitment to the individual pursuit of happiness, and the prospect of territorial growth. John Adams, in 1775, had gloomily if not quite correctly observed that "Rome never introduced the terms Roman empire until the tragedy of her freedom was completed. Before that, it was only the republic or the city."[70] What about the American empire?

Thomas Jefferson boldly united his agrarian egalitarianism with the drive toward westward expansion in his concept of the "empire of liberty." As early as 1779 he used that formula.[71] After the turn of the century, he more often returned to that concept, and refined it in the process. The American West furnished Jefferson a means for transcending Montesquieu's theory of republicanism. Its function was twofold: first, the West offered the famous safety valve for the continuation of an agrarian society predicated on the condition of independence and equality; second, westward expansion would push back European influence, whether British, Spanish, or French, and reduce the need for military preparedness, with its threats to the utmost diffusion of power. The first of these functions is reflected in Jefferson's pronouncement, in 1805, that "by enlarging the empire of liberty, we multiply its auxiliaries, & provide new sources of renovation, should its principles, at any time, degenerate, in those portions of our country which gave them birth."[72] The second function of continental expansion Jefferson described to Andrew Jackson on the occasion of the Louisiana Purchase; that purchase, he said, removed "the intrigues of foreign nations to a distance from which they can no longer produce disturbance between the Indians and us." He added that "the world will here see such an extent of country under a free and moderate government as it has never yet seen."[73] Years later, from the serenity of his retirement, Jefferson addressed one of the architects of the Louisiana Purchase on the French side, Barbé de Marbois: "I have much confidence that we shall proceed successfully for ages to come, and that, contrary to the principle of Montesquieu, it will be seen that the larger the extent of country, the more firm its republican structure, if founded, not on conquest, but in principles of compact and equality. My hope of its duration is built much on the enlargement of the resources of life going hand in hand with the enlargement of territory, and the belief that men are disposed to live honestly, if the means of doing so are open to them."[74]

Hamilton's concept of empire, it comes as no surprise to us, was sharply contrasted to Jefferson's, and no other single instance brought this out as clearly as the Louisiana Purchase. Hamilton disagreed with both points of Jefferson's design for empire: agrarianism and isolationism. Western expansion for the sake of maintaining America's agrarian structure he held both undesirable and unlikely, perhaps the former more than the latter. In retrospect, Hamilton's failure to foresee the speed and energy of westward expansion may appear a notable misjudgment by a statesman who had given several startling examples to justify Washington's comment that his judgment was "intuitively great."[75] Yet upon closer analysis, it appears that Hamilton's depreciation of the importance of the western territory is less the result of an erroneous interpretation of facts or trends than of his desire to deflect America's development from a path still dangerous. It is certainly correct to say, as Gerald Johnson has done, that one basis of the Hamiltonian philosophy of a strong central government was the assumption that the "means of physical coercion would proceed at least abreast of territorial expansion."[76] Hamilton held that the "western region acquired, together with New Orleans, was "not valuable to the United States for settlement."[77] The reasons are to be found in Hamilton's continued adherence to Montesquieu's apprehensions about the government of very large territories. It was Hamilton's opinion that considering "the present extent of the United States, and that not one sixteenth part of its territory is yet under occupation, the advantage of the acquisition, as it relates to actual settlement, appears too distant and remote to strike the mind of a sober politician with force." This was a matter of speculation "for many years, if not centuries to come." Nevertheless disbelief was mingled with apprehension. Should "our own citizens, more enterprising than wise, become desirous of settling this country, and emigrate thither, it must not only be attended with all the injuries of a too widely dispersed population, but by adding to the great weight of the western part of our territory, must hasten the dismemberment of a large portion of our country, or a dissolution of the Government."[78] Indeed, as Douglass Adair has said, Hamilton, in the last year of his life, was "pertinaciously holding to the dogma that no free republic could be established and maintained in a large geographical area."[79]

During the whole of his political career, Hamilton limited his westward ambitions to the acquisition of the mouths of the Mississippi, and New Orleans. Possession of that strategic place would vastly improve the United States's position in the maritime balance of power and definitively stave off the danger of disaffection among the western settlers. From his first detailed analysis of that problem in 1790 to the debate of 1803 following Louisiana's cession from Spain to France, conflict with the power holding New Orleans seemed to Hamilton—as it was to appear to

Jefferson—inescapable, and its outbreak only a matter of prudent timing. In what I consider Hamilton's ablest, most brilliant state paper on foreign policy, his advice to Washington on the occasion of the Nootka Sound controversy between Spain and England in September 1790, control of the Mississippi emerges as a central interest of the United States. Securing the navigation of the Mississippi, Hamilton advised Washington, "may be regarded in its consequences as essential to the unity of the Empire." Revealing his hopes for the growth of the nation's strength, he admitted "that when we are able to make good our pretensions, we ought not to leave in the possession of any foreign power, the *territories* at the mouth of the Mississippi, which are to be regarded as the key to it."[80] In his conversations with the British Major George Beckwith, Hamilton made no bones about his desire for the possession of New Orleans—"whatever individual interests may be opposed to it, the general advantage of the States points it out most evidently," Beckwith recorded.[81] Similar views were expressed on various occasions in succeeding years, and the conquest of the lower Mississippi valley was part of Hamilton's project of 1798/99 to open up Spanish America jointly with Great Britain.[82] When matters concerning Louisiana reached an acute state in 1802, Hamilton repeated that he had "always held that the *unity of our empire* and the best interests of our nation require that we shall annex to the United States all the territory east of the Mississippi, New Orleans included."[83] He felt the opportunity for war ripe and urged it ably in his *Pericles* article early in 1803.[84] Hamilton's view of the extreme improbability of a voluntary cession of Louisiana by France, upon which his argument for war was based, cannot be said to have been disproved by the turn of events. The fortuitous character of the Louisiana Purchase is a matter of historical record, and subsequent research has not been able to controvert Hamilton's conclusion of July 1803, that the "unforseen operation of events" rather than American policy was responsible for it—even if we discount his denunciation of the "feebleness and pusillanimity" of America's "miserable system of measures" as a polemical exaggeration.[85]

When Hamilton spoke of the Mississippi, he looked toward the sea, toward the Gulf of Mexico, rather than toward the vast lands beyond. One of his most revealing utterances was his reference, in 1790, to the Spanish possessions on "our right" and the British possessions (Canada) on "our left"![86] In other words, Hamilton's inner eye was as a matter of course directed toward Europe! His concept of empire corresponded to Washington's hope that some day this country "will have some weight in the scale of Empires."[87] It surely was poles apart from Jefferson's westward-looking "Empire of Liberty," agrarian, pacifist, isolationist.

Hamilton's anticipation of America's future must be seen against this background. His vision of the American empire was adumbrated in his very first political writing, in December 1774. "If," Hamilton proudly addressed his Tory opponent, "by the necessity of the thing, manufactures should once be established and take root among us, they will pave the way, still more, to the future grandeur and glory of America."[88] A few months later, and still more than a year before independence, Hamilton permitted himself another glance into the future, a glance that revealed the nature of greatness in an age of commerce and sea power: "If we take futurity into the account, as we no doubt ought to do, we shall find, that, in fifty or sixty years, America will be in no need of protection from Great-Britain. She will then be able to protect herself, both at home and abroad. She will have a plenty of men and a plenty of materials to provide and equip a formidable navy." Hamilton predicted that though America would owe a debt of gratitude to the mother country for past services, "the scale will then begin to turn in her favour, and the obligation, for future services, will be on the side of Great-Britain."[89]

Hamilton carried his vision of America's "future grandeur and glory" through the War for Independence. On July 4, 1782, he concluded his *Continentalist* with the reflection that "there is something noble and magnificent in the perspective of a great Fœderal Republic, closely linked in the pursuit of a common interest, tranquil and prosperous at home, respectable abroad."[90] The most revealing of Hamilton's looks into the future was to come a few years later, in the eleventh *Federalist* paper. There he referred to points of view "of a striking and animating kind" from which the need for an American Union might be considered. These ideas, he feared, might lead "too far into the regions of futurity, and would involve topics not proper for a newspaper discussion." Here the tradition of reasons of state and their character as *arcana imperii* makes itself strongly felt! "I shall briefly observe," Hamilton began (in a train of thought which actually led him quite far), "that our situation invites and our interests prompt us to aim at an ascendant in the system of American affairs." He postulated on the basis of the geographical division of the world into Europe, Asia, Africa, and America four political systems, "each having a distinct set of interests." Europe, Hamilton complained, had encroached upon the other parts of the world for too long. There was no reason why she should retain her superiority as "Mistress of the World."[91] "Let Americans," he finally exclaimed, "disdain to be the instruments of European greatness! Let the thirteen States, bound together in a strict and indissoluble union, concur in erecting one great American system, superior to the controul of all trans-atlantic force or influence, and able to dictate the terms of the connection between the old and the new world!"[92]

This call to greatness for the United States was only superficially clothed in the terminology of self-determination. If Hamilton vindicated the independence of the "American system" from European domination, in the same breath he announced the United States's ascendancy in the Western Hemisphere. His subsequent speculations about encroaching on South America as well are clearly and logically anticipated in *The Federalist*.[93] Furthermore, the implications of Hamilton's plan to throw Europe back upon herself were not by any means as isolationist as Jefferson's designs. Hamilton perceived that the balance of power was more than the internal mechanism of a state system like the European one. If Hamilton incited America to dictate to Europe the terms of the connection between the old and the new world, there was clearly the implication of a global balance of power in which America would gain a safe preponderance.

This intercontinental character of the balance of power emerges unequivocally from Hamilton's concept of national power in an age of commerce. The calculus of sea power dominated Hamilton's strategy of foreign policy in all those years in which he influenced, officially or unofficially, governmental policies. As early as 1781, in the *Continentalist*, he had proclaimed that "as a commercial people, maritime power must be a primary object of our attention";[94] and in the *Federalist*, the precepts to be followed in the years to come were set forth in greater detail. Hamilton painted a vivid picture of the apprehensions already aroused among the maritime nations of Europe regarding "our too great interference in that carrying trade, which is the support of their navigation and the foundation of their naval strength." This comment throws light on the strategic reasons for Hamilton's support of the shipping interests in the eastern states. Hamilton warned against the design of foreign powers to deprive America "as far as possible of an ACTIVE COMMERCE in our own bottoms. This would answer," he continued, "the threefold purpose of preventing our interference in their navigation, of monopolising the profits of our trade, and of clipping the wings, by which we might soar to a dangerous greatness."[95] Though John Adams is traditionally and rightly credited with the creation of America's first naval force, and though Hamilton's own thirst for military glory repeatedly propelled him to seek the command of an American army rather than navy, we ought to take note of Hamilton's advocacy of the establishment of a federal navy, which, "if it could not vie with those of the great maritime powers, would at least be of respectable weight, if thrown into the scale of either of two contending parties."[96] Obviously, the overwhelming preponderance of the British navy was very much in his mind. Yet Hamilton went on to anticipate a time when the United States might gain a preponderant influence at least within the Western Hemisphere, when the Union could hope "ere long to become the

Arbiter of Europe in America; and to be able to incline the ballance of European competitions in this part of the world as our interest may dictate."[97]

Hamilton's design for the foreign policy of the United States may be summed up in very few words, which appear with slight variations in Cabinet papers, in public writings like *Camillus*, and in the Farewell Address: to guide the United States through her period of present infancy to future strength and greatness. "Our national government is in its infancy," Hamilton wrote in 1790 in his Cabinet paper to Washington on the Nootka Sound issue; since "our infancy" was "the time for clipping our wings," he counseled the nation in the debate on Jay's Treaty that this was not a time to try its strength.[98]

It would go beyond the scope of this essay to investigate the details of Hamilton's reaction to the Franco-British contest that dominated American foreign policy in the 1790's. Ironically, Jefferson took a more favorable view of America's present strength and independence than did Hamilton. It was Jefferson who availed himself of a classic weapon of power politics in the age of commerce—mercantilistic discrimination. It was the very toughness of Jefferson's policy, adumbrated in his great report on commerce of 1793, which was eventually to lead to the Embargo of 1807.[99] Hamilton, on the other hand, was impressed with the role of British credit in the affairs of America.[100] That role in his eyes, became ever more essential and indeed irreplaceable as the convulsions of the French Revolutionary Wars eliminated first Paris and then Amsterdam from the position as competitors of London in the contest for American business connections.[101] There must be added Hamilton's anticipation of conflict with Spain over control of the Mississippi, which would presuppose an understanding of some sort with Britain, and, as the years went by, the horror of the French revolutionary design of universal domination, as Hamilton conceived it, which enhanced England's position as the stronghold of resistance.[102]

These are the considerations that explain, though they do not condone, Hamilton's sometimes treasonable accommodation with

Britain.[103] Yet Hamilton's conviction of the need for British support for the new nation must not be allowed to create the impression that he regarded America as a permanent satellite of England, or that ideological affinities impinged upon his notion of America's best interests. Few scholars have given attention to one of the most instructive "inconsistencies" in Hamilton's design for empire: how could a man bent on the constant appeasement of Britain devise the *Report on Manufactures* with its theory of the protection of infant industries?[104] The "inconsistency" disappears, of course, if Hamilton's policies are seen in the same long-term perspective that he himself applied to them; if it is realized that Hamilton considered himself a leader of an as yet underdeveloped country and that his prime aim was to secure the credit needed to push its industrialization, the essential prerequisite of a truly strong maritime empire. Just as Hamilton had defended the Federal Constitution in the *Federalist*, despite his misgivings, he defended Jay's Treaty in the *Camillus* essays, despite his strong disappointment.[105]

Hamilton's plans for ultimate greatness notwithstanding, temporary accommodation appears most strongly in his constant unwillingness to enter permanent alliances with any nation, even Great Britain. In contrast to Jefferson's true isolationism, Hamilton's and Washington's, as expressed in the Farewell Address, is no more than the vindication of the independence of action fitting a nation that has not resigned itself to playing the role of permanent ally. In Hamilton's Cabinet paper of 1790 on the Nootka Sound question, the importance of which has been noted before, the central message of the Farewell Address had been adumbrated. There Hamilton first discarded the argument that gratitude tied America's policy to that of France and Spain (anticipating his more famous, because more widely known, *Pacificus* papers of 1793). He set off the "vague" obligations of gratitude between nations from those of good faith, which were "precise and determinate." He challenged the view that linked America's "permanent interest" to an "intimate connection" with France and Spain, arguing that the "reality of such an interest" was a thing "about which the best and ablest men of this country" were far from being agreed. He admitted that there were some who, "if the United States were at perfect liberty, would prefer an intimate connection between them and Great Britain as most conducive to their security and advantage"; but the "most general opinion," he concluded, was "that it is our true policy, to steer as clear as possible of all foreign connection, other than commercial and in this respect to cultivate intercourse with all the world on the broadest basis of reciprocal privilege."[106]

How did Hamilton define his own option? "An attentive consideration of the vicissitudes which have attended the friendships of nations, except in a very few instances, from very peculiar circumstances, gives very little countenance to systems which proceed on the supposition of a permanent interest to prefer a particular connection. The position of the United States, detached as they are from Europe admonishes them to unusual circumspection on that point. The same position, as far as it has relation to the possessions of European powers in their Vicinity, strengthens the admonition."[107] Hamilton at no time showed the desire to make America, with respect to England, a second Portugal. It was characteristic rather than exceptional when, at a time of near-war with France, he replied to new instances of British depredations on American shipping with a combination of proud defiance and prudent foresight:

It is of the true policy as well as of the dignity of our government, to act with spirit and energy as well toward Great Britain as France. I would *mete* the same measure to both of them, though it should ever furnish the extraordinary spectacle of a nation at war with two nations at war with each other. One of them will quickly court us, and by this course of conduct our citizens will be enthusiastically united to the government. It will evince that we are neither *Greeks* nor *Trojans*. In very critical cases bold expedients are often necessary.[108]

Hamilton's commitment to the vision of empire was recognized by a man whose known hostility makes his judgment all the more worth considering—John Adams. "If there ever was an 'Hamiltonian Conspiracy,' " he wrote to a correspondent who had queried him about Federalist projects of secession, "I have reason to think that its object was not 'a Northern Confederation.' Hamilton's Ambition was too large for so small an Aim. He aimed at commanding the whole Union, and He did not like to be shackled even with an Alliance with G. Britain. . . . No! H had had wider views! If he could have made a tool of Adams as he did of Washington, he hoped to erect such a Government as he pleased over the whole Union, and enter into Allyance with France or England as would suit his Convenience."[109]

The Pursuit of Greatness

The context has now been established in which Hamilton's quest for fame and glory should be viewed. This quest reached beyond the military domain into the field of political achievement. Little attuned to the tradition in which Hamilton saw himself, some students of Hamilton have granted his thirst for military glory—admittedly very great—while limiting his political strivings to a will to power.[110] For Hamilton, of course, the psychology of military leadership applied itself to political situations as well, and in particular, to that situation of extreme crisis, the founding of a nation. The character of political leadership required for the founding of institutions, as Bertrand de Jouvenel has observed in his typology of political authority, comes close to the demands of military authority, and a celebrated notation of Hamilton's gains significance in this context.[111] It is a quotation from Demosthenes' *First Philippic*: "As a general marches at the head of his troops, so ought wise politicians, if I dare to use the expression, to march at the head of affairs; insomuch that they ought not to wait the *event*, to know what measures to take; but the measures which they have taken, ought to produce the *event*."[112]

It may be worth reminding ourselves that Hamilton's greatest antagonist, Thomas Jefferson, turned to the Hamiltonian concept of statesmanship on the occasion of the Louisiana Purchase. The initiative and leadership then displayed by the chief "executive" (strictly speaking, the functions of initiating and executing policy are different) was not provided for in the Constitution as Jefferson interpreted it. But on this occasion, Jefferson endorsed the notion of responsibility above and beyond the written law; he endorsed the "duty in officers of high trust, to assume authorities beyond the law." It was a duty "incumbent on those only who accept great charges, to risk themselves on great occasions, when the safety of the nation, or some of its very highest interests are at stake." It was difficult to draw the line where to act on one's own responsibility, "but the good officer," Jefferson concluded, "is bound to draw it at his own peril, and throw himself on the justice of his country and the rectitude of his motives."[113] There was then, in Jefferson's statesmanship rather than in the principles associated with his name, an awareness of "great charges" and of "great occasions" that was similar to Hamilton's pursuit of greatness. It testifies to Hamilton's gift of judging character that he detected in Jefferson two ingredients of statesmanship that formed, in spite of many and profound differences, a common bond between the two men: Jefferson, like Hamilton, was not "capable of being corrupted";[114] Jefferson, like Hamilton, was willing to allow "scope for the executive," willing to initiate rather than merely "execute" policy.

Hamilton's perspicacious friend Gouverneur Morris observed several years after Hamilton's death: "General Hamilton was of that kind of men, who may most safely be trusted, for he was more covetous of glory than of wealth or power."[115] Present-day political thought, exclusively attuned to the dimensions of wealth and power, is ill-equipped to grasp the relevance of this judgment. I believe it is a relevant judgment; though I would add that it seems more appropriate for the founder of a nation and the maker of its laws, both of which Hamilton was in a very real sense, than for the practitioner of "normal" politics *or* the servant of the Constitution, both of which he was not. Indeed, the measure of Hamilton's success, as well as of his failures, may perhaps be taken from the way in which he understood himself, as "a founder of an empire," as one impelled by "the love of fame, the ruling passion of the noblest minds."

Hamilton's enduring achievement is to be found in his fight to establish the bases of a new nation, a new empire. This fight he carried to success in three stages (if we set apart Hamilton's enthusiastic military engagement in the War of Independence): first, in his struggle against the defects of the Confederation in the years culminating in the Philadelphia Convention of 1787; second, in his monumental effort to win acceptance of a Constitution that he considered a compromise between the demands of republican government and the requirements of strength and stability;[116] third, in the establishment of the new nation's system of public credit, with its vast impact on the course of social development as well as foreign affairs. Hamilton's failures are to be found on two levels. First, he failed as a practitioner of "day-to-day" politics, as a manager of "party politics," precisely because of his lonely and domineering eminence as a "founder"— with distaste as well as lack of talent for the daily compromises of "regular" politics, and particularly popular politics. Three diplomats of the French Directory discerned the cardinal point of Hamilton's character. Referring to his *"soif de la gloire"* they added: *"La passion de la celebrité dominant chez lui, il neglige de captiver des préjugés par des dehors, mais il aime à se soumettre des esprits par la superiorité des talens."*[117] Second, Hamilton failed as a servant of the Constitution (in ways that have scandalized many students of later days, who grew up *within* the framework of constitutional democracy), because the purpose of steering the new nation in the right direction prevailed, for a self-appointed founder of an empire, over strict adherence to constitutional rules. Two of his most controversial actions may be explained, perhaps, in this context: his unconstitutional and treasonable role in his dealings with Major Beckwith, recently put into the limelight by Julian Boyd's study of *Number 7*; and his efforts to disregard constitutional provisions in the State of New York in connection with the presidential elections of 1800, which foundered on the rock of John Jay's unwillingness to shove aside the constitution.[118] It has been shown how, on the latter occasion, Hamilton invoked the salvation of "the substantial interests of society" against "a strict adherence to ordinary rules." Attempting to explain these two initiatives by illuminating the way Hamilton understood himself does not mean denying the extreme gravity of the dilemmas they posed for a republican society that guarded itself by constitutional rules against the exercise of arbitrariness.

If "the ruling passion of the noblest minds" and the consciousness of being the founder of an empire indeed provide essential clues for interpreting Hamilton's thought, we may find additional help, perhaps surprisingly, by turning to Abraham Lincoln. Lincoln combined a deep commitment to the ideals of democracy—which sets him apart from Hamilton—with an introspective understanding of greatness and the thirst for fame that makes the two men again appear close to one another. In one of the most remarkable documents of American political thought, Lincoln's speech on "The Perpetuation of our Political Institutions," given early in 1838 to the Young Men's Lyceum in Springfield, Illinois, Lincoln discussed the fact that the time of founding the nation was irretrievably gone. At the time of establishing the government, Lincoln said, "all that sought celebrity and fame, and distinction," expected to find them in successfully demonstrating the *"capability of a people to govern themselves*. If they succeeded, they were to be immortalized; their names were to be transferred to counties and cities, and rivers and mountains; and to be revered and sung, and toasted through all time. If they failed, they were to be called knaves and fools, and fanatics for a fleeting hour; then to sink and be forgotten." They succeeded, Lincoln continued; but the game was caught, and with the catching, ended the pleasures of the chase. Nevertheless, though "this field of glory" was harvested, new reapers would arise, and it would be to deny "what the history of the world tells us is true, to suppose that men of ambition and talents will not continue to spring up amongst us." And these men would "as naturally seek the gratification of *their ruling passion*" [my italics] as others had done before them. Lincoln denied that that gratification could be found in supporting and maintaining an edifice that had been erected by others. Many "great and good men" might be found, whose ambition would aspire to nothing beyond a seat in Congress, a gubernatorial or a presidential chair; *but such belong not to the family of the lion, or the tribe of the eagle,* [.] What! think you these places would satisfy an Alexander, a Caesar, or a Napoleon? Never! Towering genius disdains a beaten path. It seeks regions hitherto unexplored. It sees *no distinction* in adding story to story, upon the monuments of fame, erected to the memory of others. It *denies* that it is glory enough to serve under any chief. It *scorns* to tread in the footsteps of *any* predecessor, however illustrious. It thirsts and burns for distinction; and, if possible, it will have it, whether at the expense of emancipating slaves, or enslaving freemen.[119]

Hamilton indeed belonged to the family of the lion, or the tribe of the eagle. There is no better way to understand Hamilton, his triumphs and his failures, than to ponder Lincoln's words.

LIST OF SHORT TITLES

This list contains full publication data for books and articles cited in short form in the Notes. Publication data for references cited in one chapter only are given in full in the Notes.

Adair, "Authorship"
> Douglass Adair. "The Authorship of the Disputed Federalist Papers, Part II," *William and Mary Quarterly*, 3rd series, I (July 1944), 235–64.

Adair, "Fame"
> Douglass Adair. "Fame and the Founding Fathers," in E. P. Willis, ed., Fame and the Founding Fathers. Papers and comments presented at the Nineteenth Conference on Early American History, March 25–26, Moravian College. Bethlehem, Pa., 1967, pp. 27–50.

[Adair], "Note"
> [Douglass Adair.] "A Note on Certain of Hamilton's Pseudonyms," *William and Mary Quarterly*, 3rd series, XII (Alexander Hamilton Bicentennial Number, April 1955), 282–97.

Adams, *Diary*
> The Diary and Autobiography of John Adams. Ed. L. H. Butterfield. 4 vols. Cambridge, Mass., 1962.

Adams, *Works*
> The Works of John Adams. Ed. Charles Francis Adams. 10 vols. Boston, 1850–56.

Adams, W. Paul
> W. Paul Adams. "Republikanismus und die ersten amerikanischen Einzelstaatsverfassungen: Zur ideengeschichtlichen und verfassungsgeschichtlichen Komponente der amerikanischen Revolution, 1775–1780." Ph.D. dissertation, Free University of Berlin, 1968.

Bacon
> Francis Bacon. Essays. Ed. Richard Whateley. London, 1886.

Bailyn, "Origins"
> Bernard Bailyn. "The Origins of American Politics," in *Perspectives in*

American History, I (1967), 7–120. Republished as a book, New York, 1968.

Becker
Carl Becker. The Declaration of Independence. 2d ed., New York, 1942.

Binkley
Wilfred E. Binkley. American Political Parties. Their Natural History. New York, 1943.

Blackstone
William Blackstone. Commentaries on the Laws of England. 8th ed., 4 vols. Oxford, 1778.

Brown
Robert E. Brown. Charles Beard and the Constitution. Princeton, 1956.

Burgh
James Burgh. Political Disquisitions. 3 vols. London, 1774–75.

Clark
Harry H. Clark, ed. Thomas Paine. Representative Selections. New York, 1944.

Corwin, *Higher Law*
Edward S. Corwin. The "Higher Law" Background of American Constitutional Law. Ithaca, 1955. First published in the *Harvard Law Review*, Vol. XLII (1928–29).

Cox
Richard H. Cox. Locke on War and Peace. Oxford, 1960.

Cropsey, *Polity and Economy*
Joseph Cropsey. Polity and Economy. The Hague, 1957.

Dunbar
Louise B. Dunbar. "A Study of 'Monarchical' Tendencies in the United States from 1776 to 1801," *University of Illinois Studies in the Social Sciences*, X, No. 1 (March 1922).

Elliot
Jonathan Elliot, ed. The Debates in the Several State Conventions on the Adoption of the Federal Constitution. Washington, D.C., 1836.

Farrand
Max Farrand. The Records of the Federal Convention of 1787. 4 vols. Rev. ed., New Haven, 1937.

Federalist
The Federalist. Ed. Jacob E. Cooke. Middletown, Conn., 1961. Also published as a Meridian Paperback, 1961.

Ford, *Essays*
P. L. Ford, ed. Essays on the Constitution of the United States. Brooklyn, New York, 1892.

Ford, *Pamphlets*
> P. L. Ford, ed. Pamphlets on the Constitution of the United States. Brooklyn, New York, 1888.

Gilbert
> Felix Gilbert. To the Farewell Address: Ideas of Early American Foreign Policy. Princeton, 1961.

Gordon and Trenchard
> Thomas Gordon and John Trenchard. Cato's Letters. 3d ed. 4 vols. London, 1733.

Haraszti
> Zoltan Haraszti. John Adams and the Prophets of Progress. Cambridge, Mass., 1952.

Harrington
> James Harrington. Oceana. Ed. S. B. Liljegren. Heidelberg, 1924.

Hartz
> Louis Hartz. The Liberal Tradition in America. New York, 1955.

Hendel
> Charles W. Hendel, ed. David Hume's Political Essays. New York, 1953.

Hobbes
> Thomas Hobbes. Leviathan. Blackwell edition. Oxford, n.d.

Hume
> David Hume. Philosophical Works. 4 vols. Edinburgh, 1826.

Jouvenel, "Essai"
> Bertrand de Jouvenel. "Essai sur la politique de Rousseau," in Jouvenel, ed., Du Contrat social de Jean-Jacques Rousseau. Geneva, 1947.

Kenyon, "Hamilton"
> Cecelia M. Kenyon. "Alexander Hamilton: Rousseau of the Right," *Political Science Quarterly*, LXXIII (June 1958), 161–78.

Koch, *Power*
> Adrienne Koch. Power, Morals, and the Founding Fathers: Essays in the Interpretation of the American Enlightenment. Ithaca, 1961.

Koch and Peden
> A. Koch and W. Peden, eds. The Life and Selected Writings of Thomas Jefferson. Modern Library. New York, 1944.

Locke
> John Locke. Second Treatise of Government. Everyman's Library. New York, 1924.

Machiavelli
> Niccolò Machiavelli. The Prince and The Discourses. Ed. Max Lerner. Modern Library. New York, 1940.

Madison, *Writings*
   The Writings of James Madison. Ed. Gaillard Hunt. 9 vols. New York, 1900–1910.
Mansfield
   Harvey C. Mansfield, Jr. Statesmanship and Party Government—A Study of Burke and Bolingbroke. Chicago, 1965.
Marshall
   Geoffrey Marshall. "David Hume and Political Scepticism," *Philosophical Quarterly* (St. Andrews, Scotland), IV (July 1954), 247–57.
Mason
   A. T. Mason. "The Federalist—A Split Personality," *American Historical Review*, LVII (April 1952), 625–43.
Miller
   John C. Miller. Alexander Hamilton, Portrait in Paradox. New York, 1959.
Mitchell, I, II
   Broadus Mitchell. Alexander Hamilton. Vol. I, Youth to Maturity, 1755–1788. New York, 1957. Vol. II, The National Adventure, 1788–1804. New York, 1962.
Montesquieu, *Spirit*
   The Spirit of the Laws by the Baron de Montesquieu. Ed. Franz Neumann. New York, 1949.
Paltsits
   Victor H. Paltsits. Washington's Farewell Address. New York, 1935.
Papers
   The Papers of Alexander Hamilton. Harold C. Syrett, Editor, and Jacob E. Cooke, Associate Editor. New York, 1961– (15 vols. published through 1969).
Parsons
   Memoir of Theophilus Parsons . . . by his son, Theophilus Parsons. Boston, 1859.
Rossiter, *Hamilton*
   Clinton L. Rossiter. Alexander Hamilton and the Constitution. New York, 1964.
Rossiter, *Seedtime*
   Clinton L. Rossiter. Seedtime of the Republic. New York, 1953.
Rousseau, *Contrat social*
   Jean-Jacques Rousseau. Contrat social. Edition classiques Garnier. Paris, n.d.
Rush
   Benjamin Rush. Observations on the Government of Pennsylvania (1777), in The Selected Writings of Benjamin Rush. Ed. Dagobert Runes. New York, 1947.

Schachner
  Nathan Schachner. Alexander Hamilton. New York, 1946.
Sidney
  The Works of Algernon Sydney. London, 1772.
Smith
  Adam Smith. An Inquiry into . . . the Wealth of Nations. Modern Library. New York, 1937.
Spurlin
  Paul Spurlin. Montesquieu in America 1760–1801. Baton Rouge, 1940.
Stourzh, *Franklin*
  Gerald Stourzh. Benjamin Franklin and American Foreign Policy. Chicago, 1954. 2d ed., 1969.
Strauss, *Natural Right*
  Leo Strauss. Natural Right and History. Chicago, 1953.
Warren-Adams Letters
  Letters of John Adams and Mercy Warren. Collections of the Massachusetts Historical Society, vols. 72 and 73. Boston, 1917 and 1923.
Washington
  The Writings of George Washington. Ed. John C. Fitzpatrick. 39 vols. Bicentennial Edition. Washington, D.C., 1931–44.
Weinberg
  Albert K. Weinberg. Manifest Destiny. Baltimore, 1935.
White, "Bacon's Imperialism"
  Howard B. White. "Bacon's Imperialism," *American Political Science Review*, LII (1958), 470–89.
Wolfers and Martin
  Arnold Wolfers and Laurence W. Martin. The Anglo-American Tradition in Foreign Affairs. New Haven, 1956.
Wood
  Gordon S. Wood. The Creation of the American Republic, 1776–1787. Chapel Hill, 1969.
Works
  The Works of Alexander Hamilton. Ed. Henry Cabot Lodge. 12 vols. Federal Edition, New York, 1904.

NOTES

INTRODUCTION

1. Hamilton appears as a participant in such a dialogue in the most recent monograph dealing with his political and constitutional ideas, Rossiter, *Hamilton.*

2. J. M. Smith in a book review in the *William and Mary Quarterly,* 3rd series, XXV (1968), 293. The manuscript of this book was completed before the publication of Gordon S. Wood's significant work on *The Creation of the American Republic 1776–1787* (Chapel Hill, 1969). Its findings would seem to corroborate rather than challenge the views presented in this study.

3. The distinction made here pursues avenues not quite dissimilar to those used by W. H. Greenleaf, *Order, Empiricism and Politics: Two Traditions of English Political Thought, 1500–1700* (New York, 1964), yet it is not identical with it. David Lowenthal has spoken of the "great empirical tradition within political philosophy," which "has its high points in Aristotle, Machiavelli, Montesquieu, and Tocqueville." Review essay of B. Moore, Jr., *Social Origins of Dictatorship and Democracy,* in *History and Theory,* VII (1968), 257–78, here 278, n. 15.

4. Hugo Grotius, *De Iure belli ac pacis libri tres,* in The Classics of International Law series published by the Carnegie Institution (Washington, D.C., 1913–25), II, 29 (Prolegomena, sect. 57).

5. Quoted from Locke's "Some Thoughts concerning Reading and Study for a Gentleman" by Cox, p. 192. Although Rousseau expressed it differently, he seems to have had something similar in mind when he criticized Montesquieu for having "refrained from discussing the principles of political right; he [Montesquieu] was satisfied with treating of the positive law of established governments; and nothing in the world is more different than these two studies." From Rousseau's *Emile,* bk. V, quoted by Mario Einaudi, *The Early Rousseau* (Ithaca, 1967), p. 36. Cf. Hobbes on his task in the *Leviathan*: the matters in question "are not of *fact,* but of *right,* wherein there is no place for *witnesses."* Hobbes, Conclusion, p. 466.

6. Rush, p. 78. Once this dichotomy is recognized, we understand why John Adams in his dispute with John Taylor of Caroline proudly justifies his theory of balanced government by saying: "I had fortified myself behind the intrenchments of Aristotle, Livy, Sidney, Harrington, Dr. Price, Machiavel, Montesquieu, Swift, &c. You should have battered down these strong out-works before you could demolish me." Adams, *Works*, VI, 492.

7. *Papers*, V, 81. See *Federalist*, No. 1, p. 5; No. 8, p. 45; No. 13, p. 81; No. 26, p. 164; No. 37, pp. 233–34; No. 49, pp. 338–39; No. 63, p. 426.

8. Wolfers and Martin; Kenneth Waltz, *Man, the State and War* (New York, 1959); Howard B. White, "Note sur les rapports entre la civilisation et la politique étrangère," *Diogène*, XXVII (1959), 3–28; White, "Bacon's Imperialism"; and Cox. Gordon Wood's book concentrates in traditional fashion on the domestic aspects of the Founders' political ideas.

9. Mansfield, p. 60.

10. Sir Henry Maine, *Ancient Law* (New York, 1888), p. 226. Originally published in 1861.

CHAPTER I

1. Blackstone, I, 212. See also Daniel J. Boorstin, *The Mysterious Science of the Law. An Essay on Blackstone's Commentaries* (Cambridge, Mass., 1941), p. 26.

2. The possible significance of Priestley's *Essay* for Thomas Paine's *Common Sense* has been pointed out by Gilbert, p. 41.

3. Blackstone, I, 250–51.

4. *Farmer Refuted, Papers*, I, 136. Cf. I, 83.

5. See below, pp. 34ff.

6. Blackstone, I, 192. My italics.

7. *Farmer Refuted, Papers*, I, 122.

8. Quoted by Corwin, *Higher Law*, p. 46. The case was *Calvin's Case*; Hamilton's reference to it is in *Papers*, I, 91.

9. See, for example, Daniel J. Boorstin, *The Genius of American Politics* (Chicago, 1953), pp. 76ff. For an earlier illustration of this view, see Gilbert Chinard's edition of *The Commonplace Book of Thomas Jefferson* (Baltimore, 1929), p. 54.

10. Adams, *Diary*, III, 309. There is no evidence to discount Adams's report. See also his notes of the discussions leading to the Declaration, *ibid.*, II, 128–30. Adams and other supporters of the natural rights argument won this point, which was embodied in the preamble of the Declaration of Rights.

11. Blackstone, I, 245. My italics in the last two lines.

12. Rossiter, *Seedtime*, p. 393, quoting from the *South-Carolina-Gazette*, October 18, 1769; Rossiter attributes this article "probably" to Christopher Gadsden (*ibid.*, p. 532, n. 167); however, in 1771 the author was identified as John McKenzie by his opponent, William Drayton, in Drayton's collection

of polemic articles from the *Gazette, The Letters of Freeman* (London, 1771), Preface. For Van Tyne's comment see *The Causes of the War of Independence* (Boston, 1922), pp. 236–37. I am dealing with this in more detail in my paper "William Blackstone: Teacher of Revolution," in *Jahrbuch für Amerikastudien*, XV (1970).

13. *Farmer Refuted, Papers*, I, 136.

14. Boorstin, *Genius*, pp. 77–78, 79.

15. *Farmer Refuted, Papers*, I, 121–22.

16. See the words of a Virginian whom Becker quotes (p. 133): "Shall we Proteus-like perpetually change our ground, assume every moment some new strange shape, to defend, to evade?"

17. Edmund S. Morgan, ed., *Prologue to Revolution. Sources and Documents on the Stamp Act Crisis* (Chapel Hill, 1959), p. 56.

18. See James Otis, *The Rights of the British Colonies Asserted and Proved* (1765). "The supreme power in a state, is *ius dicere* only:—*ius dare*, strictly speaking, belongs only to God." Quoted by Corwin, *Higher Law*, p. 6, n. 11. On this subject see the important and quite neglected study by Otto Vossler, "Studien zur Erklärung der Menschenrechte," *Historische Zeitschrift*, CXLII (1930), 516–45. This conception survived in America longer than in England, for reasons lucidly discussed by Vossler.

19. Corwin, *Higher Law*, p. 79. This view was stressed on the other side of the ocean by Lord Camden, one of England's most eminent jurists (*ibid.*, p. 84).

20. Blackstone, I, 41. Quoted by Hamilton, *Papers*, I, 87.

21. *Farmer Refuted, Papers*, I, 86–87.

22. *Ibid.*, pp. 97–98.

23. *Federalist*, p. 207. See also No. 15, p. 95.

24. Farrand, I, 472 (Yates's notes). See also *Federalist*, No. 22, p. 139.

25. *Federalist*, No. 28, p. 176. Cf. below, p. 62.

26. The merging of conceptions of common and natural law is best discussed by Roscoe Pound, *The Spirit of the Common Law* (Boston, 1921), pp. 85–111.

27. See the provisions on religious worship in several of the revolutionary state constitutions, in particular Art. III of the Massachusetts Declaration of Rights.

28. See Strauss, *Natural Right*, p. 227. The "paradoxical proximity" of the conclusions reached from different premises by C. B. Macpherson, *The Political Theory of Possessive Individualism* (Oxford, 1962) to those of Leo Strauss has been noted by Isaiah Berlin, "Hobbes, Locke, and Professor Macpherson," *The Political Quarterly*, XXXV (1964), 444–68.

29. See Strauss, *Natural Right*, pp. 221–22.

30. The distinction made by Locke in sect. 19 is made irrelevant or is contradicted in sects. 90, 232, and 242. See also Strauss, *Natural Right*, pp.

224–26. This interpretation would refute Corwin's interpretation of the difference between Hobbes and Locke concerning the state of nature. *Higher Law*, pp. 66–67.

31. "On the Origin of Justice and Property," in Hendel, p. 36.

32. *Boston Gazette*, Jan. 21, 1771, *The Writings of Samuel Adams*, ed. H. A. Cushing, 4 vols. (New York, 1904–8), II, 151.

33. James Bowdoin, in Elliot, II, 129.

34. *Federalist*, No. 43, p. 291. See also Blackstone, I, 244–45.

35. Blackstone, I, 193.

36. *Full Vindication, Papers*, I, 51.

37. *Farmer Refuted, Papers*, I, 155.

38. *Federalist*, No. 28, p. 178. Cf. also Madison in No. 41, pp. 70–71 and in No. 43, p. 297.

39. *Farmer Refuted, Papers*, I, 92f.

40. *Ibid.*, p. 96.

41. Blackstone, I, 162.

42. *Farmer Refuted, Papers*, I, 97.

43. There is only one direct, and insignificant, reference to Locke in Hamilton's writings. It is an invitation to the Westchester Farmer to peruse "Grotius, Puffendorf, Locke, Montesquieu, and Burlemaqui." *Farmer Refuted, Papers*, I, 86. I thus disagree with Miller, p. 15, that Hamilton made John Locke "his political Bible."

44. Blackstone, I, 250–51.

45. Locke, sect. 149, quoted by Blackstone, I, 161–62. It is worth noticing that Locke uses in this section the expression "supreme power" of the people four times. In the crucial section 240 on the question who shall judge whether the prince or the legislative body acts contrary to their trust, Locke speaks also of power rather than rights, and so does Blackstone, above, p. 12.

46. *Ibid.*, p. 162.

47. *Ibid.*, pp. 244–45. See also Blackstone's comments on the "principle of necessity" in 1660 and 1688, *ibid.*, p. 152.

48. *Farmer Refuted, Papers*, I, 136.

49. Sir Ernest Barker has written: "It would pass the wit of any philosopher to reconcile a supreme, irresistible, absolute, and uncontrolled sovereignty with a controlling system of natural law and an absolute system of natural rights." Barker, *Essays on Government*, 2d ed., (Oxford, 1951), p. 136. Yet lawyers like Blackstone apparently have a keener eye than students of political theory for the difference between legal remedies, which are non-existent with respect to controlling the holder of sovereignty, and moral remedies, which may take the form of illegal, but legitimate resistance. The most revealing passage for the reconciliation that Sir Ernest holds impossible, is in Hobbes, p. 225, second paragraph.

50. Blackstone described sovereign power as "supreme, irresistible, ab-

solute, uncontrolled." Arbitrary is omitted. Our positivist approach to the theory of sovereignty has made us blind to the eighteenth-century understanding of the difference between absolute sovereignty and arbitrary power, beautifully expressed by James Otis: "To say the parliament is absolute and arbitrary, is a contradiction. The parliament cannot make 2 and 2, 5; Omnipotency cannot do it." Quoted by Wright, *American Interpretations of Natural Law*, p. 68, n. 2. Also apt is a comment of Lord Fortescue, who edited his ancestor's *Governance of England*: when Coke said that an Act of Parliament against Magna Charta was void, he meant only the moral part of it, "for no Act of Parliament can alter the Nature of Things, make Vertue Vice or Vice Vertue." From *The Difference between an Absolute and Limited Monarchy; as it more particularly regards the English Constitution*; quoted by Charles F. Mullett, *Fundamental Law and the American Revolution 1760–1776* (New York, 1933), p. 63.

51. Charles H. McIlwain, *The American Revolution: A Constitutional Interpretation* (New York, 1923), p. 192.

52. Elisha P. Douglass, *Rebels and Democrats. The Struggle for Equal Political Rights and Majority Rule During the American Revolution.* (Chapel Hill, 1955), p. 7. Douglass refers to Carl Becker, but he overstates Becker's position. Becker stresses the "ostensible purpose" of the Declaration in laying "before the world" the causes of separation (Becker, p. 6). Yet Becker does not limit his explanation of the natural rights philosophy to foreign propaganda, though he perhaps overstresses the *ad hoc* character of the Americans' use of natural rights.

53. Locke, sect. 8; also sects. 7, 9, 13, 15.

54. *Papers*, I, 176–77.

55. See B. F. Wright, *American Interpretations of Natural Law* (Cambridge, Mass., 1931), pp. 68, 138, n. 3. For Winthrop, supposed author of the Agrippa letters, see Ford, *Essays*, "Agrippa," No. XVII, p. 111.

56. See John W. Gough, *The Social Contract* (Oxford, 1936), pp. 172–73.

57. Blackstone, I, 47–48.

58. "Of the Original Contract," in Hendel, p. 60.

59. *Farmer Refuted, Papers*, I, 126.

60. See Barker, *Essays on Government*, p. 90.

61. *Ibid.*, p. 100. This is not satisfactorily brought out in Thad Tate, "The Social Contract in America, 1774–1787—Revolutionary Theory as a Conservative Instrument," in *William and Mary Quarterly*, 3rd Series, XXII (1965), 376. Tate makes no mention of Blackstone at all. I must disagree with Wood, pp. 268–69, who seems to think that the image of the contract was borrowed from the mercantile world. *Staendische* traditions as well as the impact of Calvinistic federal theology would seem more important: See the significant studies by Erich Angermann, "Ständische Rechtstradition-

en in der amerikanischen Unabhängigkeitserklärung," *Historische Zeitschrift,* vol. 200 (1965), 61–91, and Gerhard Oestreich, "Die Idee des
religiösen Bundes und die Lehre vom Staatsvertrag," in W. Berges and C.
Hinrichs, eds., *Zur Geschichte und Problematik der Demokratie,* Festschrift
for Hans Herzfeld (Berlin, 1958), pp. 11–32.

62. See his remarks in the Federal Convention on June 29, 1787, as rendered by Rufus King: "Men are naturally equal—societies or Nations are
equal when independent—it is as reasonable that States shd. inter into a
League departing from the Equality of States, as that men shd. inter into
the Social Compact and agree to depart from the natural Equality of man."
Farrand, I, p. 477. See also the "Phocion" essays of 1784, *Papers,* III, 533f,
549, 550–51; IV, 126.

63. *Farmer Refuted, Papers,* I, 88.

64. Quoted by Hamilton, *ibid.,* p. 88. See Blackstone, I, 124. "Absolute"
was italicized both by Blackstone and Hamilton, "rights" only by Hamilton.
Hamilton's emphasis on man as a "free agent" (*Papers,* I, 92) is also taken
from Blackstone (I, 125). The pagination of the edition of Blackstone used
in this essay is identical with that used by Hamilton.

65. *Farmer Refuted, Papers,* I, 90.

66. *Ibid.,* p. 91.

67. See Randolph G. Adams, *Political Ideas of the American Revolution*
(Durham, N.C., 1922).

68. *Farmer Refuted, Papers,* I, 91–92.

69. *Ibid.,* p. 99.

70. Barker, *Essays on Government,* pp. 144–45.

71. Blackstone, I, 257. Cf. the American doctrine of the different composition of the "sovereign" concerning external sovereignty and domestic
sovereignty, in *United States* v. *Curtiss-Wright Export Corp.,* 299 U.S. 304
(1936).

72. Blackstone, I, 237; see also pp. 223, 245.

73. Farrand, I, 324. The most colorful image of national sovereignty in
1776 was given by Rufus King: "The States were not 'sovereigns' in the
sense contended for by some. They did not possess the peculiar features of sovereignty. They could not make war, nor peace, nor alliances, nor treaties.
Considering them as political Beings, they were dumb, for they could not
speak to any foreign Sovereign whatever. They were deaf, for they could not
hear any propositions from such Sovereign." *Ibid.,* p. 323. John Adams held
a contrary opinion. In his *Defence of the Constitutions of Government of
the United States of America,* he held that the Confederation Congress was
"not a legislative assembly, nor a representative assembly, but only a diplomatic assembly." Adams, *Works,* IV, 579. This elicited polite but emphatic
disagreement from Jefferson, who attributed both an executive and a legislative character to Congress—some "parts of the whole sovereignty of our

states" having been "yielded to congress." *Ibid.*, n. 1 (Letter to Adams, Feb. 23, 1787).

74. *Papers*, IV, 77.

75. The Hamiltonian doctrine of national sovereignty (as of 1776) was first judicially expressed by Justice Patterson in *Penhallow* v. *Doane*, 3 Dall. 54 (1795) at 80–81; the final doctrine in *United States* v. *Curtiss-Wright Export Corp.*, 299 U.S. 304 (1936) at 316–17. Corwin quotes Rufus King's words given above (n. 74) and remarks that "it is significant that nobody challenged this position"; he does not mention Hamilton. See E. S. Corwin, *The President. Office and Powers* (New York, 1940), p. 399, n. 9.

76. Examine, e.g., *Federalist*, No. 75, on the president's power in foreign affairs.

77. "Letters of H. G.," *Papers*, V, 294.

78. Marshall, p. 10.

79. *Works*, II, 379–80.

80. "Tully" Essays, *Works*, VI, 421.

81. A view presented, e.g. by T. E. Utley in "Principles and Empiricism," *Cambridge Journal*, VI (January 1953), 200. For a comparison in Hamilton's lifetime, see Allan M. Hamilton, *The Intimate Life of Alexander Hamilton* (London, 1910), p. 76. For a—very pertinent—contrast, see Robert R. Palmer, *The Age of Democratic Revolution*, vol. I, *The Challenge* (Princeton, 1959), p. 189.

82. *Federalist*, No. 16, pp. 104–5.

83. *Federalist*, No. 25, p. 163.

84. Cabinet Paper, May 28, 1790, *Papers*, VI, 436.

85. To Rufus King, July 25, 1792, *Works*, X, 3. For details of this affair, see *The Life and Correspondence of Rufus King*, ed. Charles King, 6 vols. (New York, 1894), I, 408ff.

86. Unpublished letter to the Collector of Charleston, Isaac Holmes, June 17, 1794. Oliver Wolcott Papers, Connecticut Historical Society, Hartford, Conn.

87. *Works*, VI, 162.

88. *Federalist*, No. 85, p. 594.

89. May 7, 1800, *Works*, X, 371–74.

90. Philip Schuyler to John Jay, May 7, 1800. Quoted from *The Correspondence and Public Papers of John Jay* (New York, 1893), IV, 273, by Dixon Ryan Fox, *The Decline of Aristocracy in the Politics of New York* (New York, 1918), p. 3. Fox misinterprets Hamilton's request by stating that he asked for a redistricting of the state.

91. Jay's comment is in *Works*, X, 374. Editor Lodge felt "the proposition in this letter was one entirely unworthy of Hamilton." *Ibid.* Also Schachner, p. 394, Mitchell, II, 467–68, and Rossiter, *Hamilton*, p. 192.

92. To John Colvin, Sept. 20, 1810. Koch and Peden, pp. 606–7.

93. To Col. Edward Carrington, Jan. 16, 1787, in *ibid.*, p. 411.

94. To James Madison, Jan. 30, 1787, in *ibid.*, p. 413. Also to Col. Smith, Nov. 13, 1787, *ibid.*, p. 436. On the French Revolution, to William Short, Jan. 3, 1793, in *ibid.*, pp. 521–22.

95. See those of Pennsylvania (1776), Art. XIV; North Carolina (1776), Art. XXI; Vermont (1777), Art. XVI; Massachusetts (1780), Art. XVIII; and New Hampshire (1784), Art. XXXVIII. There is no attempt at analysis in Robert Allen Rutland, *The Birth of the Bill of Rights* (Chapel Hill, 1955).

96. Paper read by George Mason at a meeting of the Fairfax (Va.) County Independent Company in June 1775, discussing frequent elections of its officers. Reproduced in Kate Mason Rowland, *The Life of George Mason*, 2 vols. (New York, 1892), I, 430. Neither Rowland nor Helen Hill, *George Mason, Constitutionalist* (Cambridge, Mass., 1938), say whom Mason referred to. The most nearly satisfactory description of the ancestry of Mason's ideas (as stated in the Declaration of Rights) is Hugh Blair Grigsby in *The Virginia Convention of 1776* (Richmond, Va., 1855), p. 164: "Some of its expressions may be gleaned from Sidney, from Locke, from Burgh."

97. Burgh, III, 298. Burgh cited "Daven. II. 72." Indeed, Burgh quoted exactly what Charles D'Avenant, better known to students of mercantilism than of political ideas, had to say on first principles in his discourse "On the Plantation Trade," in *The Political and Commercial Works of Charles D'Avenant*, collected and revised by Sir Charles Whitworth, 5 vols. (London, 1771), II, 72. On Burgh's work, see below, p. 67.

98. The third volume of Burgh's *Disquisitions* came out in London only in the summer of 1775 and was reprinted in Philadelphia in September, 1775; that means that Mason's reference to the "deepest politician" in June 1775 may reflect the reading of *Cato's Letters*, or perhaps of Sidney's *Discourses*. Search in Mason's papers in the Library of Congress, in the Pennsylvania Historical Society, and in the New York Public Library has produced no evidence on this question.

99. Gordon and Trenchard, I, 108–9 (No. 16). See also below, Ch. II, p. 66.

100. Sidney, Ch. II of *Discourses Concerning Government*, sect. 13, p. 124; sect. 24, p. 194; sect. 31, p. 265.

101. *Ibid.*, Ch. III, sect. 25, p. 406.

102. Blackstone, I, 192.

103. Cf. Herbert Butterfield, *The Statecraft of Machiavelli* (London, 1940), p. 147. Bolingbroke was another important English writer who admittedly received the idea of recurring to first principles from Machiavelli. *Ibid.*, p. 145. But he was far less outspoken than Sidney. Sidney's revolutionary candor and martyrdom for liberty both endeared him and made him more useful to Americans. On Sidney's influence in America, see Caroline

Robbins, "Algernon Sidney's Discourses Concerning Government: Textbook of Revolution," *William and Mary Quarterly*, 3rd series, IV (July 1947), 267–96. Montesquieu and Hume shared the opinion that British liberty would sometime perish and that England would end in an absolute monarchy. Montesquieu, *Spirit*, Bk. XI, ch. 6, pp. 161–62. Hume, "Whether the British Government Inclines More to Absolute Monarchy or to a Republic," in Hendel, p. 75. Blackstone only mentioned Montesquieu's opinion, evidently considering it too hasty a prediction. Blackstone, I, 16.

104. Machiavelli, pp. 397–98.

105. *Ibid.*, p. 399.

106. Sidney, Ch. II, sect. 28, p. 233; also Ch. III, sect. 27, p. 419.

107. "Sentiments of the Town of Roxbury on the Constitution of Civil Government proposed by Conventions," May 1780, in Oscar and Mary Handlin, eds., *The Popular Sources of Political Authority, Documents on the Massachusetts Constitution of 1780* (Cambridge, Mass., 1966), p. 793. I owe this reference to the doctoral dissertation of my student W. Paul Adams (p. 539).

CHAPTER II

1. Art. IV, Sect. 4. The implications of the guarantee of a republican government (and therefore of the prohibition of monarchy) for the theory that "freedom for the thought that we hate" (Justice Holmes in *United States* v. *Schwimmer*) is a principle of the Constitution, have been thoughtfully examined by F. B. Wiener, " 'Freedom for the Thought That We Hate': Is It a Principle of the Constitution?," *American Bar Association Journal*, XXXVII (March 1951), 177–80, 241–45. For a more recent and thorough discussion of this so largely neglected clause, see Arther E. Bonfield, "The Guarantee Clause of Article IV, Section 4: A Study in Constitutional Desuetude," *Minnesota Law Review*, XLVI (1961–62), 513–72.

2. Farrand, II, 101.

3. *Ibid.*, I, 83.

4. Adams, *Works*, IV, 359. See also E. Handler, *America and Europe in the Political Thought of John Adams* (Cambridge, Mass., 1964), pp. 49–50.

5. He was speaking specifically of Virginia. Madison, *Writings*, IX, 358–60. (Note on Suffrage, written during the Virginia Convention of 1829–30.) For this and some of the other references on this subject I am indebted to the essay by Douglass Adair, " 'Experience Must Be Our Only Guide': History, Democratic Theory, and the United States Constitution," in R. A. Billington, ed., *The Reinterpretation of Early American History. Essays in Honor of J. E. Pomfret* (San Marino, Calif., 1966), pp. 129–48, esp. pp. 139–40.

6. Washington, XXIX, 190 (to James Madison, March 31, 1787). My italics.

7. Farrand, I, 310; see also pp. 288f, 299, 303.

8. *Works*, X, 425–26 (Feb. 27, 1802). For a more moderate statement see the letter to E. Carrington of 1792, *ibid.*, IX, 534.

9. *Ibid.*, X, p. 458. (To Theodore Sedgwick, July 10, 1804).

10. "Of the Origin of Government," in Hendel, p. 42.

11. *Farmer Refuted, Papers*, I, 164.

12. *Full Vindication, ibid.*, 48.

13. *Farmer Refuted, ibid.*, p. 99.

14. *Full Vindication, ibid.*, p. 47.

15. *Farmer Refuted, ibid.*, p. 100.

16. *Ibid.* Hamilton did not give the title of Hume's essay, "That Politics May Be Reduced to a Science." See Hendel, pp. 15–16.

17. *Full Vindication, Papers*, I, 53. Cf. Hendel, p. 16.

18. "The hardest of all servitudes is to be subject to a republic." *Discourses*, bk. II, ch. ii, p. 287. In the same essay Hume explicitly mentioned Machiavelli. See Hendel, p. 17. See also Montesquieu, *Spirit*, bk. X, ch. vii, p. 139.

19. See Stourzh, *Franklin*, p. 28.

20. Clark, pp. 17–18. Sir William Meredith (d. 1790) wrote political pamphlets in the early 1770's, including a letter to William Blackstone on the Wilkes case, and to Chatham on the Quebec Bill.

21. To Mercy Warren, Jan. 8, 1776. *The Warren-Adams Letters*, I, 201. Cf. Stourzh, "Die tugendhafte Republik—Montesquieus Begriff der 'vertu' und die Anfaenge der Vereinigten Staaten von Amerika," in H. Fichtenau and H. Peichl, eds., *Oesterreich und Europa. Festgabe fuer Hugo Hantsch* (Graz-Vienna-Cologne, 1965), pp. 247–67. For a collection of newspaper references to an anticipated republican form of government in late 1775 and early 1776, see George M. Dutcher, "The Rise of Republican Government in the United States," *Political Science Quarterly*, LV (June 1940), 206. The beginnings of republican government in the United States have now been carefully analyzed by W. Paul Adams. For John Adams's "divine science," see Adams's *Works*, IX, 339.

22. Adams, *Works*, X, 378. Cf. the illuminating discussion in the unjustly neglected book by Correa M. Walsh, *The Political Science of John Adams* (New York, 1915), p. 27.

23. Notes for his speech of July 12, 1788, at the New York Ratifying Convention, *Papers*, V, 149.

24. *Ibid.*, pp. 149–50.

25. See the careful disclaimers of an English republican at heart, James Burgh, I, 9; II, 18.

26. [James Winthrop], "Letters of Agrippa," in Ford, *Essays*, p. 106. Similarly, the conservative Theophilus Parsons pointed out in 1778 that "all republics are not FREE." The "Essex Result," one of the most succinct state-

ments of a conservative ideal of a free republic, is reprinted in Parsons, p. 365. The most thorough recent discussion of the "Essex Result" is in J. R. Pole, *Political Representation in England and the Origins of the American Republic* (London, 1966), pp. 182ff.

27. Madison's notes on Hamilton's speech in the Federal Convention, June 18, 1787, in Farrand, I, 288.

28. Adams, *Works*, X, 378. Cf. the first three chapters of Adams's *Defence* dealing with democratic, aristocratic, and monarchical republics! *Works*, IV, 303–78.

29. *Federalist*, No. 39, p. 251.

30. On the Americans' acquaintance with Montesquieu, see Spurlin.

31. Johnson's ambiguous definitions were not changed in subsequent editions. The prevailing confusion is best illustrated by the political literature on Venice, a state in which power was lodged in more than one person, but by no means in the people. Venice is sometimes described as a "free state" and a republic, sometimes as an aristocracy or an oligarchy. See the contradictory references in Burgh, I, 71; III, 288–89, 399, 410.

32. This has been conclusively shown by W. Paul Adams.

33. See the important article by J. R. Pole, "Historians and the Problem of Early American Democracy," *American Historical Review*, LXVII (1961–62), 626–46.

34. Edited by S. E. Morison, the spelling left as written in 1798, reprinted in *William and Mary Quarterly*, 3rd series, XIII (April 1956), 215.

35. *Papers*, V, 150. The numbers enumerating the different parts of the argument in his speech have been omitted.

36. To Gouverneur Morris, May 19, 1777, *Papers*, I, 255. The term "representative democracy" was used by Philip Mazzei in an article for John Pinckney's Williamsburg *Virginia Gazette*, supposedly published in the winter of 1774–75, though the original seems to be not extant. See "Philip Mazzei on American Political, Social, and Economic Problems," ed. and tr. by Howard R. Marraro, *Journal of Southern History*, XV (1949), 357. I owe this reference to my student Mrs. Angela Adams. Wood, p. 595, mentions Hamilton's use of the term in 1787, but seems unaware of these earlier occurrences.

37. See above, p. 16. Also *Papers*, II, 654; and see Blackstone, I, 49.

38. See Daniel Defoe, *The Original Power of the Collective Body of the People of England, Examined and Asserted* (London, 1702). On the radical implications of his ideas and the use of this work by early English Radicals in the 1760's, see Paul Ritterbusch, *Parlamentssouveränität und Volkssouveränität in der Staats- und Verfassungsrechtslehre Englands, vornehmlich in der Staatslehre Daniel Defoes* (Leipzig, 1929), pp. 108–9. Bolingbroke, *A Dissertation upon Parties*, 7th ed. (London, 1739), pp. 202, 211, 269ff.

39. Adams, *Works*, III, 480.

40. *Papers*, I, 255. Paine's definition is in Part II, ch. iii, of *The Rights of Man* (in Clark, p. 193). What has been said in the text regarding Hamilton's early use of the concept and its background adds to and perhaps modifies Robert R. Palmer's findings in his well-known "Notes on the Use of the Word 'Democracy' 1789–1799," *Political Science Quarterly*, Vol. LXVIII (1953), esp. pp. 223–24. See also Martin Diamond, "The Federalist," in Leo Strauss and Joseph Cropsey, eds., *History of Political Philosophy* (Chicago, 1963), p. 580.

41. Farrand, I, 290. Madison's notes. See also *Papers*, IV, 73.

42. Farrand, III, 397–98. Farrand also gives Pickering's query and other documents in connection with the accusations of monarchism leveled at Hamilton. *Ibid.*, 354, 368, 369, 395, 399, 410, 432, 466, 480. See also Dunbar, ch. V.

43. Farrand, III, 398.

44. Hamilton's error and Madison's comments on it are discussed by Mitchell, I, p. 625, n. 40. Yet incongruously, the author elsewhere takes Hamilton's claim of a change of mind at the end of the Convention at face value, though the admittedly erroneous explanation in Hamilton's letter to Pickering is his only source. *Ibid.*, p. 398. Hamilton's draft in *Papers*, IV, 262.

45. See Hamilton's outline in Farrand, I, 304, 309–10.

46. *Ibid.*, p. 290. Blackstone (I, 192) called an elective monarchy the most desirable form of government, if men remained true to first principles.

47. In No. 60 Hamilton deals with the "different ranks and conditions in society." *Federalist*, p. 405.

48. Edwin Mims, Jr., in his remarkable and unfortunately neglected study *The Majority of the People* (New York, 1941), p. 96.

49. *Federalist*, No. 22, p. 139. And p. 146. See also No. 9, where Hamilton equates "republican government" with "popular systems of civil government." *Ibid.*, pp. 51–52. In *Federalist*, No. 31, p. 198, Hamilton wrote: "In republics strength is always on the side of the people." It is interesting to note that Hume, to whom Hamilton was so indebted, spoke of "pure republics" in the sense of democracy in his essay "On the First Principles of Government," Hendel, p. 27.

50. *Federalist*, No. 84, pp. 578–79.

51. See Hamilton's striking affirmation of the sovereign prerogative of the Executive on strictly Blackstonian lines. In fact, Hamilton explicitly refers to Blackstone's chapter on the Royal Prerogative! *Federalist*, No. 69, pp. 467–68.

52. *Federalist*, No. 36, p. 224. True to his teacher, he equated the delegation of sovereignty with its alienation. *Ibid.*, No. 32, p. 200.

53. *Ibid.*, No. 75, pp. 504–5.

54. *Papers*, IV, 131.

55. C. H. McIlwain, *Constitutionalism and the Changing World* (New York, 1939), pp. 64–65. I must take issue with Professor McIlwain when he

charges this confusion about popular sovereignty to Hobbes and Blackstone as well as to Austin. Blackstone, I hope to have shown, was infinitely more rigorous and careful a thinker than he has been given credit for.

56. The complexity of the problem is illustrated by the logical pitfall in Carl J. Friedrich's approach. He regards the "constituent power" of the people as a power beyond and outside the constitutionally provided amending process: "It is the power to make a revolution. We say 'power' deliberately, rather than 'right.' For it is a purely factual, norm-creating thing, this power to establish a constitution or a pattern of government." Yet when Professor Friedrich continues to argue that his formulation has an advantage over the Lockeanism of the American Revolution, whose doctrine "failed to make it explicit that the constituent group as defined can come into play *only* against arbitrary power, but not against a functioning constitutionalism," he is open to two criticisms, one logical, the other historical. First, if the constituent power must be applied only against arbitrary government, there is an element of moral judgment involved which denies the assertion that the power of the people is a "purely factual, norm-creating thing." It may be *creating legal* norms, but it presupposes norms of legitimacy. Second, the natural rights theories of the American Revolution did apply only as a remedy for arbitrary, i.e., abusive employment of sovereign power. See Friedrich *The New Image of the Common Man* (Boston, 1950), pp. 130f.

57. *Federalist*, No. 10, pp. 61f; similarly No. 14, pp. 83–84, and No. 39, p. 251. Cf. examples of Hamilton's bias toward identifying republic with democracy in No. 31, pp. 197–98, No. 78, p. 527. The vocabulary Hamilton used in the Federal Convention is revealing; see Ferrand, I, 290, 300, 304. Also in the New York Ratifying Convention: "In free republics . . . the will of the people makes the essential principle of government; and the laws which control the community receive their tone and spirit from the public wishes." *Papers*, V, 37; see also p. 43.

58. Adams, *Works*, X, 378. Consistent with this is Adams's treatment of forms of government in his *Defence*. The novel and somewhat tenuous character of Madison's distinction is apparent in No. 63 of *The Federalist*, which was most likely written by Madison. (See Adair, "Authorship," p. 261; F. Mosteller and J. L. Wallace, *Inference and Disputed Authorship: The Federalist* [Reading, Mass., 1964], p. 263.) There Madison fell back upon the watered-down assertion that "the difference most relied on, between the American and other republics, consists in the principle of representation." (p. 427.) Jefferson's identification of republic with democracy is eloquent; it is worthwhile to add his most exact definition of a republic: "Indeed, it must be acknowledged, that the term *republic* is of very vague application in every language. Witness the self-styled republics of Holland, Switzerland, Genoa, Venice, Poland. Were I to assign to this term a precise and definite idea, I would say, purely and simply, it means a government by its citizens in mass, acting directly and personally, according to rules established by the

majority; and that every other government is more or less republican, in proportion as it has in its composition more or less of this ingredient of the direct action of the citizens. Such a government is evidently restrained to very narrow limits of space and population. . . . The further the departure from direct and constant control by the citizens, the less has the government of the ingredient of republicanism." Letter to John Taylor of Caroline County, Va., May 28, 1816, in Koch and Peden, pp. 669–70. John Marshall defined the proposed Federal Constitution as a "well-regulated democracy." See his forceful speech in defense of the Constitution in the Virginia Ratifying Convention, in Elliot, III, 222, 224.

59. See Sidney, Ch. III, sect. xxvii, p. 419; Montesquieu, *Spirit*, bk. XI. On the meaning of "Gothic" government, see Francis D. Wormuth's excellent study, *The Origins of Modern Constitutionalism* (New York, 1949).

60. See Hamilton's use of "free" government in *Federalist*, No. 24, p. 152; No. 25, p. 161; No. 29, p. 182.

61. See, for example, Madison in *Federalist*, No. 49, p. 340.

62. Benjamin Hichborn, "Oration Delivered at Boston, March 5, 1777," in H. Niles, ed., *Principles and Acts of the Revolution in America* (1822), p. 47. For the reasons of the rise of the claim for "democracy" and examples during the American Revolution see Merrill Jensen, "Democracy and the American Revolution," *Huntington Library Quarterly*, XX (August 1957), 321–41.

63. Quoted by Lord Acton in his "Political Causes of the American Revolution," in Douglas Woodruff, ed., *Essays on Church and State by Lord Acton* (New York, 1953), pp. 302–3.

64. Adams, *Defence*, in *Works*, V, 453.

65. For its ancestry, see Friedrich A. Hayek, *The Constitution of Liberty* (Chicago, 1960), pp. 162ff. See also Corwin, *Higher Law*, p. 8.

66. Adams, *Novanglus*, in *Works*, IV, 106; also pp. 194, 204. It has been mistakenly asserted that Adams "doubtlessly derived the expression from Bracton's *Non per hominem sed per legem et Deum.*" Samuel Eliot Morison, *Freedom in Contemporary Society* (Boston, 1956), p. 28, n. 19. Professor Morison shares the widely held misconception that John Adams wrote this phrase into Art. XXX of the Massachusetts constitution. Adams was not, however, responsible. See his *Works*, IV, 230, and Haraszti, p. 28. The rule of law was the essence of Rousseau's definition of "republic": "*Je n'entends pas seulement par ce mot une aristocratie ou une démocratie, mais en général tout gouvernement guidé par la volonté générale, qui est la loi. Pour être légitime, il ne faut pas que le gouvernement se confonde avec le souverain, mai qui'il en soit le ministre: alors la monarchie elle-meme est république.*" *Contrat social*, bk. II, ch. vi, n. 1.

See also the equation of republican government with a "government of laws, not of men" by E. Pendleton of Virginia in Elliot, III, 39. See also

Noah Webster, "An Examination into the Leading Principles of the Federal Constitution," in Ford, *Pamphlets*, p. 37, and R. H. Lee, "Letters of a Federal Farmer," *ibid.*, p. 324.

67. To James Duane, Sept. 3, 1780. *Papers*, II, 413.

68. For the significance of "Phocion" as Hamilton's choice for a pseudonym, see the very important article by [Adair], "Note," p. 285.

69. *Papers*, III, 484. The legal issues involved in the discrimination against Loyalists in the state of New York, and Hamilton's role, culminating in his defense of Tory interests in the case of *Rutgers* v. *Waddington*, have been authoritatively and exhaustively dealt with in Julius Goebel, Jr., *The Law Practice of Alexander Hamilton, Documents and Commentary*, I (New York, 1964), part III, "The War Cases," pp. 197ff.; see esp. pp. 219–23, 293–94.

70. "Would not a different doctrine," he said, "involve the contradiction of *imperium in imperio?*" *Papers*, III, 489. This is the origin of a passage in No. 15 of *The Federalist* to the effect that the enemies of the Constitution aimed at "sovereignty in the Union, and complete independence in the members. They still, in fine, seem to cherish with blind devotion the political monster of an *imperium in imperio.*" *Federalist*, p. 93.

71. *Papers*, III, 549. My italics.

72. *Ibid.*, p. 540.

73. *Ibid.*, p. 549.

74. *Ibid.*, p. 550.

75. *Ibid.*, p. 551.

76. *Federalist*, p. 483.

77. *Ibid.*, No. 78, p. 528.

78. *Ibid.*, p. 525.

79. *Ibid.*, p. 527.

80. Sir Ernest Barker, *Traditions of Civility* (Cambridge, 1948), p. 341.

81. *Federalist*, p. 524.

82. *Ibid.*

83. *Ibid.*, No. 75, p. 504. Cf. also the formulation in *The Continentalist* of 1782, concerning tax laws: "The genius of liberty reprobates everything arbitrary or discretionary in taxation. It exacts that every man by a definite and general rule should know what proportion of his property the state demands." *Papers*, III, 104. See also Madison, *Federalist*, No. 57, pp. 386–87.

84. "Tully" Essays, *Works*, VI, 418f. For the significance of the pseudonym, see [Adair], "Note," pp. 284–85.

85. John Adams: "The great question therefore is, What combination of powers in society, or what form of government, will compel the formation, impartial execution, and faithful interpretation of good and equal laws . . . ?" *Works*, IV, 406.

86. *Federalist*, No. 28, p. 176.

87. *Ibid.*, No. 6, p. 32.

88. *Papers*, V, 20.

89. *Warren-Adams Letters*, I, 202.

90. Farrand, II, 123.

91. Zera Fink's excellent book *The Classical Republicans* (Evanston, Ill., 1945) rightly stresses Sidney's indebtedness to Machiavelli in many things, yet is mistaken in implying that Machiavelli's and Sidney's notions of virtue are identical (p. 154, n. 28). Sidney's notion of virtue is Aristotelian, whereas Machiavelli's is not (see Sidney, Chap. II, sect. 27, p. 229). Since Fink's pathbreaking book, a number of more recent studies have traced the development of early modern republican thought in England: Caroline Robbins, *The Eighteenth Century Commonwealthman*, (Cambridge, Mass., 1959), Felix Raab, *The English Face of Machiavelli* (London, 1964), and J. G. A. Pocock, "Machiavelli, Harrington, and English Political Ideologies in the Eighteenth Century," *William and Mary Quarterly*, 3rd series, XXII (October, 1965), 547–83.

92. Machiavelli, *Discourses*, bk. I, ch. xxxvii, pp. 208–9; see also bk. I, ch. vi, p. 126; ch. xvii, p. 167; ch. lv, pp. 252–57; and bk II, ch. vii, p. 301; ch. xix, p. 345. Under such conditions a rule of laws could exist. See *Discourses*, bk I, ch. xxxiv, p. 203; ch. xiv, p. 229; ch. lviii, p. 261.

93. Montesquieu, *Spirit*, bk. v, ch. ii, pp. 40–41. Montesquieu was most articulate in stressing the peculiar and novel character of his notion of political virtue in an "Author's Explanatory Note" at the beginning of the books: "For the better understanding of the first four books . . . it is to be observed that what I distinguish by the name of virtue, in a republic, is the love of one's country, that is, the love of equality. It is not a moral, nor a Christian, but a political virtue; and it is the spring which sets republican government in motion, as honor is the spring which gives motion to monarchy." *Ibid.*, p. lxxi. See also bk. III, ch. v, p. 23, n. j. The passionate, rather than rational, character of Montesquieu's political virtue explains how "virtue" became a democratic, rather than aristocratic, quality; for according to the classics, virtue consisted in the tempering of passions, of which only the best men were capable, whereas all men were full of passion. The gulf between the classics and Montesquieu strikingly appears in the following passage: "Virtue in a republic is a most simple thing; it is a love of the republic; it is a sensation, and not a consequence of acquired knowledge, a sensation that may be felt by the meanest as well as by the highest person in the state." *Ibid.*, bk. V, ch. ii, p. 40. See also Stourzh, "Die tugendhafte Republik" (n. 21 above), pp. 249–50.

94. See in particular his *Thoughts on Government*, *Works*, IV, 194.

95. *Warren-Adams Letters*, I, 222. Two of his letters to Mercy Warren, January 8 and April 16, 1776, are most remarkable documents, showing the

complete sway of Montesquieu's ideas over Adams's mind. In 1760 Adams had begun to read *The Spirit of the Laws* carefully, as evidenced by the copy he used, which I inspected at the Massachusetts Historical Society in Boston (it is now in the possession of Mrs. Arthur Adams, Charles River Village, Mass.). See also Adams, *Diary*, I, 123, n. 19, and 142.

96. *Defence*, in *Works*, VI, 206–7.

97. Smith, p. 552.

98. See Stourzh, *Franklin*, pp. 18, 23, 96–98, 116, 120, 182.

99. The ramifications of the British tradition of radical Whiggism and its republican heritage in the American colonies was pointed out in Robbins's book on the Commonwealthmen. The influence of *Cato's Letters* in the colonies, first noticed by Rossiter, *Seedtime*, p. 141, is stressed by Milton M. Klein in his edition of *The Independent Reflector* by William Livingston and others (Cambridge, Mass., 1963), pp. 21–22. It has been systematically investigated by Jacobson in the introduction of his selection from Gordon's and Trenchard's writings, *The English Libertarian Heritage* (Indianapolis, 1965), pp. xlviii–lx, and by Bernard Bailyn: in his introduction to *Pamphlets of the American Revolution* (Cambridge, Mass., 1965), pp. 29–30, 34; in the expanded introduction published separately as *The Ideological Origins of the American Revolution* (Cambridge, Mass., 1967), especially pp. 35–37; and in Bailyn, "Origins." I take exception to the labeling of the tradition to which *Cato's Letters* belonged as "libertarian"—an adjective used both by Jacobson and by Bailyn. "Libertarian" may be, and has been, as diversely used as the word "liberal"; the term certainly is not appropriate to denote that Gordon and Trenchard were at the left of Whig political thought. The term "radical Whig" used by Jacobson (p. vii) seems most appropriate— better than the expression "Commonwealthmen" used by Robbins, since many radical Whigs did not oppose the mixed constitution of the settlement of 1688–89. It also seems more appropriate to speak of radical Whigs than of dissenting tradition as does Richard Buel, Jr., in "Democracy and the American Revolution: A Frame of Reference," in *William and Mary Quarterly*, 3rd series, XXI (1964), 166–67 n. 1. I also cannot agree with the recent assertion by Staughton Lynd in his *Intellectual Origins of American Radicalism* (New York, 1968), p. 27, that what he calls the "dissenting radicalism" of people like Burgh, Priestley, Paine, and Catherine Macaulay "represented the return to an essentially religious outlook." The nature of "virtue" and "disinterestedness" as a "passion" is best revealed in a piece not included in Jacobson's selection: "When the Passions of Men do good to others, it is called Virtue and Publick Spirit." (Gordon and Trenchard, II, 53, No. 40.) I drew attention to this passage in a paper delivered December 30, 1957, at the AHA Meeting in New York entitled "Alexander Hamilton, The Theory of Empire Building."

100. See Burgh, I, 9; II, 18, 41, 378. Burgh's complex attitude toward republican government is not discussed by Oscar and Mary Handlin, "James Burgh and American Revolutionary Theory," *Proceedings of the Massachusetts Historical Society,* LXXIII (1961), 38–57.

101. See Introduction.

102. Koch and Peden, p. 280 (Query XIX).

103. To James Madison, Dec. 20, 1787. *Ibid.,* p. 441.

104. One of the most perceptive pro-Constitution writers apart from the authors of *The Federalist* was Noah Webster: "The system of the great Montesquieu will ever be erroneous, till the words *property or lands in fee simple* are substituted for *virtue,* throughout his *Spirit of Laws.*

"*Virtue,* patriotism, or love of country, never was and never will be, till mens' natures are changed, a fixed, permanent principle and support of government. But in an agricultural country, a general possession of land in fee simple, may be rendered perpetual, and the inequalities introduced by commerce, are too fluctuating to endanger government. An equality of property, with a necessity of alienation, constantly operating to destroy combinations of powerful families, is the very *soul of a republic.*" "An Examination into the leading principles of the Federal Constitution" (Philadelphia, 1787), "by a Citizen of America." Ford, *Pamphlets,* p. 59.

105. May 19, 1777. *Papers,* I, 254–56.

106. *Ibid.* On the issue of a change in Hamilton's political ideas between 1777 and 1787 Miller, pp. 50–51, seems to me nearer to the mark than Rossiter, *Hamilton,* p. 118, note.

107. Early in 1776, a defender of the old order in Virginia, Carter Braxton, pointed to the danger and the inappropriateness of introducing a democratic form of government in Virginia: "The truth is, that men will not be poor from choice or compulsion, and these [democratic] Governments can exist only in countries where the people are so from necessity." Virginia, he argued, had been modelled on the example of the British Constitution, and that constitution, if "brought back to its original state" would still be the best to follow. Braxton displayed an unusual discrimination respecting the difference between private virtue and Montesquieu's public virtue. See his "Address to the Convention of ... VIRGINIA" by a native of the *Colony,* reprinted in Peter Force, ed., *American Archives, Fourth Series,* VI (1846), 748–54. See Stourzh, "Die tugendhafte Republik," (n. 21 above), p. 256. In 1784, Jeremy Belknap observed that a republic could succeed only if property was equally distributed, and he did not find it so in any of the states. Quoted in Jackson Turner Main, *The Social Structure of Revolutionary America* (Princeton, 1965), p. 224, from a letter of Belknap's to E. Hazard, "Belknap Papers," Massachusetts Historical Society, *Collections,* 5th series, II (1877), 313. A Connecticut newspaper reported in 1787 that the "consid-

erable fortunes" acquired by commerce in Massachusetts prevented "the general manners of the people from being so strictly republican ... as in Connecticut." From *Conn. Gazette*, Nov. 9, 1787, quoted by Main, pp. 224–25.

108. Farrand, I, 466.

109. *Papers*, V, 23, also p. 62.

110. *De l'étude de l'histoire et de la manière d'écrire l'histoire*, in *Collection complète des oeuvres de l'Abbé Mably*, 15 vols. (Paris, 1794–95), XII, 43–44, 65. This is one of three of Mably's works used in *The Federalist* (No. 20, p. 127, by Madison). Other references to Mably are in Hamilton's No. 6 (p. 36) and in Madison's No. 18 (p. 114). Mably was also referred to by Elbridge Gerry, "Observations on the New Constitution," in Ford, *Pamphlets*, pp. 4–5; and by Noah Webster, *ibid.*, p. 37.

111. *Observations sur le gouvernement et les lois des Etats-Unis d'Amerique* in *Collection complète*, VIII, 345, 355, 365, 386–87, 431. My italics. Hamilton commented on the poverty of the Swiss in his letter to James Duane of Sept. 3, 1780, and in *The Continentalist, Papers*, II, 403, 656–57. In 1798 he referred to the Swiss cantons as the "boast of republicans," as the model to which republicans were glad to appeal "in proof that a republican government may consist with the order and happiness of society." "The Stand," *Works*, VI, 280. Questionable in terms of the direct influence on the Constitution attributed to Mably (Art. IV, sect. 4, being called a *lex Mably*) as well as in terms of the place allocated to Mably in relation to the French Enlightenment is the essay by Mitchell Franklin: "Influence of the Abbé de Mably and of Le Mercier de la Rivière on American Constitutional Ideas Concerning the Republic and Judicial Review," in R. Pound, E. N. Griswold, and A. E. Sutherland, eds., *Perspectives of Law. Essays for Austin Wakeman Scott* (Boston, 1964), pp. 96–130.

112. *Papers*, III, 103.

113. Farrand, I, 288. Madison's notes. The emphasis on the effects of industry is omitted in the other, briefer, accounts of Hamilton's speech and in the outline in his own notes; yet there is no reason to suppose that Madison invented this statement, which is completely within the context of the argument. A significant facet of Hamilton's thought is omitted if his argument is paraphrased thus: "Societies naturally divide into two basic political divisions—the few and the many." In Koch, *Power*, p. 62.

114. Farrand, I, 432. According to Yates's notes, which seem preferable here since Madison was very active in debate. For a general evaluation of Yates's and Madison's renderings of this speech, see Arnold A. Rogow, "The Federal Convention: Madison and Yates," *American Historical Review*, LX (January 1955), 324–26.

115. *Papers*, V, 42. Italics mine.

116. Montesquieu, *Spirit*, bk. V, ch. iii, p. 41. It is important to understand that Montesquieu's advocacy of equality for republics does not mean "extreme equality." See *ibid.*, bk. VIII, ch. iii, p. 111.

117. In *The Continentalist* of 1782, Hamilton extolled Hume as "a very ingenious and sensible writer!" *Papers*, III, 77. Years later, he again referred to "the profound and ingenious Hume." *Defense of the Funding System*, *Works*, VIII, 459. See also Goebel (n. 69 above), p. 617.

118. Hendel, pp. 133–34.

119. *Federalist*, pp. 61–62. See the explicit critique of Montesquieu's principles of government in Madison's essay "Spirit of Government" (1792), *Writings*, VI, 93–95. However, only two weeks after this essay was published, Madison lauded the "life of the husbandman" for that combination of "*health, virtue, intelligence,* and *competency*" which would produce a "Republican Distribution of Citizens" (the title of the essay). *Writings*, VI, 96.

120. William Vans Murray, "Virtue," No. 8 of "Political Sketches: by a citizen of the united states," in *The American Museum and Repository*, 2d edition (September 1787), p. 231. Hamilton is listed as a subscriber to the volume of the *American Museum and Repository* in which Murray's political sketches appeared. They were written in 1784 and 1785 when Murray was at the Inner Temple in London. Murray was later to achieve reputation as American minister to Holland and member of the second peace mission sent by John Adams to France. His sketches were actually a polemic against Mably's book on America. For details, see Alexander De Conde, "William Vans Murray's 'Political Sketches': A Defense of the American Experiment," *Mississippi Valley Historical Review*, XLI (June 1954), 623–40. De Conde does not see Mably's ideas in the framework of a great tradition of political philosophy, in which alone they—and the criticism directed against them—can be properly understood. A highly interesting reaction to the challenge of virtuous republicanism is Theophilus Parsons, "Essex Result." Parsons wanted a Massachusetts constitution of great durability, i.e. one that would provide for many contingencies: "It may be said, the virtuous American would blast with indignation the man, who should proffer him a bribe. Let it now be admitted as a fact. We ask, will that always be the case? The most virtuous states have become vicious." Parsons, p. 378.

121. See what seems to me the most lucid of all modern interpretations of Rousseau's politics, Jouvenel's "Essai," pp. 84–86, 93–94, 126.

122. One should see Benjamin Constant's classic piece, "De la liberté des anciens comparée avec celle des modernes," in Charles Louandre, ed., *Oeuvres politiques de Benjamin Constant* (Paris, 1874), pp. 258, 268f.

123. See Hobbes, Part II, ch. xix, p. 122. See also Strauss, *Natural Right*, p. 197.

124. Hobbes, p. 5.

125. "Of Commerce," in Hendel, p. 134.

126. *Papers*, V, 43.

127. Paltsits, p. 151 (Washington's Final Manuscript). Hamilton's Original Major Draft speaks of "a main & necessary spring," *ibid.*, p. 192.

CHAPTER III

1. See, for example, Kurt Kluxen, *Das Problem der politischen Opposition. Entwicklung und Wesen der englischen Zweiparteienpolitik im 18. Jahrhundert* (Freiburg, 1956), p. 126.

2. Farrand, I, 378 (Yates's notes).

3. In the New York Ratifying Convention. *Papers*, p. 126.

4. See, for example, *Works*, III, 4; also *Federalist*, No. 78, pp. 529–30.

5. To John Laurens, April 1779, *Papers*, II, 35. Emendations in brackets were supplied by John C. Hamilton in his edition of *The Works of Alexander Hamilton* (1851).

6. *Papers*, I, 94–95. Hamilton indicates as his source "Hume, vol. I, Essay 5th." It is the essay "Of the Independency of Parliament"; in later editions than those accessible to Hamilton, it was placed sixth, after the essay "Of the Origins of Government." The italics in the first paragraph, with the exception of the first italicized word, are Hamilton's (unless the italicizing was changed in later editions of Hume that I used); those in the second paragraph are Hume's. See Hendel, p. 68.

7. *Full Vindication, Papers*, I, 53–54.

8. *Ibid.*, pp. 92, 100.

9. *Ibid.*, p. 156.

10. Washington, X, 363. Report to the Committee of Congress with the Army, Jan. 29, 1778; the signed report as well as two drafts are in Hamilton's handwriting. *Papers*, I, 421.

11. Farrand, I, 381. For this debate, Yates's notes are preferable; Madison evidently got his notes from Yates.

12. *Papers*, V, 36, 85.

13. To James Monroe, Oct. 5, 1786. James Madison, *Letters and Other Writings*, 4 vols. (Washington, D.C., 1865), I, 251.

14. April 29, 1789, *The Diary and Letters of Gouverneur Morris*, ed. Anne C. Morris, 2 vols. (New York, 1888), I, 69.

15. It is ironic that Patrick Henry, the great patriot, should have launched in the Virginia Ratifying Convention a panegyric on the British Constitution as based on self-love: "I beseech gentlemen to consider whether they can say, when trusting power, that a mere patriotic profession will be equally operative and efficacious as the check of self-love. In considering the experience of ages, is it not seen that fair, disinterested patriotism, and professions

of attachment to rectitude, have never been solely trusted to by an enlightened, free people? . . . The real rock of political salvation is self-love, perpetuated from age to age in every human breast, and manifested in every action." (Elliot, III, 164.) For Hamilton, see, e.g., *Works*, V, 474. See also Madison in *Federalist*, No. 37, p. 239.

16. Blackstone, I, 40.

17. *Papers*, II, 655f.

18. *Papers*, V, 102. Similarly, he had noted in *The Federalist* (No. 17, p. 107): "It is a known fact in human nature, that its affections are commonly weak in proportion to the distance or diffusiveness of the object."

19. Farrand, I, 381 (Yates's paraphrase). See also *ibid.*, p. 285; *Federalist*, No. 1, p. 4; *Papers*, I, 97; *Works*, X, 20. This connotation is clearest in another passage of Hamilton's speech of June 18 as noted by Madison: the states "constantly pursue internal interests adverse to those of the whole. They have their particular debts—their particular plans of finance &c. all these when opposed to, invariably, prevail over the requisitions & plans of Congress." Farrand, I, 284.

20. Montesquieu, *Spirit*, bk. III, ch. iii, p. 21. See also Machiavelli, *Discourses*, bk. I, ch. xvi, pp. 163–64.

21. *Defence*, in *Works*, VI, 150; see also IV, 406, and V, 457.

22. *Papers*, V, 39–40. See also "Conjectures about the New Constitution," *Papers*, IV, 276.

23. *Federalist*, No. 68, p. 461. See also No. 27, p. 172; No. 76, pp. 509–10. It would be interesting to pursue in greater detail the issue raised in Pope's verse. It provided a formula with which political scientists could adorn their usually less graceful prose. Pope's lines are frequently encountered in eighteenth-century political writings. Hume took issue with Pope in the essay "That Politics May Be Reduced to a Science." John Adams in his *Thoughts on Government* (1776), understandably thought that "Pope flattered tyrants too much." *Works*, IV, 193. Priestley, though a progressive thinker, approved of Pope in his *Essay on the First Principles of Government*. See Elie Halévy, *The Growth of Philosophic Radicalism* (Boston, 1955), p. 128. William Plumer, a New Englander, said in 1784: "I do not feel hostile to either democracy, autocracy, or monarchy. I am inclined to think the people are much more interested in the good administration than in the theory or form of government—Or, as Pope expresses it, 'That government is best which is administered best.' " Quoted by Dunbar, p. 57.

It is important to note that "constitution" and "form of government" were used synonymously in the early years of the United States, the former slowly superseding the latter. Thus Hamilton in May, 1777 thanked a New Yorker for "the pamphlet containing your form of government." *Papers*, I, 248.

24. *Papers*, I, 184.

25. Farrand, I, 378. (Yates's notes). See also *ibid.*, p. 373, for Madison's transcription: "Those who pay are the masters of those who are paid."

26. *Federalist*, No. 73, p. 493; No. 79, p. 531.

27. Jefferson's "Anas," in Koch and Peden, p. 126.

28. Blackstone, I, 335f.

29. "Of the Independency of Parliament," in Hume, III, 47.

30. Farrand, I, 376 (Madison's notes). This is one of the few cases where Madison's and Yates's transcriptions differ radically. Madison's rendering of the reference to Hume is more accurate if compared with Hume's text, which Hamilton had in mind. Yates obviously did not quite grasp Hamilton's reference to Hume, for he noted it down as follows: "Hume's opinion of the British Constitution confirms the remark, that there is always a body of firm patriots, who often shake a corrupt administration." *Ibid.*, p. 381. Yates shows that Hamilton also referred to a part of Hume's passage that does not appear in Madison's transcript—that the crown would dominate the Commons "when assisted by the honest and disinterested part of the House." For the greater part of this day's discussion, Yates's notes are preferable, Madison apparently having been prevented from writing and afterwards filling in from Yates. However, at the end of the debate when Hamilton made this point, he may have been attentive; or Madison's more accurate transcription may simply reveal that he knew Hume's essay and argument well, whereas Yates did not.

31. Blackstone, I, pp. 337 and 336.

32. Montesquieu, *Spirit*, bk. XX, ch. ii, p. 317.

33. See Smith, pp. 385ff.

34. *Ibid.*, p. 423.

35. E.g., *Federalist*, No. 78, p. 528; *Papers*, III, 534.

36. See above, p. 70. See Hamilton's comparison of "an enlightened view" of one's interest with "a spirit of romantic gratitude," in *Works*, IV, 323.

37. Hume, *Treatise of Human Nature*, in *Philosophical Works*, II, 169.

38. *Federalist*, No. 78, p. 527.

39. *Ibid.*, No. 35, p. 218.

40. *Ibid.*, p. 221.

41. *Ibid.*, p. 220.

42. A. N. Holcombe speaks of Hamilton's "theory of social dichotomy" in *Our More Perfect Union* (Cambridge, Mass., 1950), p. 60. Before Hamilton is taken to task for his lack of insight into the real tendencies of America, it is well to remember that Madison shared the same view on the direction in which American society would move: "In future times a great majority of the people will not only be without landed, but any other sort of, property. These will either combine under the influence of their common situation; in which case, the rights of property & the public liberty, [will not be secure in

their hands] or which is more probable, they will become the tools of opulence and ambition, in which case there will be the equal danger on another side." Farrand, II, 203–4.

43. Outline for his speech of June 18, Farrand, I, 308–9.

44. See also below, p. 117.

45. This reminds one of Karl Mannheim's well-known concept of the socially unattached intelligentsia (*die freischwebende Intelligenz*). See Mannheim, *Ideology and Utopia* (London, 1946), pp. 136–46.

46. *Federalist*, No. 35, p. 220f. One of the most amusing episodes that shows the political predilections of the learned professions at the time of the Founding Fathers is the bitter political quarrel between Fisher Ames and his brother, Dr. Nathanael Ames. Samuel Eliot Morison has superbly dealt with the implications of this episode for a one-sided, "economic" interpretation of history, in "Squire Ames and Fisher Ames," reprinted in Morison, *By Land and By Sea* (New York, 1953), 200–218.

47. *Federalist*, No. 35, p. 219.

48. See Brown, pp. 37, 53.

49. *Federalist*, p. 482. See also "Essex Result," in Parsons, pp. 364–65.

50. Blackstone, I, 49. Mason (p. 637) has said that in *Federalist* No. 71, "one encounters Rousseau's sentiments." Though Hamilton had looked at Rousseau's *Contrat social*, it is much more likely that he had Blackstone in mind when he wrote these lines.

51. As B. F. Wright, Jr., has well said, "that standard device of the demagogue—the scapegoat—is missing in *The Federalist*." See his introductory essay to his edition of *The Federalist* (Cambridge, Mass., 1961), p. 82. This essay remains to date the profoundest discussion of *The Federalist* as a piece of political theory.

52. *Federalist*, p. 219. My italics. Only the neglect of this argument explains Wright's statement, in an earlier important essay, on Hamilton's writing in *The Federalist*: "To be sure, he did not hesitate to reiterate his belief in the frailties of men, but he did not state the remainder of his doctrine— that men of wealth and learning can be more trusted than can the poor and ignorant." B. F. Wright, Jr., "*The Federalist* on the Nature of Political Man," *Ethics*, LIX, No. 1, Part II, p. 27. See also Wright's introduction to his edition of *The Federalist*, p. 29.

53. *Federalist*, No. 36, p. 223.

54. Hartz, p. 80.

55. Quoted by Sir Lewis Namier, "Human Nature in Politics," in his *Personalities and Powers* (London, 1955), p. 1.

56. Harrington's *Oceana*, printed in 1656, is the earliest work in which I have found the use of the term "national interest" (p. 19). A study of Harrington shows the origin of that formula in a concern for political theory, and not, as Charles A. Beard suggested, as a result of the transition from

feudal or territorial-dynastic to commercial-bourgeois thinking and politics, though Beard's stress on its republican tendency is correct. See Beard, *The Idea of National Interest* (New York, 1934), p. 22. Highly interesting is Harrington's explicit identification of "reason of state" with the "interest of the Ruler or Rulers," p. 22. See now the exhaustive study by J. A. W. Gunn, *Politics and the Public Interest in the Seventeenth Century* (London, 1969), ch. III (devoted to Harrington), pp. 109–52. For Hamilton's use of "national interests," see Farrand, I, 288; and *Federalist*, No. 23, p. 150. See also John Jay in *Federalist*, No. 64, p. 433.

57. To Robert Morris, April 30, 1781, *Papers*, II, 621.

58. January, 1790. *Papers*, VI, 68. See also the somewhat simplified statement in *Papers*, III, 494.

59. *Papers*, V, 70. See also *ibid.*, p. 72; and VII, 50, on "prejudices" in a "popular government."

60. December, 1790. *Papers*, VII, 331.

61. *Camillus*, No. 7, *Works*, V, 260–61.

62. *Camillus*, No. 21, *ibid.*, p. 453. See also Hamilton's letter to Gov. Clinton, June 1, 1783, *Papers*, III, 367–68.

63. Perhaps to Robert Morris, Dec. 1779–March 1780, *Papers*, II, 242.

64. "Whether the British Government Inclines More to Absolute Monarchy or to a Republic," in Hendel, p. 75. See also "Of the First Principles of Government," *ibid.*, p. 24. The careful study of Hume's impact on Hamilton in Alex Bein, *Die Staatsidee Alexander Hamiltons in ihrer Entstehung und Entwicklung* (Munich, 1927), pp. 165–72, has hardly been made use of in America. See, however, Rossiter, *Hamilton*, p. 306, n. 30.

65. To William Duer, June 18, 1778, *Papers*, I, 499. See also *Report on a National Bank, Works*, III, 388.

66. Drunkenness was another passion that could not be justified by the extenuating circumstances of the state of nature. On moral obligation apart from any political or prudential considerations, see the excellent study by Howard Warrender, *The Political Philosophy of Hobbes* (Oxford, 1957), pp. 62–63, 75. On suicide, see Hobbes's *A Dialogue between a Philosopher and a Student of the Common Laws of England*, in W. Molesworth, ed., *The English Works of Thomas Hobbes* (London, 1840), VI, 88.

67. For Montesquieu, see his *Lettres persanes*, No. 76. Ortega's argument is quoted from his *Obras completas*, p. 1341, by José Sánchez Villaseñor, *Ortega y Gasset, Existentialist* (Chicago, 1949), p. 117. The gratuitous crime in Gide's *Les caves du Vatican* (Lafcadio's Adventures) is discussed by Simone Weil, *The Need for Roots* (London, 1952), p. 25.

68. Montesquieu had the courage to point to the deep cleavage between moral systems that are often, under some "humanistic" label, lumped together: "In our days we receive three different or contrary educations, namely, of our parents, of our masters, and of the world. What we learn in

the latter effaces all the ideas of the former. This, in some measure, arises from the contrast we experience between our religious and worldly engagements, a thing unknown to the ancients." *Spirit*, bk. IV, ch. iv, p. 33.

69. The extraordinarily complex question of Hamilton's growing devotion to Christianity in his last years, and the impact this had on his duel with Burr, has been brilliantly and convincingly discussed by Douglass Adair and Marvin Harvey, "Was Alexander Hamilton a Christian Statesman?," *William and Mary Quarterly*, 3rd series, XII (April, 1955), 308–29.

70. *Works*, X, 474. Cf. Schachner, p. 428. I cannot agree with Schachner when he says that Hamilton threw away his shot at Burr, "not, perhaps, because of Christian principles—inasmuch as, at various stages of his career, he had evidenced no such scruples over dueling—but because, in the recesses of his conscience, he was troubled over the possibility that he might have been in the wrong." This is no valid argument. As Adair and Harvey (p. 327) have pointed out, even if Hamilton "suspected in his heart" that he had wronged Burr, "according to the code of honor, by accepting Burr's challenge to receive his fire Hamilton gained the *right* to kill Burr if he could. . . . But Hamilton was now trying desperately to live by a different and higher code." See also *Interview in Weehawken. The Burr-Hamilton Duel as Told in the Original Documents*, eds. H. C. Syrett and Jean G. Cooke, with Introduction and Conclusion by Willard M. Wallace (Middletown, Conn., 1960), pp. 102, 173. Regrettably, no account is here taken of Adair and Harvey's article just cited.

71. To Edward Stevens, Nov. 11, 1769, *Papers*, I, 4.

72. *Papers*, I, 141–42.

73. For example, *Papers*, I, 50, 127; *Works*, VI, 265–66. Hamilton said of Baron von Steuben that he had "a fondness for power and importance, natural to every man." *Works*, IX, 132. Striking, and perhaps suggestive of Hamilton's emphasis in his convention speech of June 18, are Madison's notes: "the love of power, men love power." Farrand, I, 284. Yates noted: "Men always love power," *ibid.*, p. 295. Rufus King noted: "Man loves power," *ibid.*, p. 302. See also numerous references in *The Federalist*: No. 6, p. 28 (see below, p. 149); No. 15, p. 97; No. 17, pp. 105f; No. 72, p. 492; No. 73, p. 495. Also the Farewell Address, in Paltsits, p. 150 (Washington's Final Manuscript), and p. 191 (Hamilton's Original Major Draft).

74. Locke, sects. 92 and 93 (pp. 162f).

75. Cf. above, pp. 66–67. See also the very pertinent observations on the radical Whigs' one-sided and exaggerated approach to power in W. B. Gwyn, *The Meaning of the Separation of Powers*, Tulane Studies in Political Science IX (New Orleans, 1965), 22–23. Note some of the titles of the letters of "Cato": Vol. I, No. 33, "Cautions against the natural Encroachments of Power"; Vol. II, No. 40, "Considerations on the restless and selfish Spirit of Man"; No. 43, "The Natural Passion of Men for Superiority";

No. 44, "Men not ruled by Principle, but by Passion"; Vol. IV, No. 115, "The Encroaching Nature of Power ever to be watched and checked." Gordon and Trenchard were among the few writers to have pointed out the similarity of Locke's and Hobbes's philosophy. See No. 116, p. 86. For Bolingbroke's theory that the government, by the mere fact of being in power, was bound to become corrupt, whereas the opposition, by being "out," would remain pure, see Kluxen, *Das Problem der politischen Opposition,* pp. 143ff. Burgh depicted the corruptions of power, frequently quoting *Cato's Letters,* in the most sensational ways; see, in particular, I, 106–9.

76. Cecelia M. Kenyon, "Men of Little Faith," *William and Mary Quarterly,* 3rd series, XII (January 1955), 3–43. See also the introduction to Kenyon, ed., *The Antifederalists* (Indianapolis, 1966).

77. Kenyon, "Men of Little Faith," p. 18.

78. Koch and Peden, p. 323. This is, of course, only a reformulation of the basic tenet of liberal political theory, first formulated by Hobbes, that every man is wise in his own affairs. See Hobbes, ch. VIII, p. 45: "A plain husbandman is more prudent in affairs of his own house, than a privy-councillor in the affairs of another man." Similarly, Adam Smith thought that "every man is fitter to take care of himself than of any other person." Quoted from *The Theory of Moral Sentiments,* VI, II, 1, by Cropsey, *Polity and Economy,* p. 10.

79. To E. Carrington, Jan. 16, 1787. Koch and Peden, p. 412.

80. "Speech on the state of the country under Mr. Van Buren's administration," Hanover County, Va., June 27, 1840, in *The Works of Henry Clay,* ed. C. Colton (New York, 1897), VIII, 201.

81. *Federalist,* p. 6. See also his speech of June 18 in the Federal Convention, Farrand, I, 284 (Madison's notes).

82. *Federalist,* No. 85, p. 594; cf. No. 21, p. 131.

83. To ———, Sept. 26, 1792. *Papers,* XII, 480.

84. "The Vindication No. I." *Papers,* XI, 463. This piece was most likely written in the summer of 1792 (ed. note, *ibid.,* p. 461).

85. Enclosure in a letter to Washington, Aug. 18, 1792. *Papers,* XII, 252. Cf. *Works,* V, 77. Hamilton's ambivalent use of Caesar's name is puzzling, as has been noted in [Adair], "Note," p. 295, n. 13. His repeated reference to Caesar as a demogogue clashes with the famous story told by Jefferson, that Hamilton opposed to Jefferson's trinity of Bacon, Newton, and Locke, Caesar as "the greatest man that ever lived" (Jefferson to Rush, Jan. 16, 1811, Koch and Peden, p. 609). This episode and its implications for Jefferson's and Hamilton's differing quests for fame recently were analyzed by Adair, "Fame," pp. 37–38; see also John A. Schutz and Douglass Adair, eds., *The Spur of Fame. Dialogues of John Adams and Benjamin Rush, 1805–1813* (San Marino, California, 1966), 1–3. See also below, Ch. V, n. 6, pp. 259–60.

86. Schachner, p. 51. Also Adair and Harvey, "Was Alexander Hamilton a Christian Statesman?," p. 321, n. 19.

87. To James A. Bayard, Jan. 16, 1801. *Works*, X, 417.

88. See U. Knoche, "Der roemische Ruhmesgedanke," *Philologus*, LXXXIX (1934), 102ff.

89. Gilbert Chinard, *Thomas Jefferson, The Apostle of Americanism*, 2nd ed. (Boston, 1939), p. 233. Professor Chinard plausibly explains Jefferson's exception to "honor" with Montesquieu's linking of honor with monarchy. For the text see Chinard, ed., *The Letters of Lafayette and Jefferson* (Baltimore, 1929), p. 138.

90. Nicomachean Ethics, 1123b. See the important discussion in Harry V. Jaffa, *Thomism and Aristotelianism* (Chicago, 1952), ch. VI. Hobbes, ch. XV, p. 100.

91. Hobbes, ch. XI, pp. 64–65. Ernst H. Kantorowicz has illuminatingly written about the intrusion of the Aristotelian and particularly the Averroist doctrine of the uncreatedness and infinite continuity of the world upon the Christian-Augustinian doctrine of the transitoriness of time: "The new continuity of Time did not create, but intensified, the desire for the perpetuation of man's fame and name. Fame, after all, made sense only if this world and if mankind were believed to be, in one way or another, permanent and immortal; and if Time was Life, and not Death. We may consider, perhaps, "immortal fame" in this world as the equivalent of or secular substitute for the immortal beatitude of the other world, and Dante consequently was implored by the lost souls in Inferno to keep alive their memory and their fame on earth in order to compensate for the forfeited, and often even despised, eternal beatitude of the soul." *The King's Two Bodies* (Princeton, 1957), p. 278. Kantorowicz omits, though, that in the deepest circles of the Inferno the damned despised themselves so much as to crave forgetfulness rather than remembrance.

92. Hume, *Philosophical Works*, III, 96.

93. *Ibid.*, p. 97.

94. *Federalist*, p. 488. My italics. I first called attention to Hamilton's passion for fame in my paper "Alexander Hamilton—The Theory of Empire Building," delivered at the American Historical Association meeting in New York, Dec. 30, 1957 (see Adair, "Fame," p. 40, n. 14). Independently, the significance of this passage has been stressed by Maynard Smith, "Reason, Passion and Political Freedom in *The Federalist*," *The Journal of Politics*, XXII (1960), 525–44, esp. p. 537. Smith, however, does not sufficiently differentiate between Hamilton's and Madison's contributions to *The Federalist*.

95. To a Scottish relative, May 2, 1797, *Works*, X, 259.

96. Henry Cabot Lodge, *George Washington*, 2 vols. (Boston, 1889), I, 109.

97. Samuel Eliot Morison, "The Young Man Washington," reprinted in his *By Land and By Sea* (New York, 1953). Morison rightly stresses that "Stoical magnanimity, not Christian meekness" informed some of Washington's "self-denying" actions, p. 175.

98. Sept. 1788, *Papers*, V, 221–22. Douglas Southall Freeman has commented that Hamilton's argument was made "in thorough knowledge of the man he was addressing." See his *George Washington. A Biography*, VI (New York, 1954), 148, n. 47. In a prior letter to Hamilton, Washington had argued, interestingly enough, that after all he had said about retirement from public life, "the world and posterity might probably accuse [him of] inconsistency and ambition." Aug. 28, 1788, quoted by Freeman, p. 147. The younger Pitt once raised the question, "What makes ambition virtue?," and answered, "the sense of honor." Quoted from John Marshall's *The Life of George Washington* by Robert K. Faulkner, *The Jurisprudence of John Marshall* (Princeton, 1968), p. 134.

99. To John Adams, Sept. 25, 1798, in Washington, XXXVI, 460–61.

100. Pickering Papers in the Massachusetts Historical Society, unpublished, LII, 85.

101. *Ibid.*, XLVII, 205.

102. "Helvidius" No. IV: "The strongest passions and most dangerous weaknesses of the human breast; ambition, avarice, vanity, the honourable or venial love of fame, are all in conspiracy against the desire and duty of peace." Madison, *Writings*, VI, 174.

103. "A Sketch of the Character of Alexander Hamilton," (written immediately after his death) in *The Works of Fisher Ames*, ed. Seth Ames, 2 vols. (Boston, 1854), II, 262–63. Morison called Ames the "Calhoun of New England" in his article on Ames, p. 9. Further examples of Hamilton's emphasis on that noblest passion may be adduced. For example, the description in his "Eulogium on Major-General Greene," July 4, 1789, of "the mingled emotions of a great mind—impelled by a sense of duty—allured by the hope or [*sic*] fame." *Papers*, V, 350. See also the "Address to the Supervisers of the City of Albany," Feb. 18, 1789, *Papers*, V, 258. And Hamilton's pamphlet on John Adams in 1800: "Few and feeble are the inducements to accept a place in our administration. Far from being lucrative, there is not one which will not involve pecuniary sacrifice to every *honest* man of pre-eminent talents. And has not experience shown, that he must be fortunate indeed, if even the successful execution of his task can secure to him consideration and fame? Of a large harvest of obloquy he is sure." *Works*, VII, 339.

104. Speaking of Charles Townshend in his speech on American Taxation: "But he had no failings which were not owing to a noble cause—to an ardent, generous, perhaps an immoderate, passion for fame; a passion which is the instinct of all great souls." *The Works of Edmund Burke*. Bohn ed., I,

427. Cf. Burke's own concern for glory. In 1785, speaking on the Impeachment of Warren Hastings, he said that his business was "what will acquit and justify myself to those few persons, and to those distant times, which may take a concern in these affairs and in the actors in them." *Correspondence of the Right Hon. Edmund Burke* (London, 1944), III, 41–42.

105. See, e.g., the entries in Adams, *Diary*, I, 24–25, 72–73, 82.

106. Alexis de Tocqueville, *Democracy in America*, Vintage Books ed. (New York, 1961), II, 101 (ch. IV, "That the Americans Combat the Effects of Individualism by Free Institutions").

107. *Ibid.*, pp. 109–10.

108. Louis M. Hacker, *Alexander Hamilton in the American Tradition* (New York, 1957), p. 23.

109. Farrand, II, 53. Madison's notes on G. Morris's objections to making the chief executive not reeligible.

110. Gordon and Trenchard, II, 52–53 (No. 40).

111. With regard to the United States, this problem has been masterfully explored by Weinberg.

112. *Federalist*, No. 2. The religious overtone of Jay's account of the blessings of America makes his contributions different from both Hamilton's and Madison's. This has been noted in the most satisfactory overall study to date of the political thought of all three authors: Aldo Garosci, *Il pensiero politico degli autori del "Federalist"* (Milan, 1954), p. 252. Justly, Garosci says that Jay elaborated a Romantic-historic theory of nationality without forgetting that at the origin of this nationality is a political decision. *Ibid.*, p. 256. See my review in *Political Science Quarterly*, LXXI (June 1956), 309–12.

113. Jouvenel has written of Rousseau's general will, which is nothing but his version of Montesquieu's public virtue, "La Volonté Générale ne fournit une règle de conduite juste avec l'étranger: 'Tout patriote est dur aux étrangers: ils ne sont qu'hommes, ils ne sont rien à ses yeux.' [*Émile*, p. 9.] ... On peut se demander si ce qu'on peut bien appeler le totémisme de Rousseau n'a pas joué un rôle dans ce 'recul vers les formes inférieures des vieilles sociétés militantes' ... que Taine prévoyait, et que nous voyons." Jouvenel, "Essai," pp. 119–20.

114. The argument of this chapter may by now have made clear why I cannot agree with the fundamental thesis of Kenyon's significant essay "Alexander Hamilton: Rousseau of the Right," despite my agreement on a great many points of detail. This chapter ought to be considered as an alternative interpretation. I also think that it is mistaken to speak of the "streak of political Romanticism" in Hamilton, as does Rossiter, *Hamilton*, p. 142, with the exception of the last phase of Hamilton's thought, discussed at the end of this chapter. For the same reason, I disagree with Siegfried Georg, "Staat, Verfassung und Politik bei Alexander Hamilton," in K. Kluxen and W. J.

Mommsen, eds., *Politische Ideologien und nationalstaatliche Ordnung*, Festschrift for Theodor Schieder (Munich, 1968), pp. 15–37, here 25–26.

115. As paraphrased by Yates, in Farrand, I, 381.

116. *Ibid.*, p. 289.

117. *Federalist*, No. 22, p. 142.

118. Hobbes, ch. XIX, pp. 122–23.

119. "Pacificus" No. VI, *Papers*, XV, 106. See, e.g., notes for a projected speech in support of a report on a military Peace Establishment in 1783, *Papers*, III, 383: "No individual has sufficient interest in the state to be proof against the seduction [by foreigners]." Other examples are in Farrand, I, 289, 310; *Federalist*, No. 68, pp. 459–60; "Tully," *Works*, VI, 422; and Washington's Farewell Address, in Paltsits, pp. 150 (Washington's Final Manuscript), 177 (Hamilton's Abstract of Points), and 190 (Hamilton's Original Major Draft).

120. *Federalist*, No. 22, p. 142.

121. On the dangers of state rivalry, see *ibid.*, No. 59, pp. 402–3, and No. 7, pp. 42–43. Also in the Farewell Address, Paltsits, p. 144.

122. Significant studies are Marshall; Caroline Robbins, " 'Discordant Parties'—A Study of the Acceptance of Party by Englishmen," *Political Science Quarterly*, LXXIII (1958), 505–29; and Mansfield.

123. Essay 51, "Of Faction," in Bacon, p. 545.

124. Hobbes, ch. XXII, p. 155. Rousseau, *Contrat social*, bk. II, ch. iii.

125. Edmund Burke, "Observations on a Late Publication, Intituled, 'The Present State of the Nation.' " *Works*, I, 185.

126. Edward Spelman in the Preface of his translation entitled *A Fragment Out of the Sixth Book of Polybius, containing a Dissertation upon Government in general, . . . To which is prefixed a Preface, wherein the System of Polybius is applied to the Government of England.* This work, originally published in 1743, was republished as an annex to Spelman's translation of the *Roman Antiquities* of Dionysius Halicarnassus (London, 1758), I, 369ff; quoted phrase is on p. 373. The highly significant defense of the positive aspects of party has been excerpted by Peter Campbell, "An Early Defence of Party," *Political Studies*, III (June 1955), 166–67. It was Spelman's translation of Polybius that John Adams used in his *Defence*, but I have not been able to trace a comment of Adams's on Spelman's Preface, which applied the system of Polybius to the government of England.

127. Spelman's Preface, p. 376. See now also Isaac Kramnick, *Bolingbroke and his Circle* (Cambridge, Mass., 1968), pp. 154–55.

128. *Ibid.*, pp. 374–75. An even earlier example of this approach in colonial New York is reported by Bailyn, "Origins," pp. 96–97, from the *New York Gazette* of March 1733.

129. Burke, "Thoughts on the Cause of the Present Discontents," in *Works*, I, 375. A comparison of Burke's pamphlet with Bolingbroke's *A Dis-*

sertation upon Parties yields interesting results. Burke's concept of party or connection in the public interest is closely fashioned after Bolingbroke's ideal of Country party. Bolingbroke first distinguished between party and faction: Parties were divided on "a real difference of principles and designs," as in the seventeenth century. These real differences had now disappeared, and men adhering to outworn party labels "would cease to be a party, and would become a faction. National interests would no longer be concerned; at least, on one side. They would be sometimes sacrificed, and always made subordinate to personal interests; and that, I think, is the true characteristic of faction." Bolingbroke, *Works*, 4 vols. (Philadelphia, 1841), II, 11; see also II, 63. Bolingbroke did not quite consistently adhere to his distinction between party and faction (e.g., II, 48 and 72). The following comparison of Burke's "Thoughts" and Bolingbroke's *Dissertation* yields surprising results. Burke: "Certain it is, the best patriots in the greatest commonwealths have always commended and promoted such connexions. *Idem sentire de republicâ*, was with them a principal ground of friendship and attachment; nor do I know any other capable of forming firmer, dearer, more pleasing, more honourable, and more virtuous habitudes." Burke, *Works*, I, 374. Cf. Bolingbroke: " 'Idem sentire republica,' [*sic*] to think alike about political affairs, hath been esteemed necessary to constitute and maintain private friendship. It is obviously more essential in public friendships. Bodies of men in the same society can never unite, unless they unite of this principle." Bolingbroke, *Works*, II, 26. This similarity has not been noted by Mansfield, who only mentions Burke's use of "Idem sentire" (p. 166). Contrary to the usual belief, the "Burkean" approach to party was not quite unknown in America. There was a "Constitutional Society" in Philadelphia, which proclaimed in the *Pennsylvania Gazette* of April 28, 1779, the following: "We will, as a 'party' support men and measures which will promise happiness and prosperity to the state, no matter who originates them. ... We will not support men and measures merely because of formal connection." Quoted by Eugene P. Link, *Democratic-Republic Societies, 1790–1800* (New York, 1942), p. 28.

130. Sir Lewis Namier, "Monarchy and the Party System," in his *Personalities and Powers* (London, 1955), p. 14.

131. This development had been in the making in the nineties, of course. But if John Adams was more identified with a party than Washington, he had to concede party leadership to Hamilton; thus a delay happened in the coincidence of executive rule and party leadership, which makes Jefferson's election so significant.

132. *Papers*, I, 84.

133. *Papers*, V, 85. See also the "Phocion" essays, *ibid.*, III, 496.

134. *Ibid.*, V, 70.

135. *Federalist*, No. 26, p. 168.

136. *Ibid.*, No. 65, p. 439. Similarly, Madison anticipated more than ad hoc combinations when he spoke of "preexisting parties" in *Federalist*, No. 49, p. 342.

137. Spelman's phrase quoted above, p. 111.

138. *Federalist*, No. 70, p. 475.

139. *Ibid.*, No. 81, p. 544; No. 85, p. 590.

140. "The Significance of the Section in American History," in Turner, *The Significance of Sections in American History* (New York, 1932), esp. p. 27. Of Madison's theory it has been said that with one "tremendous exception," the Civil War, "Madison's prognosis, as well as his diagnosis, has been surprisingly correct." B. F. Wright, Jr., "*The Federalist* on the Nature of Political Man," *Ethics*, LIX, No. 1, Part II, p. 26. However, the Civil War and the developments leading up to it really proved Madison's theory wanting; on the other hand, Hamilton's more pessimistic apprehensions about the sectional character of American parties were borne out.

141. An illuminating as well as amusing incident illustrates Madison's realism and shows that the liberal theory of universal corruption by power was taken with a grain of salt when concrete issues blurred universal principles of human nature. Gouverneur Morris was at the forefront of the Easterners who feared a future southern and western agrarian majority; regarding future representatives from the West he said: "The Busy haunts of men not the remote wilderness, was the proper School of political Talents. If the Western people get the power into their hands they will ruin the Atlantic interests. The Back members are always most averse to the best measures." (Farrand, I, 583.) Madison retorted that he was "not a little surprised to hear this implicit confidence urged by a member who on all occasions, had inculcated So strongly, the political depravity of men, and the necessity of checking one vice and interest by opposing to them another vice & interest. . . . But his reasoning was not only inconsistent with his former reasoning, but with itself. at the same time that he recommended this implicit confidence to the Southern States in the Northern Majority, he was still more zealous in exhorting all to a jealousy of a Western majority. To reconcile the gentln. with himself it must be imagined that he determined the human character by the points of the compass." (*Ibid.*, p. 584.)

142. *Ibid.*, p. 466 (Madison's notes).

143. *Papers*, V, 22. Also *ibid.*, p. 62.

144. *Federalist*, No. 6, p. 28; No. 7, p. 43; No. 8, p. 44; No. 12, p. 76.

145. *Ibid.*, p. 80.

146. The evidence presented for Hamilton should advise us to be cautious in taking Madison's theory for more than it is worth. A scrutiny of Hamilton's writings does not uphold Binkley's dictum that "the men who framed the Constitution" believed that "public policies would be determined by transitory majorities. . . . The fathers evidently expected such an ad hoc

combination to dissolve as soon as its purposes had been consummated."
Binkley, p. vii.

147. Paltsits, p. 189. Quoted from Hamilton's so-called Original Major
Draft, which was the basis of Washington's Final Manuscript. Hamilton's
major draft incorporated some phrases and ideas of earlier drafts by Madison
and Washington. The part to be discussed, however, is authentically Hamilton's, as a careful investigation of all the relevant documents assembled in the
work by Paltsits confirms. Despite the unusual punctuation, and although
Hamilton's formulation was obviously a rough draft, I have quoted from this
draft rather than from Washington's Final Manuscript, since the published
version of the address is better known. In the section discussed, Washington
did not make a single substantive or even large stylistic change, except to de-
lete one paragraph.

148. *Ibid.* (Hamilton's Original Major Draft.)

149. *Ibid.*, pp. 189–90. (Hamilton's Original Major Draft.) I have si-
lently corrected spelling errors. See also Hamilton's Draft for Incorporating,
p. 203, and Washington's Final Manuscript, p. 149.

150. See also above, pp. 71, 77, 84.

151. Fisher Ames, in a letter of 1802, *The Works of Fisher Ames*, ed. Seth
Ames, I, 310. Hamilton as early as 1787, in his great Convention speech, referred to the support of "so many of the wise & good" in his admiration for
the British government. Farrand, I, 288 (Madison's notes). In view of this,
Hamilton's protestations in the final paper of *The Federalist* that the accusations against "the wealthy, the well-born and the great, have been such as to
inspire the disgust of all sensible men" sound more rhetorical than he would
have liked. *Federalist*, p. 589. One should note, however, the peculiarly
Hamiltonian slant, ". . . the great"!

152. Hume, III, 576.

153. *Federalist*, p. 126. See also the reference to Sir William Temple's
work on the Netherlands on p. 127.

154. Paltsits, p. 190.

155. *Ibid.*

156. Hume, III, p. 578.

157. Cf. the arguments advanced in a Cabinet paper of 1792, *Papers*,
XII, 252. Also above, p. 98.

158. Madison, *Writings*, VI, 86. The concept of mutual checks reflects
the theory of the tenth *Federalist*. See also his letter to Jefferson of Oct. 24,
1787: "Divide et impera, the reprobated maxim of tyranny, is, under certain
qualifications, the only policy by which a republic can be administered on
just principles." Madison, *Letters and Other Writings*, I, 353.

159. Paltsits, p. 191 (Hamilton's Original Major Draft). Cf. also *Works*,
IX, 30 (*Defense of the Funding System*). Cf. John Adams's statement in his

Defence of the Constitutions: "All nations, under all governments, must have parties; the great secret is to control them. There are but two ways, either by a monarchy and standing army, or by a balance in the constitution." Adams, *Works*, IV, 587–88.

160. King wrote that in England "not only the public opinion, but what is more unconquerable, the *private interests* of many individuals" would oppose changes in the established system of national commerce. *Camillus*, No. 23, *Works*, V, 490. Adam Smith had written that an entire restoration of free trade in Great Britain was as absurd as the expectation of an Oceana or Utopia. "Not only the prejudices of the public, but what is much more unconquerable, the private interests of many individuals, irresistibly oppose it." Smith, pp. 437–38.

161. Paltsits, p. 183.

162. See Jay's *Federalist*, No. 2 (cf. also above, n. 112), and Madison's No. 49, p. 340: ". . . that veneration which time bestows on every thing, and without which perhaps the wisest and freest governments would not possess the requisite stability."

163. Hume, III, 62, 63.

164. Samuel Eliot Morison, *The Life and Letters of Harrison Gray Otis*, 2 vols. (Boston, 1913), I, 52.

165. To James Monroe, June 4, 1793, *The Works of Thomas Jefferson*, ed. P. L. Ford (Federal Edition, New York, 1904), VII, 361–62.

166. "The Stand," *Works*, VI, 274f. Cf. Hamilton's letter to William L. Smith, April 10, 1797, in a paragraph omitted in *Works*, X, 256, but quoted by Adair and Harvey, "Was Hamilton a Christian Statesman?," p. 316, n. 10.

167. "Detector," *Works*, VI, p. 319. See also "The War in Europe," *ibid.*, pp. 331–32.

168. "Lucius Crassus" Essays, *Works*, VIII, 289.

169. *Papers*, X, 249, 254, 270–71. Mitchell, II, 145–46. Cf. Machiavelli, *Discourses*, bk. II, ch. III, and Francis Bacon's essay on the "True greatness of the Kingdom of Britain." Also White, "Bacon's Imperialism," p. 477.

170. *Works*, VIII, 289.

171. To James A. Bayard, April 1802, *Works*, X, 433.

172. Hamilton's outline, Farrand, I, 311.

173. *Works*, X, 434.

CHAPTER IV

1. Hartz, p. 84.

2. Farrand, I, 401. For Pinckney's draft, see *ibid.*, IV, 28ff.

3. *Ibid.*, I, 398.

4. Farrand, I, 402. My italics.

5. *Ibid.*, pp. 466–67.

6. See Hans J. Morgenthau, *The Purpose of American Politics* (New York, 1960), pp. 11ff.

7. Elliot, III, 53.

8. *Ibid.*, p. 135.

9. John Dickinson, "Letters of Fabius," in Ford, *Pamphlets*, p. 202.

10. For a more detailed examination, see Gilbert, pp. 36; also Stourzh, *Franklin*, pp. 117ff.

11. Clark, p. 10.

12. *Ibid.*, p. 17.

13. Montesquieu, *Spirit*, bk. IX, ch. ii, pp. 127–28.

14. Leo Strauss, *The Political Philosophy of Hobbes* (Chicago, 1952), p. 161.

15. *Ibid.*

16. Aristotle, *Politics*, ed., E. Barker (Oxford, 1946), bk. VII, 1325a, p. 286.

17. *Ibid.*, 1324b, p. 285.

18. *Ibid.*, 1325a, p. 286.

19. *Ibid.*, 1334a, pp. 319–20.

20. Machiavelli, *Discourses*, bk. I, ch. vi, p. 128.

21. *Ibid.*, p. 129.

22. *Ibid.*, pp. 128–29.

23. See above all Edwin D. Dickinson, *The Equality of States in International Law* (Cambridge, Mass., 1920). See also Walter Schiffer, *The Legal Community of Mankind* (New York, 1954), p. 50; and Cox, *passim*.

24. *Works*, V, 422 (Essay XX). See also Essays XXIX and XXX, written by Rufus King, *ibid.*, VI, 77 and 88. Hamilton's partition of the Law of Nations into necessary, voluntary, conventional, and customary categories (V, 422) is taken from the Preface of Vattel's *The Law of Nations*—see the edition in the series *Classics of International Law* (Carnegie Institution of Washington, D.C., 1916), III, 11a. The quote by Hamilton given in the text paraphrases parts of Vattel's Introduction, sect. 21, III, 7–8. It is interesting to recall that Vattel openly acknowledged his debt to Hobbes's work, which "in spite of its paradoxes and its detestable principles, shows us the hand of the master—Hobbes, I repeat, was the first, to my knowledge, to give us a distinct though imperfect idea of the Law of Nations." Vattel, p. 5a. See the interesting references to the principle of the equality of states by Luther Martin and Hamilton in the Federal Convention. Farrand, I, 440, 472, 477.

25. Vattel, p. 7 (Introduction, sect. 18). Cf. Chief Justice John Marshall's pronouncement that "no principle of general law is more universally acknowledged than the perfect equality of nations. Russia and Geneva have equal rights," in the case of *The Antelope* (1825), quoted by Charles E.

Martin, *The Policy of the United States as Regards Intervention* (New York, 1921), p. 293.

26. See G. E. Lavau, "Valeur présente de la souveraineté des États," *Esprit*, XXIII (March 1955), 355–70.

27. See Quincy Wright, "International Law and Ideologies," *American Journal of International Law*, XLVIII (October 1954), 616–26.

28. Cf. Woodrow Wilson's address to the United States Senate, January 22, 1917: "The equality of nations upon which peace must be founded if it is to last must be an equality of rights; the guarantees exchanged must neither recognize nor imply a difference between big nations and small, between those that are powerful and those that are weak. Right must be based upon the common strength, not upon the individual strength, of the nations upon whose concert peace will depend. Equality of territory or of resources there of course cannot be; nor any other sort of equality not gained in the ordinary peaceful and legitimate development of the peoples themselves. But no one asks or expects anything more than an equality of rights. Mankind is looking now for freedom of life, not for equipoises of power." H. S. Commager, *Documents of American History*, 7th ed. (New York, 1963), II, 126. See also the discussion in Stourzh, "Ideologie und Machtpolitik als Diskussionsthemen der amerikanischen aussenpolitischen Literatur," *Vierteljahreshefte für Zeitgeschichte*, III (January 1955), 111.

29. Montesquieu, *Spirit*, bk. XI, ch. v, pp. 150–51.

30. Regarding English and American writers of the "empirical" tradition, beginning with Bacon, a valuable start has been made in the selections edited by Wolfers and Martin, including the very important essay by Wolfers, "Political Theory and International Relations."

31. Harrington, p. 32. For Adams's indebtedness to Harrington, see Haraszti, pp. 34–35.

32. Sidney, "Discourses upon Government," in *Works*, ch. II, sect. 22, p. 174. Sidney's concept of an expanding republican commonwealth is dealt with in the unpublished dissertation by Angelika Jaeger, "Algernon Sidney's 'Empire for Increase' " (Free University of Berlin, 1970).

33. Sidney, ch. II, sect 22, p. 174.

34. *Ibid.*, sect. 23, p. 179.

35. Machiavelli, *Discourses*, bk. I, ch. vi, pp. 129–30.

36. Hobbes, part II, ch. xxv, p. 172. On Hobbes's assertion of the primacy of foreign policy, see Leo Strauss, *The Political Philosophy of Hobbes*, pp. 162–63.

37. *Federalist*, No. 8, p. 45.

38. Aristotle, *Politics*, 1333b, pp. 318–19.

39. Machiavelli, *Discourses*, bk. I, ch. vi, p. 128.

40. Montesquieu, *Spirit*, bk. VIII, ch. xvi, p. 120. The difference between

Machiavelli's and Montesquieu's evaluation of Sparta has recently been pointed out by Gennaro Sasso, *Studi su Machiavelli* (Naples, 1967), pp. 234–35, n. 16.

41. Cf. his ideas on the defectiveness of the Agrarian Law, bk. I, ch. xxxvii, pp. 208–9.

42. Sidney, ch. II, sect. 5, p. 80, and ch. III, sect. 44, pp. 498–500. Sidney's importance in suggesting to Montesquieu prescriptions for "modern" policies the system of representation, is often ignored. But he is quoted in book XI of *Spirit of the Laws*, p. 155. An interesting study of Sidney's influence on Montesquieu is Walter Struck's *Montesquieu als Politiker. Historische Studien*, No. 228 (Berlin, 1933), pp. 281 ff.

43. See the analysis of Montesquieu's *Considérations sur les causes de la grandeur des Romains et de leur décadence* in Roger B. Oake's article "Montesquieu's Analysis of Roman History," *Journal of the History of Ideas*, XVI (January 1955), 44–59, and recently the Introduction by David Lowenthal to his translation, *Considerations on the Causes of the Greatness of the Romans and their Decline* (New York, 1965), pp. 1–20.

44. Montesquieu, *Spirit*, bk. VIII, ch. xvi, p. 120.

45. *Federalist*, No. 6, p. 30.

46. On the different stages of the polemics on "universal monarchy" see the excellent article by Adolf Rein, "Über die Bedeutung der überseeischen Ausdehnung für das europäische Staatensystem," in *Historische Zeitschrift*, CXXXVII (1927–28), 28–90.

47. *Réflexions sur la Monarchie universelle*, in *Deux opuscules de Montesquieu, publiés par le Baron de Montesquieu* (Paris, 1891), p. 20. Rein's article makes no mention of Montesquieu's work, as he omits Montesquieu in general in his discussion of the foreign policy views of the *philosophes*. The editor of the *Réflexions* thought Montesquieu might have been influenced by Fénelon's *Directions pour la conscience d'un roi*, which contained instructions on the need for alliances against any superior power manifestly tending toward *"la Monarchie universelle."* Montesquieu also owned a book of an Austrian statesman, Baron Franz von Lisola, that argued against universal monarchy. One of the most fascinating attacks on universal monarchy in English is Charles Davenant's *Essay Upon Universal Monarchy*, published with *The Ballance of Power* and *The Right of Making War, Peace and Alliances* (London, 1701). Davenant anticipated Gibbon in asking whether in a universal monarchy "afflickted Virtue" was not "without any Place or Refuge?" (p. 292).

48. Montesquieu, *Spirit*, bk. IV, ch. vii, p. 37. The crucial character of this chapter has been stressed in the doctoral dissertation by David Lowenthal, "An Inquiry Into the Moral Foundations of Montesquieu's *De l'Esprit des Lois*," New School for Social Research, New York, 1953, p. 183. See now Lowenthal's essay "Montesquieu and the Classics: Republican Govern-

ment in The Spirit of the Laws," in Joseph Cropsey, ed., *Ancients and Moderns. Essays on the Tradition of Political Philosophy in Honor of Leo Strauss* (New York, 1964), pp. 258–87.

49. Machiavelli, *Discourses*, bk. II, ch. x ("Money Is Not the Sinews of War, Although It Is Generally So Considered"). Bacon, Essay XXIX, "Of the True Greatness of Kingdoms and Estates," p. 329.

50. Hobbes, ch. XXIV, p. 164.

51. *Papers*, II, 620. My italics.

52. *Federalist*, No. 30, p. 182.

53. Montesquieu, *Réflexions*, pp. 14–15.

54. Mably, *Principes des négotiations, pour servir d'introduction au droit public de l'Europe, fondé sur les traités*, in *Collection complète*, V, 25, 26–27. My translation. For Hamilton's use of it in No. 6 of *The Federalist*, see below, p. 153. The impact of Machiavelli's *Discourses* on Mably's analysis is striking and deserves detailed investigation. It is neglected in the most recent and otherwise most thorough study by Ernst Reibstein, "Die Völkerrechts-kasuistik des Abbé de Mably," *Zeitschrift für ausländisches öffentliches Recht und Völkerrecht*, XVIII (December 1957), 229–60.

55. *Federalist*, No. 8, p. 47. See also No. 7, pp. 40–41.

56. *Ibid.*, No. 12, p. 73. See the examination of the eighteenth-century meaning of "commerce" by Walton H. Hamilton and Douglass Adair, *The Power to Govern* (New York, 1937). In their most telling description, "Commerce was then more than we imply now by business or industry. It was a name for the economic order, the domain of political economy, the realm of a comprehensive public policy" (pp. 62–63).

57. *The Continentalist*, no. IV, *Papers*, II, 671.

58. *Federalist*, no. 30, p. 192.

59. To James Duane, Sept. 3, 1780, *Papers*, II, 412.

60. *Federalist*, No. 34, p. 211. Similarly, in an earlier paper Hamilton had asked for a navy "if we mean to be a commercial people"! No. 24, p. 157.

61. Smith, p. 412. Montesquieu, *Réflexions*, p. 14.

62. Montesquieu, *Spirit*, bk. XX, ch. xxiii, p. 328.

63. *Ibid.*, ch. ii, p. 316.

64. *Ibid.*, ch. iv, p. 318.

65. *Ibid.*, bk. XXI, ch. xxi, pp. 367–68. Cf. the reference in *Camillus*, no. 23, actually written by Rufus King. *Works*, V, 487. (King wrongly cited ch. xvii.)

66. *Works*, V, 484. Written by Rufus King.

67. Montesquieu, *Spirit*, bk. XXI, ch. xx, p. 366.

68. *Ibid.*, bk. XX, ch. vii, p. 321. Similar hopes were voiced by Mably, *Principes des négotiations*, in *Collection complète*, V, 70.

69. The argument that Hamilton was not the author of the "Caesar" let-

ters directed against "Cato" has been presented convincingly by J. E. Cooke, "Alexander Hamilton's Authorship of the 'Caesar' Letters," *William and Mary Quarterly*, 3d Series, XVII (1960), 78–85. See also Rossiter, *Hamilton*, p. 316, n. 36.

70. "Letters of 'Cato,' " in Ford, *Essays*, p. 274. On the authorship of the letters of "Cato" see Linda Grant De Pauw, *The Eleventh Pillar—New York State and the Federal Constitution* (Ithaca, 1966), Appendix A, pp. 283–92.

71. The author is presumed to have been James Winthrop; see Ford, *Essays*, pp. 94, 109.

72. Gilbert, p. 49; refers to Adams, *Works*, II, 488–89.

73. James Burgh, whose isolationist opposition to "continental connections" is discussed by Gilbert (pp. 35–36), may also have influenced Adams's outlook, quite likely in a double way: directly (Adams's enthusiasm about Burgh's *Political Disquisitions* is stressed by Gilbert) as well as indirectly, as a possible and probable source for *Common Sense*. For Burgh as well as for Paine, wars were a peculiarly princely business, the business of "a couple of frantic and mischievous fiends in human shape, commonly called kings." Burgh, II, 342. These "fiends in human shape" might well have been an inspiration for Paine's ideas on "the royal Brute of Great Britain."

74. Montesquieu said that "the disadvantage of a colony that loses the liberty of commerce is visibly compensated by the protection of the mother country, who defends it by her arms, or supports it by her laws." *Spirit*, bk. XXI, ch. xxi, p. 368. What was more natural, indeed, than that the colonies should recover the liberty of commerce if the mother country ceased to dispense the compensating boon of protection? For Montesquieu, freedom of commerce was the privilege of an independent nation. Our general notions of mercantilism have tended to obscure that distinction, which was quite clear in Montesquieu's mind and also, it seems, in Adams's. A clue is given by Adams's separation of "political" and "commercial" connection in 1776. He did *not* have in mind the distinction that nowadays might be made between a treaty of alliance and a treaty of commerce. Under "political connection" he understood actual submission to the French government, replacing the British yoke by the French. "Submit to none of her authority, receive no governors or officers from her," he added (quoted by Gilbert, p. 49). About a decade later, Adams made a revealing reply to Turgot's complaint against the British "spirit of monopoly," shared by all writers except Adam Smith and Dean Josiah Tucker: "The system of monopoly and exclusion here meant is probably the Navigation Act. This system is not peculiar to England: France, Spain, Portugal, Holland, and all other nations practice it, *at least with regard to their colonies*" (my italics). Quoted in Haraszti, p. 143.

75. See the careful analysis of the treaty, which "can be regarded as Adams's work," by Gilbert, pp. 50ff. I cannot fully agree with Gilbert's an-

alysis of the background of Adams's theories on foreign policy. His extensive analysis (pp. 56–66) of the French physiocrats' and philosophes' hopes that free commerce would be an antidote to power politics omits Montesquieu, who would fit in many respects into the pattern Gilbert suggests. An example would be Montesquieu's praise of the diplomacy of a free and trading nation in the famous Chapter 27 of Book XIX of *Spirit of the Laws* (p. 312). I would like to stress more strongly than Professor Gilbert does the interdependence of forms of government and the conduct of foreign affairs. Montesquieu emphatically related commerce to forms of government, and free commerce to free nations. This interdependence was also a characteristic element of the radical Whig tradition to which Burgh and Paine, whose importance is rightly stressed by Gilbert, belonged. Monarchy was characteristically linked by the radical Whigs with the use of "standing armies"; these were among the most terrible threats to liberty. See Lois G. Schwoerer, "The Literature of the Standing Army Controversy, 1697–1699," *Huntington Library Quarterly*, XXVIII (1965), 187–212, and J. G. A. Pocock, "Machiavelli, Harrington, and English Political Ideologies in the Eighteenth Century," *William and Mary Quarterly*, 3d series, XXII (October 1965), pp. 562ff. "Trade and Naval Power the Offspring of Civil Liberty only, and cannot subsist without it"—this is the title of a pertinent chapter in Gordon and Trenchard, II, 267–78 (no. 64). James Burgh echoes *Cato*'s ideas in his chapter entitled "A Militia with the Navy, the only proper Security of a free people in an insular Situation, both against foreign Invasion and domestic Tyranny" (II, 389ff). The physiocrats, however, pleaded not for a less absolute, but only a more enlightened monarchical regime. One philosophe who most emphatically stressed the need for popular control of foreign policy and proposed a number of interesting devices (discussed by Gilbert, pp. 64–65), was the Marquis de Condorcet. He published these views in 1787 in a work that shows the impact of the American republic on the younger generation of the French Enlightenment, "Lettres d'un bourgeois de New-Haven à un citoyen de la Virginie."

76. Aug. 10, 1785, in *Works*, VIII, 298–99. In private comments on Turgot's letter to Richard Price (regarding Price's *Importance of the American Revolution*), published by Price after Turgot's death, Adams's tone is somewhat different, more aggressive, less complaining: "It is not to be doubted that the abolition of [the system of monopoly and exclusion] in all nations would be a blessing to mankind: but it is a question whether one nation who should abolish it, while the rest maintain it, would not be ruined by their liberality. National pride is as natural as self-love, or family pride, the pride of one city, county, or province.... It is, at present, the bulwark of defense to all nations. When it is lost, a nation sinks below the character of man." (Haraszti, p. 143.) "An enemy to embargoes, prohibitions, exclusions, etc. in general, I cannot swear that they are always unlawful or impolitic" (Harasz-

ti, p. 147). By 1803, after the experience of the French Revolution, Adams came to the conclusion that it was "the principle of nations as well as of princes" to aggrandize themselves as much as their power would permit. This was written on the margin of Frederick the Great's *Considerations on the Present Political Situation of Europe*, which had asserted this only regarding princes! Quoted by Alfred Iacuzzi, *John Adams, Scholar* (New York, 1952), p. 204.

77. Smith, bk. iv, ch. ii, p. 431.

78. *Federalist*, No. 6, pp. 28–29. Much of the argument and materials used in these papers of *The Federalist* Hamilton drew from his great speech in the Federal Convention on June 18, 1787.The correlation between Hamilton's outline to this speech and the papers in *The Federalist* has been established in detail in Adair, "Authorship," p. 247.

79. *Federalist*, No. 6, p. 31.

80. *Ibid.*, p. 31.

81. *Ibid.*, p. 32. Felix Gilbert has observed that "the Sixth Federalist Paper must be seen as a fundamental and thorough criticism of the currently fashionable views of the philosophes and of the physiocrats on foreign policy." Review of Schachner's biography of Hamilton in *William and Mary Quarterly*, 3d series, IV (April 1947), 238. However, this opinion stands in need of revision precisely because of the connection between forms of government and styles of foreign policy at the core of Hamilton's polemic. Hamilton was aiming at Montesquieu with the refutation of the contention that the genius of republics was pacific. Montesquieu rather than philosophes and physiocrats gravely taxed the attention of republican nation builders. For a particularly vivid example, see the speech of James Bowdoin, Jr., in the Massachusetts Ratifying Convention: "Baron Montesquieu observes, that all governments ought to be relative to their particular principles, and that 'a confederative government ought to be composed of states of the same nature, especially of the republican kind'; and instances that, as 'the spirit of monarchy is war and enlargement of dominion, peace and moderation are the spirit of a republic.' These two kinds of government cannot naturally subsist in a confederate republic." In Elliot, II, 126.

82. *Federalist*, No. 6, p. 33. Cf. Montesquieu: "It is contrary to the spirit of monarchy to admit the nobility into commerce. The custom of suffering the nobility of England to trade is one of those things which have there mostly contributed to weaken the monarchical government. *Spirit*, bk. XX, ch. xxi, p. 327.

83. *Federalist*, No. 6, p. 29.

84. *Ibid.*, pp. 29–30.

85. *Ibid.*, pp. 31–32. Cf. the actual text of *Federalist* No. 6 with Charles A. Beard's interpretation in the section on "The Economics of International Politics" in his *An Economic Interpretation of the Constitution of the*

United States (New York, 1913), pp. 183ff. Particularly instructive is Beard's rendering of Hamilton's reference to the struggle between the Habsburgs and the Bourbons (*Federalist*, No. 6, p. 33), which fully justifies the comment by Brown (p. 111): Beard "used Hamilton to prove a point that Hamilton did not prove, namely, that foreign and domestic controversies are based primarily on commercial antagonisms." See also Stourzh, "Charles A. Beard's Interpretations of American Foreign Policy," *World Affairs Quarterly*, XXVIII (July 1957), 111–48, esp. 122–25.

86. *Federalist*, No. 6, p. 33.

87. *Ibid.*, No. 4, pp. 18–19. In 1778, Jay had told the French Minister in Philadelphia the constitution of "our empire" was "inconsistent with the passion for conquest." Quoted in Weinberg, p. 19, from George Bancroft, *History of the United States of America* (New York, 1884), V, 305.

88. *Federalist*, No. 6, p. 35. Cf. Hamilton's remark in 1798 that at the close of the Revolutionary War, "the phantom of perpetual peace danced before the eyes of everybody." "The Stand," *Works*, VI, 304–5.

89. *Federalist*, p. 35. Cf. Farrand, I, 307. Hamilton's argument that neighbors are natural enemies, regardless of whether the states are republican or not, played a large role in the debates of the Virginia Ratifying Convention. The Virginia advocates of the Federal Constitution were acquainted with *The Federalist* by the time the Convention met. (See Adair, "Authorship," p. 236, n. 3). Edmund Randolph was particularly emphatic that nations bordering on each other were bound to clash in "bloodshed and slaughter." (Elliot, III, 75). Patrick Henry retorted that Randolph had forgotten "that there were no tyrants in America, as there are in Europe. The citizens of republican borders are only terrible to tyrants. Instead of being dangerous to one another, they mutually support one another's liberties." (Elliot, p. 145). In a line of reasoning not quite unlike John Jay's, Patrick Henry said: "A republic has this advantage over a monarchy, that its wars are generally founded on more just grounds. A republic can never enter into a war, unless it be a national war—unless it be approved of, or desired, by the whole community." (Elliot, p. 172). Randolph, in words reminiscent of *Federalist* No. 6, disabused Henry of his distinction between the "pacific meekness" of republics and the "barbarous ferocity" of monarchies: "The danger results from the situation of borderers, and not from the nature of the government under which they live." (Elliot, p. 197). He also argued vigorously against Henry's treating "the idea of commercial hostility as extravagant. History might inform him of its reality. Experience might give him some instruction on the subject" (Elliot, pp. 192–93).

90. Mably, *Principes des négotiations*, in *Collection complète*, V, 93. For Mably's indebtedness to the foreign policy doctrines of Machiavelli's *Discourses*, see Mably, *Principes*, pp. 18, 20ff, 30, 40.

91. *Federalist*, No. 6, pp. 35–36.

92. Montesquieu, *Spirit*, bk. IX, ch. i, p. 126.

93. *Federalist*, No. 9, p. 53.

94. *Ibid.*

95. To James Duane, *Papers*, II, 405.

96. Aristotle, *Politics*, 1265a, p. 57. Aristotle criticized Plato's provision in the *Laws* for five thousand arms-bearing citizens: "We cannot overlook the fact that such a number will require a territory of the size of Babylon or some such space . . . to support 5,000 persons in idleness, especially when we reflect that they will be augmented by a crowd of women and attendants many times as great as themselves." See also *Politics*, 1326a and 1326b.

97. See especially W. W. Tarn, "Alexander the Great and the Unity of Mankind," *Proceedings of the British Academy*, XIX (1933), 142.

98. See Cropsey, *Polity and Economy*, p. 66, on Smith's stand in "the age-old controversy as to the optimum size of the political entity," and the reference to bk. I, ch. viii, of the *Wealth of Nations*.

99. One of the most assiduous citers of Montesquieu in this respect was the author of the "Letters of 'Cato.' " Proponents of the new Constitution, like James Wilson, in the Pennsylvania Ratifying Convention, agreed on the "right" size of the individual states. The difference arose over whether the proposed Union was a confederation in Montesquieu's sense or a consolidated government. For Wilson and others, see Spurlin, p. 206. Others impressed with Montesquieu's argument were "Agrippa" (Winthrop) of Massachusetts (see Ford, *Essays*, pp. 64 and 92), Elbridge Gerry (Ford, *Pamphlets*, pp. 13–14), and A. C. Hanson (*ibid.*, p. 248), though they disagreed on the nature of the Federal Constitution.

100. Elliot, II, 126, 128–29.

101. *Federalist*, No. 9, pp. 52–53. Also in the New York Ratifying Convention, *Works*, II, 67.

102. Hume, "Idea of a Perfect Commonwealth, in Hendel, p. 157.

103. By Douglass Adair, in his article " 'That Politics May Be Reduced to a Science': David Hume, James Madison, and the Tenth *Federalist*," *Huntington Library Quarterly*, XX (August 1957), 343–60. These connections were first presented by Adair in his dissertation "The Intellectual Origins of Jeffersonian Democracy," Yale University, 1943. Independently of Adair, they were pointed out by Marshall, pp. 255–56. The study by Ralph L. Ketcham, "Notes on James Madison's Sources for the Tenth Federalist Paper," *Midwest Journal of Political Science*, I (May 1957), 20–25, is based on Adair's dissertation. Americans who openly criticized Montesquieu's principle of small size included William Vans Murray, mentioned above, one of whose sketches was entitled "Extent of Territory." See also E. Randolph and Corbin in the Virginia Ratifying Convention, Elliot, III, 85, 107–8. For later polemics against Montesquieu, repeating Madison's arguments, see Spurlin, pp. 242ff.

104. *Federalist*, No. 10, pp. 62–64.

105. *Ibid.*, p. 172.

106. *Ibid.*

107. *Ibid.*, No. 9, p. 54.

108. *Ibid.*, p. 52.

109. *Ibid.*, p. 54.

110. Mably, *Principes des négotiations*, in *Collection complète*, V, 93. My translation.

111. To James Duane, *Papers*, II, 403.

112. *Papers*, II, 656.

113. To James Duane, *Papers*, II, 401. A few months later, on February 7, 1781, he also wrote that "the republic is sick"! *Ibid.*, p. 554. This has to be contrasted with his rhetorical pleading in the New York Ratifying Convention, *ibid.*, V, 100.

114. Farrand, I, 293; for Hamilton's explanations, see *ibid.*, p. 323.

115. See the enlightening comments by Adair, "Authorship," p. 250.

116. See the pertinent remarks by Mason, pp. 639–40. See also Gottfried Dietze, *The Federalist—A Classic on Federalism and Free Government* (Baltimore, 1960), pp. 268–73.

117. E.g., *Federalist*, No. 13; No. 23, p. 149; No. 27, pp. 173f; No. 28, p. 177; No. 29, p. 181. Also, in the New York Ratifying Convention, *Papers*, V, 100.

118. *Federalist*, No. 9, p. 55. My italics.

119. *Ibid.*, p. 147. For a remarkable and important earlier invocation of the "spirit," if not the "letter," of the Confederation, and of argument by "implication," see Hamilton's report to the Continental Congress on Impost Duty, December 1782, *Papers*, III, 219; see also p. 216.

120. *Federalist*, No. 34, p. 211. Further strong statements of the theory of implied powers are in No. 30, pp. 189–90; No. 31, pp. 193–94, 196; No. 33, pp. 204ff; No. 36, p. 229. Cf. Madison in No. 44, pp. 304–5. See also Hamilton in the New York Ratifying Convention, *Papers*, V, 97–99.

121. To Lafayette, Jan. 6, 1799, *Works*, X, 337.

122. Joseph de Maistre, *Oeuvres* (Paris, 1875), I, 68, quoted by Becker, p. iii.

123. To James Duane, Sept. 3, 1780, *Papers*, II, 411. Also *ibid.*, p. 402. For his plan of a military peace establishment in 1783, see *ibid.*, III, 378–97.

124. Farrand, I, 285 (Madison's notes). The Whisky Rebellion certainly did not change Hamilton's mind, and as late as 1798 he was as insistent as ever; see his letter to H. G. Otis, Dec. 27, 1798, *Works*, X, 325–26.

125. *Federalist*, No. 23, pp. 147, 151. Cf. No. 25, pp. 162–63; No. 28, pp. 176–80.

126. *Ibid.*, No. 13, pp. 80–81; cf. also No. 28, p. 180.

127. From Washington's final manuscript. Paltsits, p. 144. It is almost identical to Hamilton's original draft, *ibid.*, p. 185. Hamilton's reference to the states as "subdivisions" is revealing in its lack of respect, and recalls his reference to the "subordinate jurisdictions" of the states in the Federal Convention. Farrand, I, 323.

128. *Federalist*, No. 34, p. 212. Cf. No. 36, p. 229.

129. Oct. 3, 1783, *Papers*, III, 468. My italics.

130. See above, p. 115.

131. *Federalist*, No. 8, p. 49.

132. *Ibid.*, No. 24, pp. 155–56.

133. *Ibid.*, p. 156.

134. *Ibid.*, p. 157. Cf. Hamilton conjuring up the specter of "encirclement" from Maine to Georgia in No. 25, p. 158.

135. Herbert Butterfield, *Christianity and History* (London, 1949), pp. 89–90.

136. The most concise modern formulation of the primacy of internal policy is Rousseau's comment on Montesquieu's discussion of the optimum size: "One sees that there are reasons for expansion and reasons for reduction; and it is not the least talent of a statesman to find between the one and the others the proportion most advantageous for the conservation of the State. Generally, one may say that *the first, being only external and relative, should be subordinated to the latter which are internal and absolute.*" Rousseau, *Contrat social*, bk. II, ch. ix, p. 266. My translation; my italics.

137. Jan. 15, 1790. See *Papers*, X, 230, n. 125.

138. *Papers*, X, 291. My italics.

139. *Ibid.*

140. Edward M. Earle, "Adam Smith, Alexander Hamilton, Friedrich List: The Economic Foundations of Military Power," in Earle, ed., (with the collaboration of Gordon A. Craig and Felix Gilbert), *Makers of Modern Strategy. Military Thought from Machiavelli to Hitler* (Princeton, 1944), p. 130. This essay remains by far the best study of Hamilton's ideas on foreign policy.

141. *Papers*, X, 262–64.

142. See the excellent and well-documented discussion in Harold T. Parker, *The Cult of Antiquity and the French Revolutionaries* (Chicago, 1937), pp. 34, 63–64, 67, 78, 93, 105f.

143. Friedrich von Gentz, *Über den ewigen Frieden* (1800). Reprinted in Kurt von Raumer, *Ewiger Friede. Friedensrufe und Friedenspläne seit der Renaissance* (Munich, 1953), pp. 468–70. My translation.

144. *Ibid.*

145. Hume, "Of Commerce," in Hendel, p. 130. One finds a trace of this in the writings of one of the most learned of the Founders, John Dickin-

son: "No nation has existed that ever so perfectly united those distant extremes, private security of life, liberty, and property, with exertion of public
force." See Ford, *Pamphlets*, p. 211.

146. As paraphrased by Madison, in his speech of June 18 (Farrand, I,
288). Hamilton seems to have quoted Necker from memory, and the quotation marks were of course supplied by Madison when taking notes. Actually,
Necker spoke of the British Constitution as "the only one in the universe,
which has left individuals in full possession of their natural strength and
dignity, and society of its power." See Jacques Necker, *A Treatise on the
Administration of Finances*, Thomas Mortimer, tr., 3 vols. (London, 1786),
I, 60. Necker's work, first published in France in 1784, was a distinguished
representative of the school of thought that hoped for a more rational and
peaceful course of international politics as a result of the growth of "commerce." See his eloquent chapter "On War": In "our days, when the general
perfection of industry, and the knowledge of commerce have rendered the
enjoyments of nations more equal; war seems to depend more on the private
ambitions of sovereigns, and the restless spirit of their counsellors" (*Ibid.*,
III, 432). Necker, a Protestant banker from republican Geneva and twice
a high dignitary of the kingdom of France, is an authentic, if so far little-
recognized spokesman for the "new diplomacy" of the eighteenth century—
presenting certain arguments that Hamilton, in *Federalist* No. 6, would
harshly criticize (see above, pp. 148ff).

CHAPTER V

1. Paltsits, p. 163 (incorporated in Washington's draft, p. 168).
2. *Ibid.*, pp. 175 (Hamilton's Abstract of Points), 182 (Hamilton's Original Major Draft), 142 (Washington's Final Manuscript), and 153 (Washington's Final Manuscript; for the same passage in Hamilton's Original
Major Draft, see pp. 193–94). My italics. Emendations in brackets were
made by Paltsits.
3. White, p. 472.
4. *Federalist*, No. 34, p. 210; "The Stand," *Works*, VI, 281, pp. 234
and 285.
5. *Papers*, IV, 140. The occasion was Hamilton's pleading for the independence of Vermont.
6. Essay 55, "Of Honor and Reputation," in Bacon, p. 574. I have mod-
ernized punctuation by replacing single quotes surrounding Latin words with
italics. See the recent important discussion of Bacon's hierarchy of honor in
Adair, "Fame." In his *Advancement of Learning*, Bacon put the honor of
the great men of philosophy and learning above that of "founders and uniters
of states and cities, lawgivers, extirpers of tyrants, fathers of the people, and
other eminent persons in civil merit" (bk. I, ch. vii, p. 1; see also bk. I, ch.

viii, p. 6). Adair discusses the implications of the different types and categories of honor pointed out by Bacon for the different kinds of fame sought by Hamilton and by Jefferson.

7. "Of Parties in General," Hume, III, 57.

8. Quoted by Cropsey, *Polity and Economy*, p. 70, from *Theory of Moral Sentiments*, p. 206.

9. Hartz, p. 46.

10. Montesquieu, vol. 2, bk. XXIX, ch. xix ("Of Legislators"), p. 170; Montesquieu cites Aristotle, Plato, Machiavelli, Sir Thomas More, and James Harrington. That he also included himself in this august group is certain from his preface, where he quoted Corregio: *Ed io anche son pittore* (And I, too, am a painter). That the notion of the great political writers as legislators was not lost in America emerges from a curious instance. On June 21, 1788, Hugh Henry Brackenridge, thinking that with the ratification by Virginia the Union had come into being, made the following remarks in Pittsburgh: "A union of nine states has taken place, and you are now citizens of a new empire: an empire not the effect of chance, nor hewn out by the sword; but formed by the skill of sages, and the design of wise men. . . . O noble pile! On the four sides of thy pedestal are the names of the patriots who framed thee. At a distance are the shades of Plato, Montesquieu, and Hume. They rise from Elysium, and contemplate a structure which they may have imagined, but could never have expected to see upon the earth." Quoted by Spurlin, p. 219. Hume is included, of course, as author of the essay "Idea of the Perfect Commonwealth."

11. John Adams to Mercy Warren, Jan. 8, 1776, in *Warren-Adams Letters*, vol. I (1743–77), p. 202. Similarly, Theophilus Parsons wrote in the "Essex Result" of 1778: "Was it asked, what is the best form of government for the people of the Massachusetts-Bay? We confess it would be a question of infinite importance: and the man who could truly answer it, would merit a statue of gold to his memory, *and his fame would be recorded in the annals of late posterity, with unrivalled lustre.*" Parsons, p. 365. My italics.

12. "Publius Letters, III," *Papers*, I, 580–81. I first called attention to the significance of this passage in my paper "Alexander Hamilton—The Theory of Empire Building" delivered at the AHA meeting in New York, Dec. 30, 1957 (see Adair, "Fame," p. 40, n. 14).

13. *Federalist*, p. 239–40.

14. *Ibid.*, p. 241.

15. *Ibid.*, p. 240.

16. Adam Ferguson, *An Essay on the History of Civil Society*. First published 1767. New edition, with introduction by Duncan Forbes (Edinburgh, 1966), p. 4.

17. For the clash between the old individual- and politics-centered view of history and the new group- and society-centered one, see Duncan Forbes, "'Scientific Whiggism': Adam Smith and John Millar," *Cambridge Journal*, VII (1953–54), 643–70. To illustrate the significance of this clash for the problem discussed in this chapter, I would like to juxtapose two eighteenth-century writers, a "modern" and an "ancient." Gilbert Stuart, in *An Historical Dissertation Concerning the Antiquity of the English Constitution* (1768), pp. 222–23 (quoted by Forbes, p. 655), said: "Historians, judging of rude times by the standards of a cultivated age, have frequently concluded that the establishments which arise in society are the result of intention and design. They seek for legislators before legislators could exist." On the opposite side was John Gillies, the noted translator of Aristotle. From a study of the rule of Frederick the Great in Prussia, he returned "with satisfaction and increased confidence" to studying the "statesmen and generals of ancient times, whose history as related by Greek and Roman writers, can no longer be deemed an amplification altogether beyond nature, since the example of Frederick will serve to convince modern incredulity of the wonderful revolution that may be produced by the exertions of one man, in the republic which he guides, or the kingdom which he governs." *A View of the Reign of Frederick* II (1789, pp. 502-3, quoted by Forbes, p. 659. Cf. also W. C. Lehmann, *John Millar of Glasgow 1735–1801* (Cambridge, England, 1960), including the text of Millar's "The Origin of the Distinction of Ranks."

18. Bertrand de Jouvenel, *Sovereignty. An Inquiry Into the Political Good* (Chicago, 1957), p. 21.

19. *Ibid.*; see also note to ch. iv of bk. IV of the *Contrat social*.

20. The notes referred to were written in the Pay Book of Hamilton's New York Artillery Company. The two main spheres of interest concerned political institutions and sexual mores. Hamilton wrote at the beginning that these notes were "selected more for their singularity than use—though some important facts are comprehended." *Papers*, I, 391. The Pay Book is now in the Hamilton Papers of the Library of Congress. The notes have been closely studied and edited, together with notes taken by Hamilton from M. Postlethwayt's *Universal Dictionary of Trade and Commerce*, by E. P. Panagopoulos, *Alexander Hamilton's Pay Book*, Wayne State University Studies, vol. 10 (Detroit, 1961). They are also to be found in *Papers*, I, pp. 373–411.

21. *Plutarch's Lives, in six volumes: Translated from the Greek. With Notes, Explanatory and Critical, from Dacier and others. To which is prefix'd the Life of Plutarch, Written by Dryden* (London, 1758), I, 96. This has been identified by the editors of the Hamilton *Papers* as the translation Hamilton used (I, 391, n. 66).

22. *Papers*, I, 396.

23. *Ibid.*

24. See above, pp. 97ff.

25. For the dating of these notes see Mitchell I, p. 100; also *Papers*, I, 373, n. 2.

26. See above, pp. 67–68.

27. *Papers*, I, 396; see also p. 392 (on Theseus) and p. 395 (on Romulus).

28. *Papers*, V, 85. My italics.

29. Jefferson's well-known remarks on the "natural aristocracy" do not refute this assertion, as a careful reading of his famous letter to John Adams of October 28, 1813, shows. See Lester J. Cappon, ed., *The Adams-Jefferson Letters*, 2 vols. (Chapel Hill, 1959), II, especially pp. 388 and 391. See also the excellent observations by John C. Livingston, "Alexander Hamilton and the American Tradition," *Midwest Journal of Political Science*, I (November 1957), 209–24, esp. 220ff.

30. "Observations on the Government of Pennsylvania (1777), in *The Selected Writings of Benjamin Rush*, ed. Dagobert Runes (New York, 1947), pp. 62–63. Rush regarded "natural distinctions of rank" as the consequence of "industry and capacity, and above all, commerce." *Ibid.*

31. See Query XIX of the *Notes on Virginia*, and Jefferson's letter to Mr. Lithson, Jan. 4, 1805, where he is doubtful about admitting to the country "at present the dissolute and demoralized handicraftsmen of the old cities of Europe." *The Writings of Thomas Jefferson*, ed. A. A. Lipscomb (Memorial Edition, Washington, D.C., 1905), XI, 56.

32. Query XIII of the *Notes on Virginia* on the separation of powers, and Jefferson's theories on "ward republics," the smallest units of government, developed in several letters between 1813 and 1816; these are discussed by Charles M. Wiltse, *The Jeffersonian Tradition in American Democracy* (Chapel Hill, 1935).

33. Jouvenel, *Sovereignty*, p. 165.

34. *Ibid.*, p. 140. My italics.

35. *Papers*, IV, 11.

36. *Ibid.*, V, 74. On the origins of the term "responsibility" in American usage of the 1780's, see the interesting observation by Douglass Adair, "The Federalist Papers, a Review Article," *William and Mary Quarterly*, 3 vols., XXII (1965), 137–38.

37. *Papers*, V, 57 and 60; see also VII, 314.

38. *Ibid.*, V, 95.

39. *Federalist*, No. 76, pp. 513–14.

40. Cecelia M. Kenyon, "Human Nature in American Political Thought," doctoral dissertation, Radcliffe College.

41. Report for the Continental Congress, Dec. 16, 1782, *Papers*, III, 222. See also Hamilton's argument against the limiting of presidential terms, in *Federalist*, No. 72.

42. The important difference between two conceptions of democratic officeholding, one based on the identity of will, the other on the concept of trust, has been lucidly discussed by Wilhelm Hennis, "Amtsgedanke und Demokratie," in a Festschrift for Rudolf Smend, *Staatsverfassung und Kirchenordnung* (Tübingen, 1962), pp. 51–70.

43. See Hamilton's exploitation of this expectation in his argument for judicial review: the judges as the standard-bearers of popular sovereignty (*Federalist*, No. 78).

44. See Ch. III, note 82.

45. *Federalist*, No. 70, p. 478.

46. *Ibid.*, No. 15, p. 96.

47. *Ibid.*, No. 74, p. 501.

48. *Ibid.*, No. 70, p. 476.

49. See above, p. 97.

50. Winston S. Churchill, *The Gathering Storm* (Boston, 1948), p. 321. Churchill precedes this with the following comment: "It is baffling to reflect that what men call honour does not correspond always to Christian ethics."

51. *Federalist*, No. 66, p. 451, speaking of the Senate. Cf. Hamilton's speech on the Senate in the New York Ratifying Convention on June 24, 1788, *Papers*, V, 73–74.

52. H. W. Stoke, *The Paradox of Representative Government*, quoted by Binkley, p. 3.

53. See the discussion above, pp. 80f, 92f. See especially Hamilton's outline of the principles of "civil obedience" for his Convention speech of June 18, 1787, in Farrand, I, 305–6; see also Madison's notes on the speech, *ibid.*, pp. 284–85.

54. *Federalist*, No. 31, p. 195. My italics.

55. New York Ratifying Convention, *Papers*, V, 85. Though there is no evidence of Hamilton's acquaintance with Burke's speech to his constituents at Bristol, the similarity of ideas is profound: "Parliament is not a *congress* of ambassadors from different and hostile interests; which interests each must maintain, as an agent and advocate, against other agents and advocates; but parliament is a *deliberative* assembly of *one* nation, with *one* interest, that of the whole.... You choose a member indeed; but when you have chosen him, he is not a member of Bristol, but he is a member of *parliament*." *The Works of Edmund Burke* (Bohn ed., London, 1881), I, 447.

56. *Federalist*, No. 30, p. 191.

57. In a report to the Continental Congress, Dec. 16, 1782, *Papers*, III, 216. See also a Cabinet paper for Washington dated May 15, 1793, in *Papers*, XIV, 459. On the European background, see the chapter on "Ratio Status: Foreign Policy in Practice" in Gilbert, pp. 76ff. On Hamilton's realism, *ibid.*, pp. 111–14.

58. *Federalist*, No. 34, p. 211. Cf. the ironic comments in No. 25, p.

161: "All that kind of policy by which nations anticipate distant danger, and meet the gathering storm, must be abstained from, as contrary to the genuine maxims of a free government."

59. To Timothy Pickering, Postmaster-General of the United States, Jan. 15, 1792. *Pickering Papers*, Massachusetts Historical Society, Boston, Mass., XIX, 250. My attention was first drawn to this letter in the excellent dissertation by Edward H. Phillips, "The Public Career of Timothy Pickering, Federalist, 1745–1802," Harvard, 1950, p. 114.

60. Circular Letter to the State Governors, June 8, 1783. Washington, XXVI, 485.

61. Hamilton to Washington, July 3, 1787, *Papers*, IV, 224; *Camillus*, No. 2, *Works*, V, 206; Hamilton to T. Sedgwick, July 10, 1804, *Works*, X, 458. There are numerous other mentions of "empire."

62. See Richard Koebner, "The Emergence of the Concept of Imperialism," *Cambridge Journal*, V (September 1952), 726–41, and Helmut Dan Schmidt, *Imperialism, The Story and Significance of a Political Word, 1840–1960* (Cambridge, England, 1964).

63. See Richard Koebner, *Empire* (Cambridge, England, 1961), pp. 1ff.

64. *Ibid.*, p. 317. Quoted from Harrington, p. 14.

65. Koebner, *Empire*, p. 58.

66. *Ibid.*, p. 59, quoted from Temple's *An Essay upon the Original and Nature of Government*, in *Works* (1720), I, 103.

67. In a letter to Lord Kames. See Stourzh, *Franklin*, p. 81.

68. For examples of the term "British Empire" before the end of the French and Indian War (now, following Lawrence H. Gipson, better called "the Great War for Empire"), see James Truslow Adams, "On the Term 'British Empire,' " *American Historical Review*, XXVII (April 1922), 485–89. Adams suggests that the political downfall of the Holy Roman Empire might have something to do with the fact that after 1763 the term "the empire" was more and more used to connote the "British Empire."

69. John Adams, *Works*, IV, 106–7.

70. *Ibid.*, pp. 173–74.

71. In a letter to George Rogers Clark, Dec. 25, 1779. Quoted by Julian P. Boyd, "Thomas Jefferson's 'Empire of Liberty,' " *The Virginia Quarterly Review*, XXIV (Autumn 1948), 549–50.

72. To the President and Legislative Council, the Speaker and the House of Representatives of the Territory of Indiana, Dec. 28, 1805, quoted by Adrienne Koch, *Jefferson and Madison: The Great Collaboration* (New York, 1950), pp. 244–45.

73. Sept. 19, 1803, quoted in *ibid.*, p. 244.

74. June 14, 1817, Koch and Peden, p. 682.

75. To John Adams, Sept. 25, 1798, in Washington, XXXVI, 461.

76. Gerald W. Johnson, *American Heroes and Hero-Worship* (New

York, 1941), p. 67. The other basis Johnson refers to is the "permanence of a substantial identity of interest among the rich and well-born."

77. Unsigned article, "Purchase of Louisiana," in the *New-York Evening Post*, July 5, 1803, identified and reprinted in Adair, "Hamilton on the Louisiana Purchase: A Newly Identified Editorial from the *New York Evening Post*," *William and Mary Quarterly*, 3rd series, XII (April 1955), 276.

78. *Ibid.*

79. *Ibid.*, p. 278, n. 13.

80. *Papers*, VII, 51, 53.

81. *Papers*, VII, 112; also p. 71.

82. See, e.g., *Camillus*, No. 2, *Works*, V, 207; and "The Stand," *Works*, VI, 284. In connection with Latin America, see, e.g., Hamilton's letter to Secretary of War McHenry of June 27, 1799, *Works*, VII, 97. Hamilton's interest in Francisco de Miranda's plans for a liberation of Latin America has received several full treatments: Bradford Perkins, *The First Rapprochement. England and the United States, 1795–1805* (Philadelphia, 1955), ch. IX, pp. 106ff; Stephen G. Kurtz, *The Presidency of John Adams* (Philadelphia, 1957), pp. 317–20; Miller, pp. 496–500; Mitchell, II, 442–47; and most recently, Robert Ernst, *Rufus King, American Federalist* (Chapel Hill, 1968), pp. 265–67.

83. To Gen. C. C. Pinckney, Dec. 29, 1802, *Works*, X, 445–46.

84. *Works*, VI, 333–36.

85. [Adair], "Hamilton on the Louisiana Purchase," p. 275. My evaluation of Hamilton's war policy in this respect is somewhat more positive than Adair's attitude of condemnation.

86. *Papers*, VII, 52f.

87. To Lafayette, Aug. 15, 1786, Washington, XXVIII, 520.

88. *Papers*, I, 56.

89. *Ibid.*, p. 129.

90. *Papers*, III, 106.

91. *Federalist*, No. 11, p. 72. Hamilton added some sardonic remarks on the theories of Cornelis Pauw (more widely associated with the Abbé Raynal) on the degeneration to which men and animals were exposed on American soil. Pauw's book, *Recherches philosophiques sur les Américains*, which Hamilton mentioned by title (without giving the author's name), was first published in 1768 and 1769, and not, as given by J. E. Cooke, in 1770. See now H. S. Commager and Elmo Giordanetti, *Was America a Mistake? An Eighteenth Century Controversy* (New York, 1967), pp. 20–21 and 75ff.

92. *Federalist*, No. 11, p. 73. This has hardly ever been recognized as a significant anticipation of the Monroe Doctrine and Henry Clay's ideas on hemispheric unity.

93. See above, n. 81.

94. *Papers*, III, 102; VII, 424.
95. *Ibid.*, p. 68.
96. *Ibid.*
97. *Federalist*, No. 11, p. 66.
98. *Papers*, VII, 49–50; *Camillus*, No. 2, *Works*, V, 207.
99. Perkins, *The First Rapprochement*, p. 27. Jefferson and Madison held "that American commerce could be used as a weapon to exact concessions from the European powers, a point of view in marked contrast to that of most Federalists, who believed that commerce was to be protected by national policy rather than made the instrument of it." Perkins quotes (*ibid.*) from a letter of Jefferson to T. Pinckney, May 29, 1797: "War is not the best engine for us to resort to, nature has given us one *in our commerce*, which, if properly managed, will be a better instrument for obliging the interested nations of Europe to treat us with justice." Jefferson's Report on Commerce is favorably discussed by Albert H. Bowman, "Jefferson, Hamilton, and American Foreign Policy," *Political Science Quarterly*, LXXI (March 1956), pp. 30ff.

100. *Camillus*, *Works*, V, pp. 256–57 and 353. For details of the credit situation, see Perkins, pp. 10ff.

101. Samuel Eliot Morison, *The Maritime History of Massachusetts*, (Boston, 1941), p. 169.

102. For Hamilton's horror of the proselytizing character of the French Revolution, see particularly "The Warning," *Works*, VI, 233; and "The Stand," *ibid.*, p. 272 ("the worst of all despotisms, a despotism over opinion"), and p. 274 ("The prominent original feature of her revolution is the spirit of proselytism, or the desire of new modelling the political institutions of the rest of the world according to her standard").

103. See, above all, Julian P. Boyd, *Number 7* (Princeton, N.J., 1964); also the significant review by S. F. Bemis in *New England Quarterly*, XXXVIII (1965), 252–55. Pertinent is Miller, p. 368; Mitchell, II, disappointingly, does not deal with the Beckwith conversations.

104. Brown, p. 53, has rightly stressed, in contrast to Beard, the potential conflict between commercial and manufacturing interests, and the frustration by commercial interests of the protective tariff advocated in the *Report on Manufactures*. Francis Lieber wrote in 1870 that if Hamilton were alive then, he would be a free trader. Lieber to Hamilton Fish, Sept. 18, 1870, quoted by Merle Curti, *Probing Our Past* (New York, 1955), p. 142.

105. Hamilton in private held Jay's Treaty an "execrable one" made by "an old woman." Bowman, "Jefferson, Hamilton, and American Foreign Policy," p. 36. By qualifying this comment as "insolent," Bowman disallows the legitimacy of defending to the utmost for prudential reasons what one may well merely regard as the lesser evil.

106. *Papers*, VII, 52.

107. *Ibid.* For the Farewell Address, see Paltsits, pp. 155–56.

108. To Timothy Pickering, June 8, 1798, *Works*, X, 294. Cf. also Hamilton's pamphlet against John Adams, where he admits the plan of a temporary connection with Great Britain against France, but never a "lasting connection." *Works*, VII, 358.

109. To B. Waterhouse, July 12, 1811, in W. C. Ford, ed., *Statesman and Friend. Correspondence of John Adams with Benjamin Waterhouse, 1784–1822* (Boston, 1927), p. 65.

110. E.g., Koch, *Power*, pp. 66–67. Dr. Koch holds (pp. 46–47) that "there is an oppressive narrowness about his interests, a single-minded preoccupation with himself, his own power, his own ambitions, prestige, reputation, manoeuvres, intrigues." Her argument is summed up as follows: "Hamilton in his conduct and thought is the embodiment of an ageless theme, the pervasive drive for power." This argument reveals a lack of appreciation of Hamilton's pursuit of fame, even if the author is mindful of Hamilton's concern for "reputation." Mitchell limits the concept of glory to military matters, correlating the primacy of political ambitions over military ones (with which I agree) to "power." Mitchell, I, 331. As to Hamilton's attitude on war, his first letter to E. Stevens seems still more in character than a polite letter written to a lady during the war, which is adduced by Mitchell (pp. 331–32). The preoccupation with Hamilton's drive for power, with its blinding effect on recognition of the pursuit of fame, tinges also Joseph Charles's portrait of Hamilton in his notable analysis of American politics in the 1790's: "A man can have only one dominant urge, and Hamilton's was for power and influence." Charles, "Hamilton and Washington: The Origins of the American Party System," *William and Mary Quarterly*, 3d series, XII (April 1955), 250. A further illustration of the point made in this chapter is R. B. Morris's omission of the crucial passage on the love of fame as "the passion of the noblest minds" from his quotation (p. 188) of *Federalist* No. 72 in Richard B. Morris, ed., *Alexander Hamilton and the Founding of the Nation* (New York, 1957), p. 188. John P. Roche has suggested that in a contemporary setting, Hamilton "would be the *eminence grise* dominating (*pace* Theodore Sorensen or Sherman Adams) the Executive Office of the President." This, too, seems to miss the full measure of Hamilton's pursuit of fame. "The Founding Fathers: A Reform Caucus in Action," *American Political Science Review*, LV (1961), 799. Rossiter, on the other hand, ascribes great significance to the motive of fame rather than power, in *Hamilton*, pp. 27–28, 230, and 268 n. 101.

111. Cf. Jouvenel, *Sovereignty*, pp. 21, 34.

112. Quote in his Pay Book, *Papers*, I, 390.

113. To J. B. Colvin, Sept. 20, 1810. *The Writings of Thomas Jefferson*, 418, 421–22. Other instances of this view—first found as early as 1785, significantly also in connection with a diplomatic negotiation—are discussed

by Charles M. Wiltse, *The Jeffersonian Tradition in American Democracy* (Chapel Hill, 1935), pp. 171–75.

114. Hamilton to J. Bayard, Jan. 16, 1801, *Works*, X, 414, also 413.

115. To Robert Walsh, Feb. 5, 1811. Jared Sparks, ed., *The Life of Gouverneur Morris with Selections from His Correspondence and Miscellaneous Papers*, 3 vols. (Boston, 1832), III, 262. See also David H. Fischer, *The Revolution of American Conservatism* (New York, 1965), p. 20 n. 57.

116. See *Papers*, V, 81. Hamilton's strategy at the New York Ratifying Convention is ably summarized by Alfred F. Young, *The Democratic Republicans of New York* (Chapel Hill, 1967), pp. 112–13.

117. Report of the Commissioners Fauchet, La Forest, and Petry to the Commissioner of Foreign Relations, Jan. 5, 1795, in F. J. Turner, ed., "Correspondence of French Ministers to the United States, 1791–1797," in *Report of the American Historical Association for the Year 1903*, II (Washington, D.C., 1904), 534. In free translation: "The passion for celebrity being dominant with him, he neglects courting people's favor by superficial gestures, but he likes to subject people's minds to his own by the sheer superiority of his talents." Cecelia M. Kenyon's observations in "Hamilton," pp. 176–77, are pertinent: "As a Legislator, Hamilton was initially successful. The conditions which existed during and shortly after the inauguration of the new government were congenial for the exercise of his special talents. Afterward, his effectiveness as politician and statesman declined with remarkable rapidity." Professor Kenyon's article is reprinted in Jacob E. Cooke, ed., *Alexander Hamilton: A Profile* (New York, 1967), pp. 166–84, here at p. 182.

118. See also above, pp. 32–33. It follows from the foregoing that my interpretation of the incident of 1800 differs from that of Professor Rossiter. Hamilton's initiative on this occasion seems more in character and less exceptional to me than to Professor Rossiter; and precisely because I think Hamilton's action may be explained by his position as a "founder," it does not seem to me conducive to an understanding of his action to argue that he, "like every other American who has faced a desperate political situation, could break out of the limits of his commitment to constitutionalism" and propose the action he did. See Rossiter, *Hamilton*, p. 192n.

119. Address Before the Young Men's Lyceum of Springfield, Illinois, January 27, 1838. Roy P. Basler, ed., *The Collected Works of Abraham Lincoln* (New Brunswick, N.J., 1953), I, 113–14. For an extensive analysis, see Harry V. Jaffa, *Crisis of the House Divided* (New York, 1959), pp. 191 ff.

ACKNOWLEDGMENTS

Work on this book originated in the late fifties, when I was Research Associate at the University of Chicago. Return to my native country and professional obligations unrelated to the theme of this book imposed an interval before work on it could be resumed. In the meantime, the most significant development in the field of Hamilton scholarship was the launching of the definitive edition of the *Papers of Alexander Hamilton* at Columbia University, under the direction of Harold Syrett and Jacob E. Cooke. Fifteen volumes, published by Columbia University Press, have appeared by 1969, covering Hamilton's most creative years and those most directly relevant to the theme of this book. I have consulted the *Papers* extensively in my research and have quoted some material from them.

In the early stages of research, I benefited from the helpfulness of the staffs of the Library of Congress, the New York Historical Society, the Connecticut Historical Society, and the Massachusetts Historical Society. During the later stages of writing and preparing the book for publication, I greatly profited from the research facilities provided by the Institute for Advanced Study at Princeton, during a stay as temporary member, and by the John F. Kennedy Institute of American Studies at the Free University of Berlin; I am grateful for the support granted by these institutions. The excellent library of the John F. Kennedy Institute possesses holdings on the history of seventeenth- and eighteenth-century America that are hardly equalled elsewhere in continental Europe. I have accumulated a heavy debt of gratitude toward the staff of the History Department of the Institute, which I directed from its inception in 1964 to my return to the University of Vienna in 1969. My particular thanks are due to my doctoral students and associates Dr. W. Paul Adams, Mrs. Angelika Jaeger, and Miss Brigitte Classen. My secretary in Berlin, Miss Ursula Möbius, has excelled in typing and retyping a manuscript written in a language that is as little her native language as it is the author's. For most valuable assistance in compiling the Index, I am grateful to Dr. Eva-Maria Loebenstein, of the Institute of History of the University of Vienna. Both the language problem and the distance between California and Central Europe have made unusually difficult the editorial task of the publisher. I would like to express my great appreciation to Mr. J. G. Bell, Editor, and Miss Betty K. Smith, Assistant Editor, of Stanford University Press, for their interest, patience, and help while preparing the manuscript for publication. Essential for completing the book have been my wife's understanding and her wise counsel at critical junctures.

I may be permitted to single out, among those scholars and friends from whom I have received encouragement and advice, three men to whom my debt is greatest: Hans J. Morgenthau, in whose Research Center at the University of Chicago this work began; Felix Gilbert, who has been and continues to be mentor to so many historians on either side of the Atlantic Ocean; and the late Douglass Adair. Adair's work, centering on the Founders' "Use of History"—as he called a program at the AHA Convention in Washington in December 1955, at which we both participated—has anticipated and influenced significant contemporary research trends in the history of political ideas in eighteenth-century America. My own approach to the theme of this book has been shaped by Adair's concern with the Founding Fathers' "Use of History." He took great interest in the progress of this book. I have never met a scholar who more generously shared his own findings, his own ideas with others. This book cannot but be dedicated to his memory.

                                                                                                G. S.

Vienna, Austria

INDEX

Acton, Lord, 96, 184–85
Adair, Douglass, 193, 238 n70, 259–60 n6
Adams, John: on natural rights, 12, 214 n10; on British Constitution, 38, 57f, 83; on republican government, 44, 47, 55–57, 63; on legislative power, 50; on virtue, 65–66; on international commerce, 167, 252ff notes 74, 75, and 76; on tasks of a politician, 175; on meaning of empire, 191; on Hamilton, 200–201; Hamilton's pamphlet against, 267 n108; mentioned, 13f, 26, 38f, 41, 77, 81, 104, 135, 150, 183
Adams, Samuel, 15, 19
Adams, Sherman, 267 n110
Adler, Alfred, 99
Africa, 196
Age of Reason, 76, 86
Age of the True Believer, 125
"Agrippa," see James Winthrop
Alexander the Great, 102, 154, 205
American Revolution, Ch. I passim, 40–44, 144
Ames, Fisher, 24, 103, 105, 236 n46, 241 n103
Ames, Dr. Nathanael, 236 n46
Amsterdam, 117–18, 198
Ancients and moderns, 7, 70–75, 94f, 130–33, 166–70, 173, 178
Anti-Federalists, 184–85
Arbitrary government, 22, 40–44, 56–62 passim, 217 n50, 225 n56
Aristocracy, 44–56 passim, 100, 104, 181, 262 n29. See also Ancients and moderns; Honor
Aristotle, 4, 57, 100, 131–39 passim, 154, 177, 213f, 256, 260f
Articles of Confederation, 57, 160
Asia, 196

Athens, 150
Atlantic Ocean, 3, 10, 41, 50, 184
Augustus, Emperor, 174
Austin, John, 15, 225 n55

Bacon, Francis: and parties, 110–11; and sinews of war, 141–42; and degrees of honor, 174–80 passim, 260 n6; Jefferson and, 239 n85; and empirical tradition, 249 n30; mentioned, 3, 133, 190, 247
Bailyn, Bernard, 2, 229 n99
Balanced government, see Free government; Limited government
Barbé de Marbois, François, 192
Barker, Sir Ernest, 59–60
Baumann, Sebastian, 189
Becker, Carl, 14, 217 n52
Beckwith, Maj. George, 194, 203
Belknap, Jeremy, 230 n107
Bills of Rights, 5, 18, 34, 53–54
Blackstone, William: and Hamilton's political theory, 6, 9–36 passim, 53, 61, 224–25 n55; on self-love, 80; on Crown's influence, 84–85; on democracy, 89; mentioned, 3, 221f, 236
Bodin, Jean, 4
Bolingbroke, Henry St. John, Viscount: and concept of representation, 50; and Whig doctrines, 96, 239 n75; on parties and factions, 110–11, 244 n129; and Machiavelli, 220 n103
Boorstin, Daniel, 13–14
Bowdoin, James, Jr., 155–56
Boyd, Julian, 203
Brackenridge, Hugh Henry, 260 n10
Braxton, Carter, 230 n107
Brissot de Warville, J. P., 168
Bristol, 263 n55

Brogan, Sir Denis, 186
Burckhardt, Jacob, 96
Burgh, James: on first principles, 35, 220;
  his republican sympathies, 67; and radical Whig tradition, 96, 229 n99, 239
  n75, 253 n75; influence on J. Adams,
  146, 252 n73
Burke, Edmund: contrasted with Hamilton, 30; on love of fame, 104; on
  parties and factions, 110–11, 243–44
  n129; theory of representation, 187;
  concern with glory, 242 n104
Burlamaqui, J. J., 216 n43
Burr, Aaron, 39, 94, 98–102 *passim*, 105,
  238. *See also* Demagoguery
Butterfield, Herbert, 165

Caesar, Julius, 98–99, 102, 119, 174,
  205, 239 n85
Canada, 190, 195
Canvassers, Board of (New York), 31
Carthage, 44, 136, 150
Cato, 99, 102
Cato's Letters (by Trenchard and Gordon),
  35, 66–67, 96, 106, 220, 229
Charles I of England, 45
Charles V, Emperor, 140
Charles XII of Sweden, 102
Charters (of American colonies), 12
Chatham, Earl of, *see* William Pitt the
  Elder
Checks and balances, 62, 82, 158. *See also*
  Diffusion of power; Mixed government
China, 135
Christian Constitutional Society, 125
Christianity, 64, 86, 93–94, 99, 104–5,
  122, 125, 173
Churchill, Sir Winston, 186
Clay, Henry, 97, 184, 265 n92
Clinton, George, 29, 31, 164
Classes, *see* Social classes
Coke, Sir Edward, 12, 18, 26, 28, 217 n50
Commerce, 71, 85–86, 136, 140–50 *passim*,
  170f, 197. *See also* Free trade
Common law, 17–18
Commonwealth (1649), 47
Commonwealthmen, 64, 229 n99
Condorcet, Marquis de, 253 n75
Congress: Confederation period, 97, 109,
  112; Hamilton on, 160, 175; Union
  period, 89, 96, 113, 205
Conservatism, 23, 169
Constitution, British: contest over nature
  of, 5, 10–16 *passim*; J. Adams on, 12,
  38, 57, 83, 191; C. Van Tyne on, 13;
  eighteenth-century understanding of, 15,
  45; principle of allegiance in, 27; T.
  Paine on, 45; Whig view of, 58; J.

Burgh on, 67; Hume on, 84; Ch. Pinckney on, 127; Hamilton on, 163, 170; J.
  Necker on, 170, 259 n146; mentioned,
  48, 112. *See also* Great Britain, Parliament
Constitution, U.S. Federal: longevity of,
  1; guarantee of republican government
  in, 2, 38–39, 46; Bill of Rights in, 18,
  53–54; and national sovereignty, 28–
  29; and Louisiana Purchase, 33, 202;
  and frequent elections, 36; Hamilton's
  judgment of, 39, 203; Hamilton's plans
  for (1787), 51–52; Hamilton and sovereignty of, 59–60; debates on (1788),
  63, 67, 89; opponents of, 96, 157; and
  parties, 112–13; and sectional interests,
  114; Hamilton and federal aspects of,
  160–61; House of Representatives in,
  87; mentioned, 5, 57. *See also* Anti-
  Federalists
Constitutionalism, 5, 57–59, 181, 203–4,
  225 n56
Convention, *see* Federal Convention; New
  York Ratifying Convention
Convention Parliament (1689), 25
Correggio, 260 n10
Corsica, 73
Crete, 69
Cromwell, Oliver, 45
Cyrus, 174

Dante, 240 n91
Davenant (D'Avenant), Charles, 220 n97,
  250 n47
David, Biblical, 178
Declaration of Independence, 5, 12, 22–28
  passim, 40, 154, 171
Declaration of Rights (1774), 12
Declarations of Rights (state constitu-
  tions), *see* Bills of Rights
Defoe, Daniel, 50
Demagoguery, 97–99, 179
Democracy: Hamilton on, 40, 48–49, 68,
  82; and republican form of government,
  46–49; Hume on, 157; D. Brogan on,
  186; representative, 49–56, 223 n36;
  liberal, 114; constitutional, 203; well-
  regulated, 226 n58. *See also* Majority
  rule; Popular government
Demosthenes, 201
Dickinson, John, 63, 129, 258–59 n145
Diffusion of power, 40, 62, 181. *See also*
  Constitutionalism; Liberalism; Whig
  tradition
Domestic policy, *see* Internal policy
Dominion theory (of British Empire), 26–
  27, 41
Dostoevski, F., 124

Draft treaty (of 1776), 146
Drayton, William H., 215 n12
Duane, James, 12

East Indies, 142
Empire, 129, 140; America as, 40, 155, 189–201; founding of an, 174–75; meaning of, 189–93
England, *see* Great Britain
Enlightenment, 76, 86, 108, 122, 231 n111
Equality, social, 66–74, 127, 181, 191–92, 230 n104. *See also* Social classes
Equality of states, doctrine of, 134–35, 218 n62
Europe: political thought in, 2–3; tradition of political testaments in, 117; monarchies in, 130; and international commerce, 145; relations of U.S. to, 146, 164–65, 195–200, 266 n99; concept of *raison d'état* in, 188; Hamilton's attitude toward, 195
Expansionism, 129, 145, 153, 192ff
Extent of territory, 110–20, 153–61, 163–64, 190–93

Factions, 110–20, 158–59, 172, 244 n129. *See also* Parties
Fame, 95–106 *passim*, 201–5, 240 n94, 267 n110. *See also* Honor
Farewell Address (1796), 74, 109–23 *passim*, 163–64, 171–72, 198–99
Federal Convention: Hamilton in, 17, 28, 51–52, 79–84 *passim*, 88, 107–8, 115, 124, 160, 162; J. Dickinson in, 63; G. Morris in, 106; Hamilton's exchange with Ch. Pinckney in, 126–27, 148; mentioned, 38–39, 46, 97
Federalists (party), 43, 123, 266 n99
Fénelon, François de, 140, 250 n47
Ferguson, Adam, 177
First principles, 6 and Ch. I *passim*
Foreign policy, primacy of, 132ff, 147, 148–53, 161, 167.
Founding Fathers, 1–2, 17, 37f, 44–45, 61–62, 74, 105, 130–33, 153, 174–77 *passim*
France: Jefferson in, 100; absolute government in, 140; expansionism of, 145; help for American colonies (1776), 146; free trade policy in, 147; republican government in, 168–69; compared with ancient Rome by Hamilton, 173; and war with Great Britain in North America, 190; and early American foreign policy, 193–203 *passim*, 267 n108; mentioned, 19, 39–43 *passim*, 109, 122, 124, 128, 157, 191. *See also* French Revolution; Louisiana Purchase

Franklin, Benjamin, 38, 41, 190
Frederick II of Prussia, 102, 254 n76, 261 n17
Free government, 40–44, 56–63, 111, 223 n31. *See also* Diffusion of power; limited government; Mixed government
Free trade, 131, 145–48, 166–68, 247 n160, 266 n104. *See also* Commerce
French Revolution, 34, 107, 121–24, 135, 162, 198, 254 n76
Freud, Sigmund, 99, 124
Fromm, Erich, 124

Gadsden, Christopher, 214 n12
Galloway, Joseph, 12
Genêt, Edmond, 122
Geneva, 191, 248 n25, 259 n146
Genoa, 255 n58
Gentz, Friedrich von, 169
George III of England, 22, 28, 43–46, 56, 179, 184–85
Georgia, 157
Gibbon, Edward, 172
Gide, André, 94
Gilbert, Felix, 117, 188, 252–53 n75, 254 n81
Gillies, John, 261 n17
Girondists, 122
Glorious Revolution (1688–89), 9, 25, 66, 110, 184–85
Gordon, Thomas, *see* Cato's Letters
"Gothic" government, 55
Government, *see* Arbitrary; Free; Limited; Mixed; Popular
Government of laws, 17, 56–63, 140, 151
Great Britain: as maritime power, 7, 136, 140, 148, 165, 221 n103; constitutional thought in, 9–11, 36; contest with colonies, 9–37 *passim*, 40–44; Peace Treaty with U.S. (1783), 58; Mably on, 69–70; Montesquieu on, 73, 135, 145, 150; Hume on, 157, 221 n103; as model for Hamilton's policy, 7, 168; and Hamilton's foreign policy concept, 190–201 *passim*; mentioned, 39, 71
—Parliament: supremacy of, 17, 26–27; Hamilton on, 78; House of Commons, corruption of, 83–85, 183; House of Lords, abolition of (1649), 47; mentioned, 41–50 *passim*, 56, 66
Greece, 70, 94, 126, 131, 139, 146, 176, 200
Gresham's Law, 147
Grotius, Hugo, 4, 216 n43

Hamilton, Alexander: contributions to revolutionary debate, 11–28 *passim*, 41–44; indebtedness to Blackstone, 13 and Ch. I *passim*; concept of law and sovereignty, 15–17, 21–22, 26–30, 54; and "government of laws," 17, 57–62, 151; indebtedness to Hume, 21, 40, 42–43, 71, 92, 101, 117–19; social conservatism of, 23–24; concept of social contract, 25–30; actions beyond legality, 30–33; and election of 1800, 32–33, 203, 268 n118; on republican government, 39, 44, 46, 51–52, 123, 182; on Federal Constitution, 39; on democracy, 40, 48–49, 51–54, 68; charge of "monarchism" against, 46, 51–52; admiration for British system, 46, 113, 163, 168, 170; on forms of government, 48–49, 83; significance of "Phocion" essays, 57; on despotism, 62, 182; on republican virtue, 70–71, 74; views on human nature, 76–125 *passim*, 149, 164, 182–86; friendship for J. Laurens, 77; on role of "corruption," 83–84; on judicial review, 87; analysis of social classes, 87–90; attitude toward Christianity, 94, 122, 125; fear of demagogues, 97–99, 179; on love of fame, 102; on monarchy, 108, 113; fears of foreign influence in republics, 109; on parties and factions, 112–20, 185; on sectional conflict, 115–20; impact of French Revolution on, 121–23; changing views on immigration, 123; exchange with Ch. Pinckney on foreign policy, 127, 148, 165; on commerce, 142–43, 150, 166–68; on causes of war, 148–53; and meaning of "Confederation," 156–61; and doctrine of implied powers, 161; on free trade, 167–68; on founding an empire, 175, 180; theory of representation, 187; concept of American empire, 189–201; and Nootka Sound controversy, 194, 198f; character, achievements, and failures, 201–5

Hamilton, Angelica, 94
Harrington, James, 4, 56–57, 64, 117, 133, 135, 175, 190, 260 n10
Hartz, Louis, 90, 126, 175
Henry IV of France, 174
Henry VII of England, 174
Henry, Patrick, 128–29, 147–48, 233 n15, 255 n89
Hichborn, Benjamin, 56
Hobbes, Thomas: view of law and sovereignty, 15–22 *passim*, 30, 49, 53–54, 61, 224 n55; on primacy of self-interest, 73–74, 93–94; on love of virtue, 100–101; on preference of monarchy, 108–9; condemnation of factions, 110–11; and state of nature, 134, 152, 160, 216 n30; and primacy of foreign policy,

137; on money, 141; "Hobbesian fear," 165; compared with Locke, 239 n75; liberal political theory and, 239 n78; Vattel on, 248 n24
Hoffer, Eric, 124
Holland, *see* Netherlands
Holland (Province of), 117–18
Honor, 65, 77, 94, 100, 173, 174–75, 183, 186, 238 n70
Human nature, 18–20, 64–65, 71–75, Ch. III *passim*, 149, 152, 176, 180f
Hume, David: on state of nature, 19; influence on Hamilton, 21, 30, 40, 42–43, 71, 92, 101, 117–19, 232 n117; and social contract, 24–25; on free government, 40–43, 62; on relation of reason to passions, 64, 86; on ancient and modern policy, 71–72, 74, 154; on human nature in politics, 77–78, 80f; on the Crown's influence on Commons, 84; on opinion, 92; on love of fame, 101; influence on Madison and Hamilton, 117–19, 157–58; on parties, 121; on private happiness and public greatness, 169–70; on legislators and founders, 174; on "pure republics," 224 n49; and A. Pope, 234 n23; mentioned, 3, 10, 90, 143, 162, 235, 260

Immigration, 123
Immortality, desire of, 100–101
Impeachment, 113
Implied powers, doctrine of, 161–62, 166
Indians, 165, 192
Industrial growth, 123, 199
Industrial Revolution, 173
Interest, meaning of, 80–87, 90–91, 186–88. *See also* National interest
Internal policy, primacy of, 131–32, 258 n136
Ireland, 42
Isolationism, 129, 192, 199, 252 n73
Italy, 47

Jackson, Andrew, 192
James II of England, 9, 13, 28, 185
Jay, John: and election of 1800, 32–33, 203; in *The Federalist*, 107, 121, 151–52, 242 n112; mentioned, 23, 146
Jay's Treaty, 91, 198–99, 266 n105
Jefferson, Thomas: *Summary View*, 14; and dominion theory of Brit. Empire, 26, 41; Presidency of, 32, 99, 102, 112; and Louisiana Purchase, 33–34, 194, 201–2; and "little rebellions," 34, 37; on human nature and social circumstances, 67, 97, 177–86 *passim*; and Lafayette, 100; on origin of parties in

America, 122; on immigration, 123; "empire for liberty," 191–92, 195f; mercantilist policy of, 198, 266 n99; isolationism of, 199; definition of republic, 225–26 n58; and great men, 239 n85, 260 n6

Jeffersonians and Jeffersonianism, 46, 104, 117–18, 122, 124–25, 172, 177, 180–86, 201–2. *See also* Republicans

Johnson, Gerald, 193

Johnson, Samuel, 47

Jouvenel, Bertrand de, 178, 181, 201

Judicial review, 52, 59, 87

Jury trial, 18

Justinian, 174

Kant, Immanuel, 24

Kantorowicz, Ernst H., 240 n91

Kenyon, Cecelia M., 96, 183, 242 n14, 268 n117

King, Rufus, 28, 31, 121, 218

Lafayette, Marquis de, 100, 162

Laurens, John, 77

Law of nature, *see* Natural law

Law, rule of, 56–63. *See also* Government of laws

Legislators, 174–80

Liberalism, 25, 90, 104, 173, 176, 182, 239 n78. *See also* Utilitarianism

Lieber, Francis, 266 n104

Limited government, 41, 96. *See also* Mixed government; Whig tradition

Lincoln, Abraham, 204–5

Lisola, Baron Franz von, 250 n47

Livy, 57

Locke, John: and principles of government, 4, 6; and self-preservation, 18; Blackstone and, 21; and law of nature, 23; and social contract, 25–26; and popular sovereignty, 53–55; and corruption by power, 95–96; mentioned, 3, 49, 73, 134, 216, 220, 239

London, 67, 198

Louis XIV of France, 140, 147

Louisiana Purchase, 33, 192–94, 201–2

Lycurgus, 141, 174, 179

Mably, Gabriel Bonnot de, 64–73 *passim*, 142, 153f, 159–62 *passim*, 168, 231 n111, 232 n120

Macaulay, Catherine, 229 n99

Macaulay, Thomas B., 90–92

Machiavelli, Niccolò: and first principles, 34–36; and Hume, 43; republican virtue and, 64–73 *passim*; on security, 81; and parties, 111; on foreign policy, 132–45 *passim*, 154; and Bolingbroke, 220

n103; on Sparta, 250 n40; mentioned, 3–6 *passim*, 100, 175, 213f, 260

McIlwain, Charles H., 54

Mackenzie, John, 13, 215 n12

Madison, James: on tendency toward monarchy, 38–39; on republican government, 47, 55; 225 n58; and Hamilton's plans in the Federal Convention, 51–52; on "perfect equality," 72; on meaning of interest, 80–81, 85f, 107; on love of fame, 103; on parties, factions, sectional conflict, and extent of territory, 110–20, 157–68, 245 n140; exchange with P. Henry on foreign policy, 128–29; and confederations, 160, 162; draft of Farewell Address, 171–72, 246 n147; on founding of states, 176; on development of social inequality, 235 n42; mentioned, 19, 46, 84, 121, 126, 231, 234f, 245

Maine, Sir Henry, 7

Maistre, Joseph de, 162

Majority, rule of, 53, 75. *See also* Democracy; Popular government

Mandeville, Bernard, 74

Mannheim, Karl, 99, 236 n45

Manning, William, 48

Manufactures, 67, 123, 166–67, 199, 266 n104. *See also* Industrial growth; Sea power

Marcus Aurelius, 102

Marlborough, Duke of, 102

Marseilles, 135

Marshall, John, 33, 161, 226 n58, 241 n98, 248 n25

Martin, Luther, 17

Marx, Karl, 99

Maryland, 17

Mason, George, 34–35

Massachusetts, 5, 15, 19, 48, 56, 155, 157

Mazzei, Philip, 223 n36

Meinecke, Friedrich, 188

Mercantilism, 144, 198, 220 n97, 252 n73. *See also* Sea power

Meredith, Sir William, 43

Milton, John, 124

Minos, 141

Miranda, Francisco de, 265 n82

Mississippi River, 164, 193–95, 198

Mixed government, 41, 52, 55, 62, 111. *See also* Free government; Limited government

Monarchy, 38–52 *passim*, 83, 107–8, 110, 119–20, 130, 151–52, 158

Moderns political theory, *see* Ancients and moderns

Monroe Doctrine, 265 n92

Montesquieu: and definition of republic,

47; and republican virtue, 64–69, 71–74, 81, 89, 107, 228 n93, 230 n107; on commerce, 85, 91, 140–46, 148; on extent of territory, 117, 153, 190–93; on peacefulness of republics, 131; on republican government and foreign policy, 138–60 *passim*, 168; and confederations, 162, 166; on legislators, 175; political science and, 177; on forms of government and conduct of foreign policy, 253 n75; mentioned, 3f, 94, 133, 171, 213, 216, 221, 237, 250–60 *passim*
More, Sir Thomas, 260 n10
Morison, Samuel E., 102, 122
Morris, Gouverneur, 39, 68, 80, 106, 202, 245 n141
Morris, Robert, 92, 106, 202
Morristown, N. J., 67
Mount Vernon, 102
Murray, William Vans, 232 n120, 256 n103

Napoleon I of France, 122, 205
National interest, 91, 187–88, 236 n56. *See also* Interest
Nationalism, 106–7, 121–25
Natural law, 3, Ch. I *passim*, 60, 134
Natural rights, 3–4, 6, Ch. I *passim*, 133, 176, 225 n56. *See also* State of nature
Navigation Acts, 148, 252 n74. *See also* Sea power
Necker, Jacques, 170, 259 n146
Nero, 101
Netherlands, 19, 44, 117, 130, 150, 225 n58, 232 n120. *See also* Holland (Province of)
"New Diplomacy," 259 n146
New England, 66, 241 n103
New Hampshire, 5, 220 n95
New Jersey, 67
New Orleans, 193–94
Newton, Sir Isaac, 4, 239 n85
New York: colony of, 14, 41; city of, 23, 189; state of, 28f, 31–33, 54, 57–58, 145, 157, 164, 173, 203; Hamilton on constitution of, 49–50, 68
New York Ratifying Convention (1788), 5, 44, 48–49, 62, 69–74 *passim*, 79–82 *passim*, 89, 91, 115, 180, 182
Nietzsche, Friedrich, 124
Nootka Sound, 194, 198–99
North Carolina, 157, 220 n95
Numa Pompilius, 174, 178–79

Ortega y Gasset, José, 94
Otis, James, 24, 215 n18, 217 n50

Paine, Thomas, 12, 28, 43, 50, 129–30, 138, 146–50 *passim*, 229, 252f

Palmer, Robert R., 3, 219 n81, 224 n40
Pareto, Vilfredo, 99
Paris, 162, 198
Parsons, Theophilus, 232 n120, 260 n11
Parties, political, 110–20, 122, 244 n129. *See also* Factions
Passions, hierarchy of, 95
Pauw, Cornelis, 265 n91
Peace Treaty (of Versailles, 1783), 58
Peking, 96
Pennsylvania, 29, 61, 157, 220 n95, 256 n99
Perfectibility, social, 36
Pericles, 151
Philadelphia, 67, 162
Physiocrats, 148, 253 n75, 254 n81
Pickering, Timothy, 51–52, 73, 103, 105
Pinckney, Charles, 126–28, 147–48, 165, 188
Pitt, William, the Elder (Earl of Chatham), 220 n20
Pitt, William, the Younger, 241 n98
Plato, 69, 73, 131, 141, 154, 256 n96, 260 n10
Plumer, William, 234 n23
Plutarch, 179–80
Poland, 44, 46, 135, 225 n558
Political science: J. Adams on, 44, 63; Hamilton on, 76; mentioned, 3–4, 78, 135, 175, 177–78, 190
Political theory, classical and modern, *see* Ancients and moderns
Political testaments, 117
Polybius, 11
Pope, Alexander, 234 n23
Popular government, 48–56, 120. *See also* Democracy; Majority rule
Portugal, 142, 200
Power, 95–102, 201, 267 n110. *See also* Diffusion of power
Price, Richard, 214 n6
Priestley, Joseph, 10
Property, 70–71, 80, 91, 126, 230 n104 and 107, 235 n42
Prussia, 261 n17
Public opinion, 121, 247 n160
Pufendorf, Samuel, 134
Puritanism, 3, 63, 104

Radicalism, 23
Raison d'état, *see* Reasons of state
Randolph, Edmund, 255 n89
Raynal, Abbé, 265 n91
Reason, Age of, 76, 86
Reasons of state, 188, 237 n56
Renaissance, 11, 36, 47
Representative Democracy, *see* Democracy
Representative government, 50, 55–56, 139, 158

Republican government: guarantee in Federal Constitution, 38; criteria for defining, 44–45; eighteenth-century understanding of, 44–75 *passim*; Madison on, 47, 55, 225 n58; principle of virtue and, 63–75; demagogues and, 98; foreign corruption in, 106–9; extent of territory and, 116–20, 153–61, 168–69; immigration and, 123; international commerce and, 143–46, 150; Hamilton on responsibility in, 182–86. *See also* Democracy; Free government; Government of laws; Mably; Machiavelli; Montesquieu

Republicans (party), 43. *See also* Jeffersonians and Jeffersonianism

Revolution, Age of Democratic, 3. *See also* French Revolution; Glorious Revolution; Industrial Revolution

Rivington, James, 23

Romanticism, political, 242 n114

Rome, 42, 44, 70, 82, 126, 132–40 *passim*, 146, 154, 172–73, 178, 191

Romulus, 174, 178–79

Rousseau, J. J., 24, 48–49, 64, 71–74, 107–11 *passim*, 138, 154, 168, 178, 213 n5, 236 n50, 242 n113, 258 n136

Rule of law, 56–63. *See also* Government of laws

Rush, Benjamin, 4, 6, 67, 181

Russia, 248 n25

Schuyler, Philip, 33

Sea power, 136, 141, 145–48, 167–68, 193–94. *See also* Commerce; Manufactures; Navigation Acts

Seabury, Samuel, 15–16, 42, 112

Sectionalism and sectional conflict, 114–15, 118–19

Self-preservation, principle of, 19–21, 64, 135

Shakespeare, William, 173

Shays, Daniel, 34

Sidney, Algernon, 3, 35–36, 49, 55, 64, 66, 133, 135–39, 220, 228

Smith, Adam, 66, 85, 91, 121, 143, 148, 154, 167, 174, 239 n78, 247 n160, 252 n74

Social classes, 69–74, 87–90. *See also* Equality, social

Social contract (or compact), 24–30, 82, 176, 217 n61

Sociology, 99, 177–78

Solomon, 178

Solon, 126, 174

Sorensen, Theodore, 267 n110

South America, 196

South Carolina, 13, 126

Sovereignty, 16–17, 22, 27–29, 52–54, 59– 60, 62, 110, 112, 216 n49, 218 n71. *See also* Blackstone; Hobbes; McIlwain

Spain, 43, 142, 165, 191–99 *passim*

Sparta, 44, 69–73 *passim*, 82, 126, 133–39 *passim*. *See also* Lycurgus

Spelman, Edward, 111

Staatsformenlehre, 3

Stamp Act, 50

State of nature, 18–19, 134, 152, 160, 216 n30. *See also* Natural law, Natural rights

States, equality of, 134–35, 218 n62. *See also individual states by name*

Steuben, Baron von, 238 n73

Stoicism, 99, 102

Story, Joseph, 56

Strauss, Leo, 131

Stuarts (royal family), 108, 184

Supreme Court, 28. *See also* Judicial review

Swift, Jonathan, 214 n6

Switzerland, 69–73 *passim*, 159

Taine, Hippolyte, 242 n113

Taylor, John, 213 n6

Temple, Sir William, 190

Territory, *see* Extent of territory

Tocqueville, Alexis de, 4, 93, 104–5, 126, 213 n3

Townshend, Charles, 241 n104

Trade, *see* Commerce; Free trade

Trajan, 101

Treaty of Peace (1783), *see* Peace Treaty

Trenchard, John. *See Cato's Letters*

Trial by jury, 18

Tucker, Josiah, 252 n74

Turgot, A. R. J., 252 n74, 253 n76

Turner, Frederick Jackson, 114

United Provinces, *see* Netherlands

Utilitarianism, 25, 80–87, 173, 176

Van Tyne, Claude, 13

Vattel, Emmerich de, 134, 248 n24

Venice, 46, 133, 136, 150

Vermont, 54

Virginia, 34, 128, 157

Virtue, 63–75, 81, 83, 100–101, 106–9 *passim*, 126, 129, 138, 140–41, 155, 186

Voltaire, 69

War of Independence, 167, 195, 203

Warren, Mercy, 229 n95

Washington, George: on monarchy, 39; and striving for fame, 102; judgment of Hamilton, 103, 105, 192; and Hamilton's fear of party spirit, 115–18; on American empire, 189, 195; J. Adams on Hamilton's relationship to, 210; mentioned, 31, 67, 78–79, 80, 98, 104,

109, 112, 194, 198f. *See also* Farewell
    Address
Webster, Noah, 230 n104
Western Hemisphere, 196–97
West Indies, 164f
Whig tradition: 2f, 66–67, 96–97; Hamil-
    ton and, 57–58; views on corrupting in-
    fluence of power, 95, 176, 182–86; and
    foreign policy, 146
Whisky Rebellion (Pa.), 29, 61

White, Howard B., 172
Williamson, Hugh, 38
Wilson, James, 26, 28, 41, 256 n99
Wilson, Th. Woodrow, 249 n28
Wilsonianism, 135
Winthrop, James ("Agrippa"), 24, 145–
    46, 256 n99
Wolsey, Cardinal, 151

Yates, Robert, 79, 81, 231 n114, 235 n30